Bread Machine Cookbook

A Practical Recipe Guide With Specific Quick and Easy Recipes to Have Homemade Bread With Your Bread Machine.

By

Michelle Crocker

Table of content

INTRODUCTION 7

CHAPTER 1: EASY BAKING WITH BREAD MACHINE 10

1.1 MAIN INGREDIENTS FOR BAKING 12
1.2 BREAD MACHINE CYCLES 16
   1.2.1 Kneading Cycle 16
   1.2.2 Rest Cycle 16
   1.2.3 Rise Cycle 17
   17
   1.2.4 Punch Cycle 18
   1.2.5 Baking Cycle 18
1.3 HOW EASY ARE BREAD MACHINES TO USE? 20
1.4 CHOOSING THE RIGHT BREAD MACHINE 22
1.5 MISTAKES TO AVOID WHILE USING THE BREAD MAKER 24
1.6 BENEFITS OF USING BREAD MACHINE 25

CHAPTER 2: BASIC BREADS 27

2.1 EVERYDAY WHITE BREAD 27
2.2 HONEY WHOLE-WHEAT BREAD 29
2.3 MOLASSES WHEAT BREAD 30
2.4 100 PERCENT WHOLE-WHEAT BREAD 31
2.5 FRAGRANT HERB BREAD 33
2.6   ROSEMARY BREAD 34
2.7 SPICY CAJUN BREAD 36
2.8 AROMATIC LAVENDER BREAD 37
2.9 HONEY-SPICE EGG BREAD 39
2.10 CINNAMON SWIRL BREAD 41

CHAPTER 3 : GRAIN, SEED & NUTS BREADS 43

3.1 WHOLE-WHEAT SEED BREAD 43
3.2 MULTIGRAIN BREAD 44
3.3 TOASTED PECAN BREAD 46
3.4 MARKET SEED BREAD 47
3.5 CHEESY CHIPOTLE BREAD 48
3.6 ROASTED GARLIC ASIAGO BREAD 50
3.7 CHEDDAR CHEESE BASIL BREAD 52
3.8 JALAPEÑO CORN BREAD 53
3.9 RICH CHEDDAR BREAD 54
3.10 FETA OREGANO BREAD 56

CHAPTER 4: FRUIT BREADS 57

4.1 Warm Spiced Pumpkin Bread 58

4.2 Black Olive Bread 60

4.3 Robust Date Bread 62

4.4 Yeasted Carrot Bread 64

4.5 Sauerkraut Rye Bread 66

4.6 Savory Onion Bread 67

4.7 Simple Sourdough Starter (No-Yeast Whole Wheat Sourdough Starter) 69

4.8 Basic Sourdough Bread 72

4.9 Cranberry Pecan Sourdough 75

4.10 Dark Chocolate Sourdough 76

CHAPTER 5: CREATIVE COMBINATION BREADS 77

5.1 Zucchini Pecan Bread 77

5.2 Raisin Bran Bread 79

5.3 Lemon Poppy Seed Bread 80

5.4 Panettone Bread 82

5.5 White Chocolate Cranberry Bread 84

5.6 Eggnog Bread 86

5.7 Chocolate Chip Peanut Butter Banana Bread 87

5.8 Chocolate Sour Cream Bread 89

CHAPTER 6: KETOGENIC BREADS 90

6.1 Basic Low-Carb Bread 90

6.2 Almond Flour Yeast Bread 92

6.3 Almond Milk Bread 94

6.4 Gluten-Free White Bread 95

6.5 Brown Rice Bread 96

6.6 Brown Rice & Cranberry Bread 97

6.7 Italian Panettone 99

6.8 Italian Bread 101

CHAPTER 7: BREAD & OTHER BAKERY PRODUCTS 102

7.1 Strawberry Jam 102

7.2 Tomato Sauce 104

7.3 Apple Pie 106

7.4 Blueberry Jam 107

7.5 Peach Jam 108

7.6 Grape Jelly 109

7.7 Crab Apple Jelly 110

7.8 Pizza Dough 111

OVEN RECIPES TO BREAD MACHINE CONVERSION 113

CONVERSION TABLES 116

.... **118**

CONCLUSION **119**

RECIPE INDEX **122**

This document is geared towards providing exact and reliable information regarding the topic and issue covered. The publication is sold with the idea that the publisher is not required to render accounting, officially permitted, or otherwise qualified services. If advice is necessary, legal or professional, a practiced individual in the profession should be ordered.

From a Declaration of Principles which was accepted and approved equally by a Committee of the American Bar Association and a Committee of Publishers and Associations.

The information provided herein is stated to be truthful and consistent, in that any liability, in terms of inattention or otherwise, by any usage or abuse of any policies, processes, or Instructions contained within is the solitary

Introduction

Homemade bread is nutritious and tasty, but to make it from scratch requires a huge amount of work. It requires a lot of effort, time, and patience to combine the ingredients, knead the dough, wait for it to rise, knead it again, and then bake it, but it does not have to be always this way. The bread maker can do all the hard work, and you have only to taste and appreciate the wonderful taste of homemade bread. If one is not yet persuaded and wonders if it is wise to invest in such an appliance, all the recipes in this book can reassure you of its merit. The bread-making process is slow and labor-intensive, and as many people do not have the patience to go through the entire process in this time, bread machines have become a requirement.

Although a person can still buy bread from markets, it would always be a better choice to bake bread at home, as bread can be optimized as per the tastes and health needs of the individual/family. A home machine for baking bread is a bread machine that transforms all the ingredients into tasty bread. The wonderful thing about an automated bread maker is that all these steps are

completed for you. Basically, a bread-making appliance is a portable electric oven that contains a single wide bread tin. The tin is still a little unique; it has a bottom axle that attaches to the electric motor below it. Within the tin, a small metal paddle spins on the axle. A waterproof seal holds the axle, so the bread mixture cannot leak. Bread has always been eaten along with all sorts of food, rendering it mandatory for all occasions, whether it be lunch, brunch, or dinner. Using a bread maker is better than purchasing the bread at a store.

Tore-bought bread is full of synthetic chemicals, but you only need natural ingredients at home with a bread machine. You may even incorporate specific ingredients, including grains or seeds, to make it much better; apart from flour, you will need yeast and water. Homemade bread is even tastier given the fact that you must always use fresh ingredients, and you can personalize ingredients according to the particular preference. Even if that's not enough, after traditional bread-making, many dishes have to be washed too. One has to put in the ingredients with a bread machine, and after the bread is baked, clean the tin.

Current bread machines bring a lot of special controls that allow several bread specialties to be prepared. For individuals who are intolerant or sensitive to such foods, such as gluten, a bread machine may be especially useful. This book will provide you with all sorts of recipes. These devices can also be used for recipes other than bread, such as jelly, fruit jam, scrambled eggs, tomato sauce, and casseroles, and even some desserts, with a couple of ingredients variations. All you have to do is use fresh ingredients and walk away.

Chapter 1: Easy Baking with Bread Machine

Since the beginning of baking, freshly made bread is the best thing ever. The only trouble is, time and commitment are required. Many individuals have never baked bread in their lives and will never think of doing so, but much of that has begun to shift with the new advent of automated bread-making machines. Today millions convert their homes into bakeries, and every day one can enjoy their own freshly made bread at a fraction of the price they might spend in a shop. There are different explanations for why an individual should suggest using a bread maker instead of any other choices that he has access to.

Bread machines in cafes, households, workplaces, etc., have often been more comfortable people's choice. The majority of available bread makers on the market are automatic.

Bread machines reduce effort and time by helping their customers. An ingredient may be added to it by a baker, homemaker, or any other user. It completes its work automatically, without any control on the part of its consumer. Bread machines allow consumers to do other required things, such as preparing the main course, dinner, etc., while reducing the workload.

It is necessary to remember, though, that not all bread machines are automated. Many Pricey bread makers only give automatic functions. To finish the bread-making method, you just need all the necessary ingredients. Bread makers are often simple to use and manage, much like ovens for bread makers. Assume an individual doesn't know how to bake or doesn't even want to bake; bread machines are the ideal substitute for those people. In addition, it is often likely that individuals wish to bake a certain form of bread at home, like French bread, but does not know how to use an oven for baking one. A bread maker allows us to produce such bread in these situations, while alternate cycles or settings also come with it.

The dough must go through 5 phases if you make bread the conventional way, primarily as mixing, kneading, rising, punching down, proving, and baking, but it's all in one move with the bread maker. All ingredients you have to add to the system, adjust the cycles, and let it do its thing. Each time, you'll get accurate outcomes.

1.1 Main Ingredients for Baking

Baking powder, produced from starch and tartar cream, is a fermenting agent that allows the batter to grow. It has an acidic ingredient incorporated into it, so one does not need to integrate something else for raising the flour. A bitter-tasting food can result from too much baking powder, whereas too little results in a hard cake with very little volume.

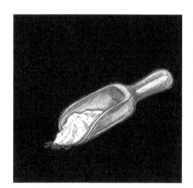

Baking soda is a simple sodium bicarbonate which has to be mixed with yogurt, honey, or cocoa, as an acidic ingredient. It's a fermenting product much like baking soda. Using baking soda too much will make the cake rough in texture. Baking soda and baking powder can lose their strength more easily than you would know. If the packages are not fresh, inspect them before using them. Place a couple of teaspoons of white vinegar in a tiny bowl to test the baking soda and incorporate a teaspoon of baking soda. It can vigorously foam out, and it will take some moments for the frothing to subside. The more bubbles, the stronger the baking soda would be. You should substitute the baking soda for fresh baking soda if there is no action, or it just ends up with a couple of tiny bubbles. To check the baking powder, add a spoon full of baking powder into a cup.

Fill the bowl with hot water to cover the baking powder; if it continues to burst furiously, it's safe to include it in the recipes. When weighing, do not add a wet spoon into the baking powder bag for better results.

The water can trigger the baking powder left unused in the can, and each time, it will not be as pleasant to use. If you can see lumps in the baking soda, it's typically a warning that humidity has made its way in the baking soda.

Butter, as a stable fat, butter is ideally used for baking than any other fat material. In fact, butter adds taste, with a melting point only below body temp. Hence certain cookies and bakery items appear to "melt in the

mouth."

Cornstarch has many uses based on the kind of recipe it's being incorporated in. Cornstarch is commonly either a binder or thickener, although it may be an anti-caking agent as well.

 It's perfect to use to thicken custards sauces or in gluten-free cooking.

Eggs have many uses, but most significantly, they add volume to foods and are a binding agent, ensuring they hold together the final product.

For glazing, flavor, thickening, and binding, you can use the entire egg or just use the egg yolks and egg whites for different reasons. Egg whites, providing moisture and strength. Egg yolks contribute to shape and flavor.

Flour has a very crucial part in making bread. Its major quality is that it binds all the products together.

It transforms into gluten as flour protein is mixed with heat and moisture.

Different flour varieties have different protein amounts and are ideal for various bakery products.

Milk provides softness, moisture, taste, and lightens color to baked goods.

It provides a double function since it adds structure and strength to the batter or dough and provides tenderness, flavor, and moisture.

Sugar, in every particular recipe, sugar is executing a variety of functions. It provides texture, moisture, and holds the form.

Although operating in combination with eggs, fat, and liquid materials, it is also just another rising agent. Sugar gives "crunch" to certain cookies and cakes.

1.2 Bread Machine Cycles

Like in any other bread making, the bread machine also goes through cycles to make you the flavorful bread.

1.2.1 Kneading Cycle

The first cycle is kneading, and perhaps the most significant step in baking bread that includes yeast. Kneading combines all the ingredients absolutely well and is probably the bread machine's noisiest period. It will also take anywhere between 15 to 45minutes for this cycle. The time it takes depends on the bread machine, and the sort of bread one is making. In most machines at the bottom of the baking tin, kneading propellers completely combine everything.

1.2.2 Rest Cycle

The rest cycle makes the dough rest until it begins kneading again. Autolyzing is the scientific baking word for this. Essentially, it helps the moisture surrounding the dough to soak in the starch and gluten completely. It can take this process from only a couple of minutes to over 35 minutes.

1.2.3 Rise Cycle

It would require this cycle if the flour has gluten in it, so it will rise and make the bread airy and soft. It is a fermentation. Depending on the bread machine, this cycle can normally take about 40 to 50 minutes. It can take considerably longer occasionally, particularly if you're making French bread.

1.2.4 Punch Cycle

The next cycle is Punch Cycle after the dough has finished the rising cycle. In this cycle, the bread machine continues to knead the dough yet again. The distinction is that it is performed even more lightly at this point, and the goal is to remove the small air pockets produced in the growing period by the fermentation of the yeast. Usually, the Punch cycle, often referred to as the shape-forming cycle, is a short cycle that takes only seconds to complete, and it is still necessary.

1.2.5 Baking Cycle

This is the most important cycle. This is the cycle in which the bread maker bakes the bread. Depending on the bread maker and the kind of bread you are making, this cycle will take anywhere from half an hour to more than 90 minutes.

Other important baking modes of the bread machine are

- Basic Bread
- Sweet Bread
- Whole-Wheat Cycle
- Gluten-Free Bread

- Rapid Bake

- Cake & Jam—yes, you can make Jellies and Jam and sauces.

1.3 How easy are Bread Machines to use?

Bread machines are very easy and simple to use. Add in ingredients specifically in an order, following the bread machine's manufacturer suggested order. In most machines, add liquids first, then in dry ingredients, or as your machine specifies. All ingredients should be at room temperature or specified otherwise.

- Choose the type of bread you want to make (whole wheat, sweet, basic, multigrain, pizza, or French).

- Choose the baking mode (bake rapid, bake, sandwich, or dough). Choosing different modes changes the sequence of kneading, mixing, rising, and baking. In dough mode, for example, the bread maker will stop without actually baking the bread. You can open up the lid, take out the dough, and roll it out however you like. After that, you have to bake in the oven rather than a bread machine.

- Choose the bread loaf size if your machine has this feature. (1 lb., 1.5 lb. or 2 lb.).

- Choose the crust type to your liking.

- Click the Timer button if your machine has one. The bread maker will show you the time it will take to bake the bread.

- Now click the Start button, and your wait begins.

- When the loaf is baked (from three to four hours), you slowly open the lid, take the heated tin out of the bread machine, wait for ten or more minutes to take out the loaf, let it cool off. In the cleaning process, you only have to wipe out the tin (which is non-stick), requiring only 30 seconds.

1.4 Choosing the Right Bread Machine

Think of yourself what the criteria will be before selecting the right kind of bread machine for yourself.

Timer: You can manually determine when to set the timer for a baking cycle. Then you have to come at the right time, to take the bread out of the maker. Otherwise, the bread would be preheated and cooked, or choose a one where the machine will calculate the time.

Size: Get the bread machine that carries a recipe comprising 3 cups of flour if one has a big family. Some can hold flour cups of up to 4 to 5-1/2.

Blades: Blades in horizontal pans do not often knead the dough too well, leaving the pan's corners with flour. A big negative is incomplete blending. However, the upright settings do a better job of mixing. Many new machines are made vertically, but some horizontal pans also offer two blades, so choose carefully.

How expensive does a bread machine be?

Some automated control machines are a bit pricey since they do not need your supervision, but some machines require your full-time attention, so keep that fact in mind.

1.5 Mistakes to Avoid While Using the Bread Maker

Here are some tips that will help you to avoid making mistakes while using a bread machine

- You must unplug the appliance before taking bread out.

- Failing to measure the ingredients precisely

- You must add ingredients accepted by the bread machine in the order suggested.

- Please consider the Kitchen's temperature.

- Not opening the lid: it's a good idea to open the lid and look at the dough, particularly in the kneading process, for about after ten minutes. Look at the dough's surface if it's too sticky and requires more flour if your finger is covered in the dough.

  If the dough looks too dry, so it needs more water. Adding products is better than taking them out, so incorporate a vigilant quantity at once. To re-adjust the texture, add a teaspoon of water or flour at a time.

- As the bread bakes, you leave paddles in the machine: You can hear the bread maker begin beating down the dough before the bread reaches the final rise process. Now open the lid, shift the flour to the side of the tin, and gently bring the paddles out.

- Enabling the loaf to rise without reshaping the dough in the final period.
- Taking the bread out before it cools, try waiting for ten to fifteen minutes before taking out the bread.

1.6 Benefits of Using Bread Machine

- It is easier to bake bread in a bread machine.
- The process is cleaner and simpler than traditional bread baking.
- Every time the bread machine produces the same consistency & exceptional taste.
- The benefit of jam and jelly making.
- You're not going to do the kneading.
- Make your fresh bread, at home, for the sandwiches.
- You can add many ingredients to make the bread to your taste.
- It is convenient for busy people.

- Saves long-term resources and money.

Chapter 2: Basic Breads

2.1 Everyday White Bread

(Prep time: 20 minutes | Total time: 2 hours 30 minutes)

Ingredients

- 3 and 3/4 cups of flour

- Lukewarm water: 1 cup

- Butter: 3 tbsp.

- Lukewarm milk: 1/3 cup

- Bread machine Yeast: 2 tsp

- Sugar: 3 tbsp.

- Salt: 1 tsp

Instructions

- In the bread machine, add all the ingredients according to your machine's order.

- Select 2 pounds' loaf, and basic setting, medium crust. Click on start.

- After it's baked, let it cool down before slicing.

2.2 Honey Whole-Wheat Bread

(Prep time: 5 minutes | Total time: 3 hours 30 minutes)

Ingredients

- Olive oil: ⅓ cup

- 4 and a half cups of whole wheat flour

- 1 and a half cups of warm water

- Honey: ⅓ cup

- Yeast: 1 tablespoon

- Kosher salt: 2 tsp

- Gluten: 1 tsp (optional)

Instructions

- In the machine, add water, then oil, and then honey. Add half flour, salt, gluten, and the rest of the flour.

- Make a well in the center add yeast.

- Select whole wheat and light crust. Press start.

- Serve fresh bread.

2.3 Molasses Wheat Bread

(Prep time: 10 minutes | Total time: 4 hours 10 minutes)

Ingredients

- Whole wheat flour: 1 and 3⁄4 cups

- Water: 3⁄4 cup

- Melted butter: 3 tablespoons

- Milk: 1⁄3 cup

- Sugar: 2 tablespoons

- Molasses: 3 tablespoons

- Fast-rising yeast: 2 and 1⁄4 teaspoons

- Bread flour: 2 cups

- Salt: 1 teaspoon

Instructions

- Add all the ingredients to the machine according to your suggested machine's order. Make sure the ingredients are at room temperature

- Use light crust, basic setting.

- Serve fresh.

2.4 100 Percent Whole-Wheat Bread

(Prep time: 10 minutes | Total time: 4 hours 10 minutes)

Ingredients

- 3 and 1/3 cups of whole wheat flour

- Powdered milk: 2 tablespoons

- 1 and a half cups of water

- Honey: 2 tablespoons

- Molasses: 2 tablespoons

- Margarine: 2 tablespoons

- Salt: 1 and a half teaspoons

- Yeast: 1 and a half teaspoons

Instructions

- Add liquid ingredients before dry ingredients or as per your machine's order.

- Mix the powdered milk and water. Heat in microwave for 30 seconds, then adds in the bread machine followed by rest of the ingredients.

- Select 2 lb. loaf and whole wheat bread press start.

- Serve fresh.

2.5 Fragrant Herb Bread

(Prep time: 10 minutes | Total time: 3 hours 5 minutes)

Ingredients

- Olive oil: 2 tablespoons

- Warm water: 1 cup

- 1 egg, lightly beaten

- Dried rosemary leaves: 2 teaspoons

- White sugar: 2 tablespoons

- 1 teaspoon of salt

- Dried oregano: 1 teaspoon

- Bread machine yeast: 2 teaspoons

- Dried basil: 1 teaspoon

- All-purpose flour: 3 cups + 2 tablespoons

Instructions

- Add all ingredients in the pan of the bread machine, as per the suggested order.

- Select large loaf, light crust. Press start.

- Serve fresh

2.6   Rosemary Bread

(Prep time: 10 minutes | Total time: 3 hours 15 minutes)

Ingredients

- Onion Powder: 1 Tablespoon

- Butter: 4 Tablespoons

- Bread Flour: 3 Cups

- 1 and 1/3 Cups of warm Milk

- One Minute Oatmeal: 1 Cup

- Salt: 1 Teaspoon

- 1 and a half Teaspoons of Bread Machine Yeast

- White Granulated Sugar: 6 Teaspoons

- Dried Rosemary: 1 Tablespoon

Instructions

- Add all ingredients to the bread machine in the suggested order by the manufacturer.

- Select 2 lb. loaf, basic and light crust.

- Press start.

- Before the baking cycle begins, sprinkle some rosemary on top and let it bake.

- Serve fresh.

2.7 Spicy Cajun Bread

(Prep time: 10 minutes | Total time: 2 hours 20 minutes)

Ingredients

- Bread flour: 2 cups

- 1/4 cup of diced green bell pepper

- Half cup of water

- 1/4 cup of chopped onion

- 2 teaspoons of soft butter

- 2 teaspoons finely chopped garlic

- Active dry yeast: 1 teaspoon

- Sugar: 1 tablespoon

- Cajun seasoning: 1 teaspoon

- Half teaspoon of salt

Instructions

- Place all ingredients into the bread machine in the suggested order by the manufacturer.

- Select white bread, dark or medium crust, and not the delay cycle.

- Press start.

2.8 Aromatic Lavender Bread

(Prep time: 10 minutes | Total time: 2 hours 55 minutes)

Ingredients

- Water: 1/3 cup

- Buttermilk: 3/4 cup

- Fresh lavender flowers, finely chopped: 1 teaspoon

- Bread flour: 3 cups

- Olive oil: 3 tablespoons

- Fresh lavender leaves, finely chopped: 2 tablespoons

- Gluten: 1 tablespoon

- One lemon: zest

- 2 and a half tsp. of bread machine yeast

- 1 and a half teaspoons of salt

Instructions

- Add all ingredients to the bread machine in the suggested order by the manufacturer.

- Select dark crust, basic cycle, and press start.

2.9 Honey-Spice Egg Bread

(Prep time: 10 minutes | Total time: 3 hours 25 minutes)

Ingredients

- 2 Fresh eggs

- Warm water: 1 Cup

- 1 and a half Tablespoons of unsalted butter

- Honey: 2 Tablespoons

- Salt: 1 teaspoon

- Powdered milk: 3 Tablespoons

- Bread flour: 3 Cups

- Active dry yeast: 2 teaspoons

- Cinnamon: 1 teaspoon

- Cardamom: 1 teaspoon

- Ginger: 1 teaspoon

- Nutmeg: 1 teaspoon

Instructions

- Place all ingredients into the bread machine in the suggested order by the manufacturer.

- Select white bread, light crust. Press start.

- Serve warm with honey or butter.

2.10 Cinnamon Swirl Bread

(Prep time: 10 minutes | Total time: 3 hours 25 minutes)

Ingredients

- 1 and a half tbsp. of butter

- Warm milk: ¾ cup

- 1 whole egg

- 1 tbsp. of brown sugar

- Half teaspoon of salt

- Instant Yeast: 1 ¾ tsp

- 2 and a half cups of bread flour

For Cinnamon Swirl

- Half tbsp. of cinnamon

- 3 tbsp. of white sugar

- Raisins: 1 ¼ cups

Instructions

- Warm the milk to 110 F. Mix with butter and stir, so it melts.

- Add to the bread machines. Add the rest of the ingredients as per the suggested order.

- Select basic. Choose crust to your liking. Select knead. Meanwhile, combine the swirl ingredients.

- After the second knead cycle's beeping, add the swirl ingredients.

- After the third kneading cycle's beeping, remove paddles and place the dough back in the machine.

- Serve fresh.

Chapter 3 : Grain, Seed & Nuts Breads

3.1 Whole-Wheat Seed Bread

(Prep time: 10 minutes | Total time: 3 hours 10 minutes)

Ingredients

- 1 and 1/3 cups of whole wheat bread flour

- 1 and 1/3 cups of water

- Honey: 3 tablespoons

- Salt: 1 teaspoon

- Softened Butter: 2 tablespoons

- Half cup of flaxseed

- 1 and a half cups of bread flour

- Half cup of sunflower seeds

- Active dry yeast: 1 teaspoon

Instructions

- Add all ingredients to the bread machine in the manufacturer's suggested order, except for sunflower seeds.

- Select basic cycle, and press start.

- Add sunflower seeds on the beeping of the kneading cycle.

- Serve fresh.

3.2 Multigrain Bread

(Prep time: 10 minutes | Total time: 2 hours 40 minutes)

Ingredients

- Multigrain Cereal: 3/4 Cup

- Softened Unsalted Butter: 3 tbsp.

- 2 and a 1/4 Cups of Bread Flour

- Warm Milk: 1 Cup

- 1 Teaspoon of Bread Machine Yeast

- Brown Sugar packed: 1/4 Cup

- 1 teaspoon of Salt

Instructions

- Add all ingredients to the bread machine in the suggested order by the manufacturer.

- Select basic cycle, Light crust, and press start.

- Serve fresh

3.3 Toasted Pecan Bread

(Prep time: 10 minutes | Total time: 3 hours 5 minutes)

Ingredients

- 2 and a half tablespoons of butter

- 1 and 1/4 cups of water

- Half cup of old-fashioned oatmeal

- bread flour: 3 cups

- Half cup chopped pecans

- bread machine yeast: 2 teaspoons

- Dry milk: 2 tablespoons

- Sugar: 3 tablespoons

- 1 and a 1/4 teaspoons of salt

Instructions

- Add all ingredients to the bread machine in the suggested order by the manufacturer.

- Select Grain and light crust. Press start.

- Serve fresh.

3.4 Market Seed Bread

(Prep time: 10 minutes | Total time: 3 hours 10 minutes)

Ingredients

- Olive oil: 2 tablespoons

- Tepid water: 1 cup

- Whole wheat bread flour: 1 cup

- 1/3 cup mixed seeds (pumpkin, sunflower, sesame, linseed, & poppy)

- 1 teaspoon of salt

- 1 and a half teaspoons of dried yeast

- Sugar: 1 tablespoon

- White bread flour: 2 cups

Instructions

- Add all ingredients to the bread machine in the suggested order by the manufacturer. Add seeds in the end.

- Select white bread cycle—press start. Check the dough's consistency if it needs more water or flour. Add one tbsp at a time. Serve fresh.

3.5 Cheesy Chipotle Bread

(Prep time: 10 minutes | Total time: 3 hours 10 minutes)

Ingredients

- 1 and a half teaspoons of salt

- Shredded Mexican Cheese: 1 cup

- Chipotle Chili powder: 1 teaspoon

- Sugar: 1/4 cup

- 1 and 1/4 cups of lukewarm water

- Bread machine yeast: 1 teaspoon

- Bread flour: 4 cups

- 3 tablespoons of dry milk

Instructions

- Add all the ingredients to the bread machine's pan in the suggested order by the manufacturer.

- Select white bread cycle, light crust. Press start.

- Do not use a delay cycle.

- Enjoy fresh.

3.6 Roasted Garlic Asiago Bread

(Prep time: 10 minutes | Total time: 3 hours 15 minutes)

Ingredients

- 1 cup of white bread flour

- Gluten flour: 1/4 cup

- 1 and a 3/4 cup of whole wheat flour

- Grated Asiago cheese: 3/4 cup

- Fresh rosemary minced: 2 teaspoons

- Dry milk: 2 tablespoons

- 3 roasted crushed garlic cloves

- Fresh basil minced: 1 tablespoon

- Fresh oregano minced: 2 teaspoons

- 4 teaspoons of active dry yeast

- 1 and 1/4 cups of water

- Honey: 1 teaspoon

- 1 teaspoon of salt

- Olive oil: 2 tablespoons

Instructions

- Add all the ingredients to the bread machine in the suggested order by the manufacturer.

- Select whole wheat cycle, crust to your liking.

- Serve fresh.

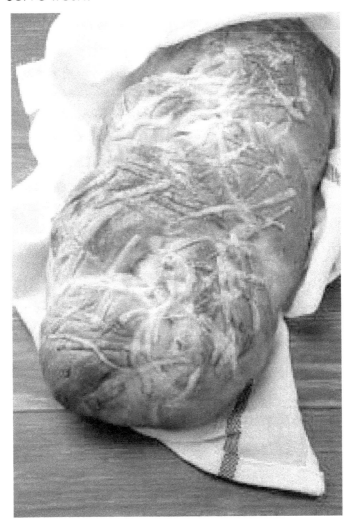

3.7 Cheddar Cheese Basil Bread

(Prep time: 10 minutes | Total time: 3 hours 10 minutes)

Ingredients

- Softened Unsalted Butter: 4 Tablespoons

- 1 and 1/8 Cups (2tbsp.) of lukewarm Milk

- 1 Cup of Shredded Cheese

- 3 Cups of Bread Flour

- Brown Sugar: 1 Tablespoon

- Basil: 1 Teaspoon

- 1 and a half Teaspoons of Bread Machine Yeast

- 1 and a half Teaspoons of Salt

Instructions

- Put all ingredients into the bread machine in the suggested order by the manufacturer.

- Select basic setting, light crust. Press start.

- Before the baking cycle, add some cheese on top of the bread loaf, if you like.

- Enjoy fresh.

3.8 Jalapeño Corn Bread

(Prep time: 10 minutes | Total time: 2 hours 50 minutes)

Ingredients

- Thawed frozen corn: 2/3 cup, drained

- Water: ¾ cup + 2 tablespoons

- jalapeño chili, chopped: 1 tablespoon

- Softened Butter: 2 tablespoons

- Sugar: 2 tablespoons

- Bread flour: 3 and a ¼ cups

- 2 and a half teaspoons of bread machine

- Cornmeal: 1/3 cup

- 1 and a half teaspoons of salt

Instructions

- Add all ingredients to the bread machine in the suggested order by the manufacturer.

- Select White cycle and Light crust—press start. Do not use a delay cycle.

- Enjoy fresh.

3.9 Rich Cheddar Bread

(Prep time: 10 minutes | Total time: 3 hours 10 minutes)

Ingredients

- 2 and a half tablespoons of Parmesan cheese

- 1 cup of warm water

- Half teaspoon of salt

- 3 and a half teaspoons of sugar

- 1 and a 1/4 cup of freshly grated cheddar cheese

- Dry mustard: 1 teaspoon

- 2 and a half tablespoons of softened butter

- 2 and a half cups of bread flour

- 1 and a half teaspoons of paprika

- Active dry yeast: 2 teaspoons

- 2 and a half tablespoons of minced onions

Instructions

- Place all ingredients in the bread machine in the suggested order by the manufacturer.

- Select white setting, crust to your liking.

- Press start and assess dough's consistency if it needs water or more flour.

- Add one tbsp. of flour or water if required.

- Serve fresh.

3.10 Feta Oregano Bread

(Prep time: 10 minutes | Total time: 3 hours 10 minutes)

Ingredients

- 1 and a half tablespoons of olive oil
- 3 cups of bread flour
- Half cup of crumbled feta cheese
- 1 cup of water
- Active dry yeast: 2 teaspoons
- Dried leaf oregano: 1 tablespoon
- Salt: 1 teaspoon
- 3 tablespoons of sugar

Instructions

- Put all ingredients in the bread machine in the suggested order by the manufacturer.
- Select basic. Press start.
- Serve fresh.

Chapter 4: Fruit Breads

4.1 Warm Spiced Pumpkin Bread

(Prep time: 10 minutes | Total time: 3 hours 10 minutes)

Ingredients

- Half cup white sugar

- Canned pumpkin: 1 cup, not pie filling

- 1/4 tsp. of salt

- Half cup of brown sugar

- 2 whole eggs

- 1 tsp. of vanilla

- 1 and a half cups of all-purpose flour

- 1 and a half tsp. of pumpkin pie spice

- Half cup of chopped walnuts

- Canola oil: 1/3 cup

- 2 tsp. of baking powder

Instructions

- Spray the bread machine pan with cooking oil.

- Add all ingredients to the bread machine in the suggested order by the manufacturer.

- Select Quick cycle, medium crust.

- After three minutes, clean the sides of the pan with a spatula.

- Start again, and serve fresh.

4.2 Black Olive Bread

(Prep time: 10 minutes | Total time: 2 hours 10 minutes)

Ingredients

- Warm water: 1 cup and half cup brine

- 1/3 -1/2 cup of brine (from olives)

- 3 cups of bread flour

- Olive oil: 2 tablespoons

- Active dry yeast: 2 teaspoons

- 1 and a half teaspoons of salt

- 1 and 2/3 cups of whole-wheat flour

- Sugar: 2 tablespoons

- Half to 2/3 cup of finely chopped olives

- 1 and a half teaspoons of dried basil

Instructions

- Mix water with brine.

- Add all ingredients, except for olives, to the bread machine in the manufacturer's suggested order.

- Select wheat or basic setting. Press start.

- Add the chopped olives to the ingredient signal.

- Serve fresh bread, and brush with olive oil.

4.3 Robust Date Bread

(Prep time: 10 minutes | Total time: 2 hours 10 minutes)

Ingredients

- Boiling water: 3⁄4 cup

- Unsalted butter: 3 tablespoons cut into half-inch pieces

- Granulated sugar: 2⁄3 cup

- Baking powder: 1 teaspoon

- 1 and a 1⁄3 cup of all-purpose flour

- Vanilla extract: 1 teaspoon

- Chopped dates: 3⁄4 cup

- Baking soda: 1 teaspoon

- Chopped walnuts: 1⁄3 cup

- Half teaspoon of salt

Instructions

- Add all ingredients to the bread machine in the suggested order by the manufacturer.

- Select basic and light crust.

- After 4 minutes, scrape the sides of the pan with a rubber spatula.

- Before baking starts, remove paddles.

- Enjoy fresh.

4.4 Yeasted Carrot Bread

(Prep time: 10 minutes | Total time: 4 hours 10 minutes)

Ingredients

- 2/3 cup of whole wheat flour

- 1 and a 1/3 cup of rolled oats

- 2 cups of bread flour

- 1 and a 1/3 tsp of salt

- 1 and a half Tbsp. of vegetable oil

- 1 cup of water

- Brown sugar: 2 Tbsp.

- 1/4 cup of dry milk powder

- 2 and a half tsp of active dry yeast

- 2/3 cup of grated carrot

Instructions

- Add all ingredients to the bread machine in the suggested order by the manufacturer.

- Select basic setting, light crust. Press start.

- Enjoy fresh bread.

4.5 Sauerkraut Rye Bread

(Prep time: 10 minutes | Total time: 3 hours 50 minutes)

Ingredients

- Bread flour: 2 cups
- 1 cup of rinsed & drained sauerkraut
- 1 and a half tablespoons of butter
- ¾ cup of warm water
- 1 and a half tablespoons of brown sugar
- 1 and a half teaspoons of active dry yeast
- 1 and a half tablespoons of molasses
- 1 and a half teaspoons of salt
- 1 teaspoon of caraway seed
- Rye flour: 1 cup

Instructions

- Add all ingredients to the bread machine in the suggested order by the manufacturer.
- Use Basic Cycle setting. Press start.
- Serve fresh bread.

4.6 Savory Onion Bread

(Prep time: 10 minutes | Total time: 3 hours 40 minutes)

Ingredients

For Caramelized Onions

- 2 sliced onions
- Butter: 1 tablespoon

For Bread

- Water: 1 cup
- Olive oil: 1 tablespoon
- Bread flour: 3 cups
- Sugar: 2 tablespoons
- 1 teaspoon of salt
- 1 and a ¼ teaspoons of bread machine

Instructions

- In a skillet, sauté onions over medium flame in butter until caramelized and brown. Turn off the heat.
- Add all ingredients to the bread machine in the manufacturer's suggested order, except for caramelized onion.

- Select Basic cycle, Press start. Do not use the delay feature. Add half a cup of onions at nut signal.

- Serve fresh bread.

4.7 Simple Sourdough Starter (No-Yeast Whole Wheat Sourdough Starter)

(Prep time: 10 minutes | Total time: 8 Days)

Ingredients

- Half a cup of cool water

- 1 cup of whole wheat or rye flour

- To feed the starter:

- Half cup of cool water (if the environment is warm) or lukewarm water (if the environment is cool)

- 1 cup of All-Purpose Flour Unbleached

Instructions

Day 1: In a one-quart glass container(preferably), mix the flour with cool water. Mix well, so there is no dry flour. Let it rest at (70 F) room temperature, loosely covered.

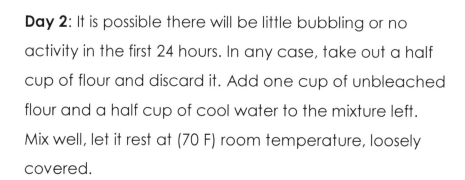

Day 2: It is possible there will be little bubbling or no activity in the first 24 hours. In any case, take out a half cup of flour and discard it. Add one cup of unbleached flour and a half cup of cool water to the mixture left. Mix well, let it rest at (70 F) room temperature, loosely covered.

Day 3: On the third day, there will be some activity like bubbling, fruity, fresh aroma, and expansion. Now you will start possibly two feedings each day. For every feeding, keep half of the mixture. Discard the rest. Add one cup of all-purpose flour and a half cup of water. Mix well with the mixture and let it sit at room temperature for 12 hours.

Day 4: Keep one cup of mixture and discard the rest. Again, add one cup of flour with a half cup of water.

Day 5: Repeat day 4. At the end of this day, it should be with a lot of bubbles and doubled with a tangy, acidic aroma. In any case, the starter has not doubled yet. Repeat the whole process after every 12 hours on the 6th and 7th day.

After the starter is ready, feed it for one last time. Discard half of it, mix the half with flour and water mix well. Let it rest at room temperature for 6-8 hours. It should be very bubbly and ready. Store in a jar for the long-term. Feed it again in the jar, let it rest for many hours at room temperature, then cover it. Cover lightly, even with a tight lid.

Keep in the fridge, feed it once a week with one cup flour and a half cup of water.

4.8 Basic Sourdough Bread

(Prep time: 10 minutes | Total time: 3 hours 22 minutes)

Ingredients

- 1 and a half teaspoons of salt

- Active dry yeast: 2 teaspoons

- 1 and a half teaspoons of sugar

- 4-6 tablespoons of lukewarm water

- 2 cups of ripe sourdough starter

- 2 and a half cups of All-Purpose Flour (Unbleached)

- 2 tablespoons of vegetable oil

Instructions

- Add all ingredients to the bread machine in the suggested order by the

  manufacturer.

- Select French bread or long-rise cycle. Press start.

- After ten minutes of kneading, check the dough and more flour or water if necessary, to make the dough smooth and soft.

- Serve fresh bread.

4.9 Cranberry Pecan Sourdough

(Prep time: 10 minutes | Total time: 3 hours 10 minutes)

Ingredients

- 1 dried package of (3 and a half ounce) sweetened cranberries

- Water: 2 tablespoons + 1 and a ¼ cup

- Salt: 2 teaspoons

- Chopped pecans: 3⁄4 cup, toasted

- Bread flour: 4 cups

- Butter: 2 tablespoons

- 2 teaspoons of yeast

- Non-fat powdered milk: 2 tablespoons

- 1⁄4 cup of sugar

Instructions

- Place all ingredients in the bread machine as per the suggested order by the manufacturer.

- Select white bread setting, medium crust. Press start. Enjoy fresh bread.

4.10 Dark Chocolate Sourdough

(Prep time: 10 minutes | Total time: 3 hours 10 minutes)

Ingredients

- Lukewarm (110 F) Water: 3⁄4 cup

- Half cup of cocoa powder

- Sourdough starter: 1 cup

- Sugar: 1 tablespoon

- dark chocolate: Half cup, finely diced

- 3 tablespoons of oil

- 2 teaspoons of salt

- Active dry yeast: 1 tablespoon

- 3 cups of bread flour

Instructions

- Add all ingredients to the bread machine in the suggested order by the manufacturer.

- Select basic cycle. Light crust. Press start.

- Check dough's consistency if it's too wet and sticky and requires more flour. Add one tbsp. of flour at a time. Serve fresh bread.

Chapter 5: Creative Combination Breads

5.1 Zucchini Pecan Bread

(Prep time: 10 minutes | Total time: 1 hour 40 minutes)

Ingredients

- 1/3 cup of Vegetable Oil

- Baking Powder: 2 tsp

- 3 whole Eggs, whisked

- Sugar: 3/4 cup

- 1 tsp of Baking Soda

- Half tsp of Allspice

- Half tsp of salt

- toasted pecan: Half cup chopped finely

- All-Purpose Flour: 2 cups

- 1 tsp of cinnamon

- Zucchini: 1 cup, shredded

Instructions

- Add oil and whisked eggs in the bread machine.

- Add flour, then add the rest of the ingredients, except for zucchini.

- Select the cake/quick cycle. Dark crust if you like.

- Press start.

- Add in the zucchini at the ingredient signal. Serve fresh.

5.2 Raisin Bran Bread

(Prep time: 10 minutes | Total time: 3 hours 10 minutes)

Ingredients

- 2 tablespoons of softened butter

- 2 and a 1/4 teaspoons of active dry yeast

- 1/4 cup of packed brown sugar

- 1 and a half cups of raisin bran

- Half teaspoon of salt

- Lukewarm water: 1 cup + 1 tbsp.

- 1/4 teaspoon of baking soda

- Half cup of raisins

- 2 and 1/4 cups of bread flour

Instructions

- Add all ingredients to the bread machine, except for raisins, in the manufacturer's suggested order.

- Select basic bread. Crust color to your liking.

- Check dough if it needs more water or flour add one tbsp. at a time.

- At the signal, add raisins. Serve fresh bread.

5.3 Lemon Poppy Seed Bread

(Prep time: 10 minutes | Total time: 3 hours 10 minutes)

Ingredients

- 3 cups of bread flour

- 1 and a half Tablespoons of dry milk

- ¾ cup of water

- 1 teaspoon of salt

- 1 and a half tablespoons of butter

- Honey: 2 Tablespoon

- Lemon extract: 2 teaspoons

- ¾ cup of lemon yogurt

- Half cup of toasted almonds, cut into slices

- Lemon peel: 1 tablespoon

- Yeast: 2 teaspoons

- Poppy seeds: 3 Tablespoons

Instructions

- Add all ingredients to the bread machine in the suggested order by the manufacturer.

- Select sweet bread cycle—press start.

- Enjoy fresh bread.

5.4 Panettone Bread

(Prep time: 10 minutes | Total time: 3 hours 10 minutes)

Ingredients

- 1 and a half teaspoons of vanilla extract

- 3⁄4 cup of water

- 2 eggs, whisked

- 3 and 1⁄4 cups of flour

- 2 tablespoons of sugar

- 1⁄4 cup of softened butter

- 1 and a half teaspoons of salt

- Half cup mixed dried fruit, chopped

- 2 tablespoons of powdered milk

- 2 teaspoons of yeast

Instructions

- Add all ingredients, except dried fruits, to the bread machine in the manufacturer's suggested order.

- Select sweet bread cycle. Light crust. Press start.

- Enjoy fresh bread.

5.5 White Chocolate Cranberry Bread

(Prep time: 10 minutes | Total time: 3 hours 10 minutes)

Ingredients

- Softened butter: 4 teaspoons
- 1 cup of milk
- 3 tablespoons of water
- 1 and a half teaspoons vanilla
- 1 whole egg
- 4 cups of bread flour
- 6 tbsp. of chopped white baking bar
- Half cup of dried cranberries
- 2 tablespoons of sugar
- 1 and a ¼ teaspoons of bread machine yeast
- 1 teaspoon of salt

Instructions

- Add all ingredients, except cranberries, to the bread machine in the suggested order by the manufacturer.
- Select white bread cycle. Light crust. Press start.

- Add cranberries at the ingredient signal.

5.6 Eggnog Bread

(Prep time: 10 minutes | Total time: 3 hours 10 minutes)

Ingredients

- 1 and a ¼ teaspoon of salt

- 4 cups of bread flour

- Half cup of dried cranberries or raisins

- Oil: 1 Tablespoon

- Half cup of milk

- 2 Tablespoons of sugar

- 1 cup of eggnog

- 1 and a ¾ teaspoons of active dry yeast

- 1 teaspoon of cinnamon

Instructions

- Add all ingredients to the bread machine in the suggested order by the manufacturer.

- Select basic cycle. Medium crust. Press start.

- Enjoy fresh bread.

5.7 Chocolate Chip Peanut Butter Banana Bread

(Prep time: 10 minutes | Total time: 3 hours 10 minutes)

Ingredients

- 3 whole Eggs

- Half cup of softened butter

- 1 and a half cups of mashed bananas (very ripe)

- 1 and 1/4 cups of sugar

- Half cup of vegetable oil

- 1 and a half cups of all-purpose flour

- 1 teaspoon of salt

- Half cup of plain Greek yogurt

- 1 teaspoon of vanilla

- 1 cup of peanut butter + chocolate chips

- 1 teaspoon of baking soda

Instructions

- Add all ingredients, except chocolate chips and nuts, to the bread machine in the manufacturer's suggested order.

- Select batter bread cycle. Press start.

- Add chocolate chips and nuts at the ingredient signal and take out the paddle.

- Enjoy fresh bread.

5.8 Chocolate Sour Cream Bread

(Prep time: 10 minutes | Total time: 3 hours 40 minutes)

Ingredients

- 3 and 3⁄4 cups of flour

- 3 tablespoons of butter

- 3⁄4 cup of sour cream

- 2 and a 1⁄4 teaspoons of yeast

- 1 tablespoon of sugar

- 3⁄4 cup of water

- Chocolate chips

- 1 teaspoon of salt

Instructions

- Place all ingredients into the bread machine in the suggested order by the manufacturer.

- Select basic cycle. Light crust. Press start.

- Serve fresh bread.

Chapter 6: Ketogenic

Breads

6.1 Basic Low-Carb Bread

(Prep time: 10 minutes | Total time: 3 hours 40 minutes)

Ingredients

- 1 and a half tsp of Bread Machine Yeast

- 1 and a half tbsp. of sugar

- ¼ cup of Vegetable Oil

- 1 cup of Water Warm

- 3 cups of low carb flour

- 3 tsp of Wheat Gluten

Instructions

- Spray the bread machine pan with cooking spray.

- Activate yeast in warm water with sugar. After 8-10 minutes, add to the pan.

- Add rest of the ingredients as well, as per the suggested order by the manufacturer.

- Select the low-carb cycle or basic. Press start Enjoy

6.2 Almond Flour Yeast Bread

(Prep time: 10 minutes | Total time: 3 hours 40 minutes)

Ingredients

- 2 and 1/4 cups of Almond Flour

- 1 and 1/4 cups of Water

- 1/3 cup of Psyllium Husk Powder

- Ground Flax Seed: 3/4 cup

- Half cup of Wheat Gluten

- 2 tsp of Coconut Palm Sugar

- 1/3 cup of seed mix

- 6 whole Eggs, lightly whisked

- 2 tbsp. of yeast

- Extra Virgin Olive Oil: 1/3 cup

- 1 tsp of Sea Salt

Instructions

- Add all ingredients to the bread machine in the suggested order by the manufacturer.

- Select a gluten-free or basic cycle. Medium crust. Press start.

- Scrap the sides of the pan with a rubber spatula after the kneading cycle.

- Enjoy fresh bread.

6.3 Almond Milk Bread

(Prep time: 10 minutes | Total time: 3 hours 20 minutes)

Ingredients

- 1 and a half teaspoons of salt

- Unsalted butter: 1 tablespoon, slice into pieces

- 2 teaspoons of fast-rising yeast

- 3 cups of almond flour

- 1 and 1⁄8 cups of almond milk

- 1 tablespoon of sugar

- 1 teaspoon of xanthan gum

Instructions

- Add all ingredients to the bread machine in the suggested order by the manufacturer.

- Select basic cycle. Medium crust and Press start.

- Enjoy fresh bread.

6.4 Gluten-Free White Bread

(Prep time: 10 minutes | Total time: 3 hours 40 minutes)

Ingredients

- Milk: 1 and 1/3 cup

- 2 eggs, whisked

- Vinegar: 1 tsp

- Oil: 6 tbsp.

- Whole wheat flour: 450 g

- Quick yeast: 2 tsp

- Salt: 1 tsp

- Sugar: 2 tbsp.

Instructions

- Mix the milk with vinegar and oil.

- Add all ingredients to the bread machine in the suggested order by the manufacturer.

- Select basic rapid or gluten-free cycle. Press start.

- Enjoy fresh bread.

6.5 Brown Rice Bread

(Prep time: 10 minutes | Total time: 3 hours 40 minutes)

Ingredients

- 4 cups of bread flour

- Half cup of cooked brown rice

- 1 and a half teaspoons of salt

- 1 and 1/4 cups of warm (110 F) water

- 2 and a ¼ teaspoons of bread machine yeast

- 1 teaspoon of sugar

Instructions

- Place all ingredients into the bread machine in the suggested order by the manufacturer.

- Select basic cycle. Medium crust. Press start.

- Enjoy fresh bread.

6.6 Brown Rice & Cranberry Bread

(Prep time: 10 minutes | Total time: 3 hours 40 minutes)

Ingredients

- 1/4 cup of non-fat milk powder

- 2 tbsp. of liquid honey

- 1/8 tsp of black pepper

- 1 and 1/4 cup of water

- 1 tbsp. of olive oil

- 3 cups of bread flour

- 3/4 cup of cooked brown rice

- 1 and 1/4 tsp of salt

- 2/3 cup of dried cranberries

- 1/4 cup of pine nuts

- 3/4 tsp of celery seeds

- 1 tsp of bread machine

Instructions

- Add all ingredients, except cranberries, to the bread machine in the suggested order by the manufacturer.

- Select basic cycle. Crust to your liking. Press start. Add cranberries at the signal ingredient.

- Enjoy.

6.7 Italian Panettone

(Prep time: 10 minutes | Total time: 3 hours 40 minutes)

Ingredients

- Half tsp of rum

- 2 tbsp. of butter

- 2 whole eggs

- 1 tsp of lemon zest

- 1/4 tsp of salt

- 1/4 cup of granulated sugar

- 1 tsp of orange zest

- Sultana raisins: 1/4 cup

- Half tsp of anise seeds

- 2 and a half cups of all-purpose flour

- Half cup of water

- 1 and a 1/4 tsp of bread machine yeast

- 2 tbsp. of candied orange, finely diced

- 2 tbsp. of citron peel

- Toasted slivered almonds: 1/4 cup

Instructions

- Add all ingredients, except raisins, peel, and nuts, to the bread machine in the manufacturer's suggested order.

- Select basic bread cycle. Press start.

- Add remaining ingredients at the ingredient signal.

- Before the baking cycle begins, brush with melted butter and let it bake.

- Enjoy fresh bread.

6.8 Italian Bread

(Prep time: 10 minutes | Total time: 3 hours 40 minutes)

Ingredients

- 1 and a half cup of water

- 1 and a half tsp of salt

- 4 and 1/4 cup of bread flour

- 2 tsp of bread machine yeast

- 2 Tbsp. of olive oil

- 2 Tbsp. of sugar

Instructions

- Add all ingredients to the bread machine in the suggested order by the manufacturer.

- Select basic cycle. Press start.

- Serve fresh bread.

Chapter 7: Bread & Other Bakery Products

7.1 Strawberry Jam

(Prep time: 10 minutes | Total time: 3 hours 10 minutes)

Ingredients

- 1 cup of sugar

- Half box of pectin

- 4 to 5 cups of fresh or frozen strawberries

Instructions

- Let the strawberries thaw and mash the berries, to make 3 cups. Mash as much chunky as you like, but preferably mash well.

- Add mashed berries, sugar, and pectin to the bread machine.

- Select jam cycle. Press start.

- After the jam has been made, let it cool in the machine for 30 to 45 minutes.

- Take it out into jars. Let it cool completely.

- Keep in the fridge overnight. Enjoy with freshly baked bread.

7.2 Tomato Sauce

(Prep time: 10 minutes | Total time: 3 hours 40 minutes)

Ingredients

- 1 tbsp. of olive oil

- 2 and ¾ cups of tomatoes (fresh and canned)

- Half tsp of garlic powder

- 1 tsp of sugar

- 1 tbsp. of onion powder

- Red-wine vinegar: a dash

Instructions

- Chop the tomatoes how much chunkier you like.

- Add all ingredients to the pan of the bread machine in the suggested order by the manufacturer.

- Select jam cycle and press start. Do not overfill your pan.

- Halfway through the process, with the help of a rubber spatula, scrape the sides of the pan.

- As the machine has completed the jam cycle, wait for it to cool down.

- Then blend in a blender to your desired texture.

- Adjust seasoning by adding any herbs or salt and pepper.

- Store in a jar.

- Serve with fresh bread and olive oil.

7.3 Apple pie

(Prep time: 10 minutes | Total time: 3 hours 10 minutes)

Ingredients

- 1 and 1/4 cups of apple pie filling

- Half cup of water

- 1 and a half teaspoons of salt

- 1 and a half tablespoons of butter

- 3 and 1/4 cups of flour

- 1 and a half teaspoons of yeast

- 3 tablespoons of dry buttermilk

- 1 and a half teaspoons of cinnamon

Instructions

- Add all ingredients to the bread machine in the suggested order by the manufacturer.

- Select sweet bread cycle—press start.

- Enjoy.

7.4 Blueberry Jam

(Prep time: 10 minutes | Total time: 3 hours 40 minutes)

Ingredients

- 1 Tbsp. of no sugar pectin

- 2 and a half cups of granulated sugar

- 5 cups of blueberries

Instructions

- If using frozen blueberries, let them thaw and mash them in a food processor.

- In a bowl, mix all ingredients and add to the pan of the bread machine.

- Select jam cycle and press start.

- Let it cool for half an hour in the machine. Pour into jars and let it rest for 3 hours.

- Keep in the fridge for four weeks.

7.5 Peach Jam

(Prep time: 10 minutes | Total time: 3 hours 40 minutes)

Ingredients

- 1 Tbsp. of no sugar pectin

- Ripe peaches: 4 cups, peeled and halved

- 2 cups of granulated sugar

Instructions

- Mash the ripe peaches with a masher. In a bowl, mix all ingredients and pour into the bread machine.

- Select jam or jelly cycle.

- Let the jam cool in the pan of the bread machine for half an hour.

- Pour into jars.

- Serve with fresh bread.

7.6 Grape Jelly

(Prep time: 10 minutes | Total time: 3 hours 40 minutes)

Ingredients

- 2 packets of Knox Gelatin

- 1 Tbsp. of lemon juice

- 2 cups of 100% grape juice

- 1 cup of sugar

Instructions

- Mix all ingredients in a bowl until sugar and gelatin dissolve.

- Add this into the pan of the bread machine.

- Select jam cycle.

- Let it cool for half an hour in the machine, then take it out.

- Pour into jars and serve with fresh bread.

7.7 Crab Apple Jelly

(Prep time: 10 minutes | Total time: 3 hours 40 minutes)

Ingredients

- 2 packets of Knox Gelatin

- 4 cups of Crabapple Juice

- 2 cups of sugar

Instructions

- Juice the apples by a juice or with a blender, add apples and water to blender and pulse and make it 4 cups. Add water to make 4 cups. Strain the juice.

- In a bowl, add all ingredients until gelatin and sugar dissolves.

- Select jam cycle and press start.

- Let it cool for half an hour in the machine, then take it out.

- Pour into jars and serve with fresh bread.

- Keep in the fridge for four weeks.

7.8 Pizza Dough

(Prep time: 10 minutes | Total time: 1 hour 40 minutes)

Ingredients

- 1 and a half tablespoons of vegetable oil

- 1 and a half teaspoons of salt

- 1 and a half teaspoons of active dry yeast

- 3 and 3/4 cups of bread flour

- 1 and a half cups of water

- 1 tablespoon + 1 teaspoon of sugar

Instructions

- Add all ingredients to the bread machine in the suggested order by the manufacturer.

- Select dough cycle. Press start.

- Let the oven preheat to 400 F.

- Take the dough out and roll it into one inch thick.

- Drizzle oil and let it rest for 10-15 minutes.

- Add pizza sauce and toppings of your choice.

- Bake for 20-25 minutes.

- Enjoy the fresh pizza.

Oven Recipes to Bread Machine

Conversion

The bread machine can label a 1-pound, 1.5 pounds, or 2-pound loaf. What it means is the "flour capacity." Review the manufacturer's booklet of the bread machine to calculate any individual bread machine's flour capability. You can check if the manufacturer's booklet calls for 3-4 cups of flour regularly, then it is your bread machine's capacity. Now you can convert oven recipes to bread machine recipes.

These are general flour capacities that yield a certain pound of bread loaf:

- The bread machine that yields 1-pound uses 2 or 2-3/4 cups of flour

- Bread machine that yields 1.5 pound uses 3-4 cups of flour

- Bread machine that yields 2-pound use 4 to 5 and a half cups of flour

Here are some measurements to help you convert the oven to bread machine recipes:

- Reduce the amount of yeast to 1 tsp

- for a 1.5-pound bread machine and

- 1 and 1/4 tsp.

- for a two-pound machine.

- Reduce the flour to three cups for a 1.5-pound bread machine and 4 cups for a 2-pound bread machine.

- Reduce the other ingredients as well, along with flour and yeast.

- If a recipe calls for 2 or different kinds of flour, add the flour quantities and use it to decrease the formula. The total amount of flour used can be either 3 -4 cups based on the bread's size.

- Use 1-3 tbsp. of gluten flour in a bread machine with all-purpose flour, or only use bread flour, which is a better option. If you are using any rye flour, must combine with 1 tbsp. of gluten flour if even the base is bread flour.

- All ingredients should be at room temperature and added to the bread machine in the manufacturer's suggested order.

- Add any nuts, raisins, dried fruits to the ingredient signal, or as the manufacturer's booklet specifies.

- If you are using only dough cycle, try to handle the dough with a little more flour after taking out from the machine, so it will be easy to handle.

- Use the whole-grain cycle if the bread machine has one, for whole-wheat, rye, and any grain flour.

- Always try to keep the recipe or any additional changes made to the recipe safe for future references.

- Use the sweet bread cycle with a light crust for rich and sweet bread.

Conversion Tables

Here are some conversion tables to help you measure recipes accurately.

FLOUR

¼ cup = 32 g
⅓ cup = 43 g
½ cup = 64 g
⅔ cup = 85 g
¾ cup = 96 g
1 cup = 128 g

BUTTER

¼ cup = 57 g
⅓ cup = 76 g
½ cup = 113 g
⅔ cup = 142 g
¾ cup = 171 g
1 cup = 227 g

SUGAR

¼ cup = 50 g
⅓ cup = 67 g
½ cup = 100 g
⅔ cup = 134 g
¾ cup = 150 g
1 cup = 201 g

BROWN SUGAR

¼ cup = 45 g
⅓ cup = 60 g
½ cup = 90 g
⅔ cup = 120 g
¾ cup = 130 g
1 cup = 180 g

ICING SUGAR

¼ cup = 30 g
⅓ cup = 45 g
½ cup = 60 g
⅔ cup = 75 g
¾ cup = 90 g
1 cup = 120 g

COCOA POWDER

¼ cup = 30 g
⅓ cup = 45 g
½ cup = 60 g
⅔ cup = 75 g
¾ cup = 90 g
1 cup = 120 g

LIQUID

¼ cup = 60 ml
⅓ cup = 90 ml
½ cup = 120 ml
⅔ cup = 150 ml
¾ cup = 180 ml
1 cup = 240 ml

CUPS	TBSP	TSP	ML
1	16	48	250
3/4	12	36	175
2/3	11	32	150
1/2	8	24	125
1/3	5	16	70
1/4	4	12	60
1/8	2	6	30
1/16	1	3	15

If you want to double the recipes:

Original Recipe	Double Recipe
1/8 tsp	1/4 tsp
1/4 tsp	1/2 tsp
1/2 tsp	1 tsp
3/4 tsp	1 1/2 tsp
1 tsp	2 tsp
1 Tbsp	2 Tbsp
2 Tbsp	4 Tbsp or 1/4
1/8 cup	1/4 cup
1/4 cup	1/2 cup
1/3 cup	2/3 cup
1/2 cup	1 cup
2/3 cup	1 1/3 cups
3/4 cup	1 1/2 cups
1 cup	2 cups
1 1/4 cup	2 1/2 cups
1 1/3 cup	2 2/3 cups
1 1/2 cup	3 cups
1 2/3 cup	3 1/3 cups
1 3/4 cup	3 1/2 cups

<u>Conclusion</u>

Everybody is occupied in this busy day and age, but no one has time to bake bread from scratch, but with a bread machine, you only have to add precisely measured ingredients, and it will bake you fresh bread. The bread machine is easy to use. If one doesn't have the time to practice and have little training, but you also want fresh bread, this really is the machine for you. The bread machine can easily turn you into a baker. You will save money, time, be in charge of the food (the food that goes into your body), and eat fresh food. The bread maker does all the labor of kneading the dough and avoids the trial and error involved with the dough's readiness. To combine and knead the bread dough, one can use a stand mixer or a food processor. But you are offered the choice of completing the baking by the bread maker. So, it's a handy appliance that saves time.

Making the bread allows you to control over the products, as opposed to buying prepared bread. The bread machines are enjoyed by many, solely for the diet element. You get to select the ingredients, monitor or use substitutes for starch, milk, and other components with a bread machine. You will ensure the family a no-preservative product with a bread machine. Many people enjoy their machines for bread and jams and will not be without one. As gluten-free bread is often best when baked in the machine, many gluten-free diets consider this an indispensable appliance. For some, it appears like the excitement of baking fresh bread from scratch wears off easily. The entire thing is rendered so much simpler by the bread machine. Place the ingredients into the bread maker, push start, select the cycle you want, and that's all one has to do. The kitchen remains tidy, and waiting for the fresh bread to be ready is all that's you have left to do.

The schedule becomes critical if you bake bread regularly and despite the rigorous routine that most of us maintain and know so well. There are many benefits of using a bread machine. Most bread machines would have built-in times to avoid mixing, enable to rise, punch down the dough, and so on. Bread Machines will bake bread as well, clearly, but mixers can't. With its many benefits, jams, jellies, and sauces may also be made.

Bread machines are very useful. For all the reasons, I would certainly suggest it. The pros outweigh the cons, and you can enjoy delicious freshly baked bread with many flavors any time you want.

Recipe Index

1

100 Percent Whole-Wheat Bread · 31

A

Almond Flour Yeast Bread · 92
Almond Milk Bread · 93
Apple pie · 105
Aromatic Lavender Bread · 37

B

Basic Low-Carb Bread · 90
Basic Sourdough Bread · 70
Black Olive Bread · 60
Blueberry Jam · 106
Brown Rice & Cranberry Bread · 97
Brown Rice Bread · 96

C

Cheddar Cheese Basil Bread · 52
Cheesy Chipotle Bread · 48
Chocolate Chip Peanut Butter Banana Bread · 87
Chocolate Sour Cream Bread · 89
Cinnamon Swirl Bread · 41
Crab Apple Jelly · 109
Cranberry Pecan Sourdough · 72

D

Dark Chocolate Sourdough · 74

E

Eggnog Bread · 86
Everyday White Bread · 27

F

Feta Oregano Bread · 56
Fragrant Herb Bread · 33

G

Gluten-Free White Bread · 94
Grape Jelly · 108

H

Honey Whole-Wheat Bread · 29
Honey-Spice Egg Bread · 39

I

Italian Bread · 100
Italian Panettone · 98

J

Jalapeño Corn Bread · 53

L

Lemon Poppy Seed Bread · 80

M

Market Seed Bread · 47
Molasses Wheat Bread · 30
Multigrain Bread · 44

P

Panettone Bread · 82
Peach Jam · 107
Pizza Dough · 110

R

Raisin Bran Bread · 78
Rich Cheddar Bread · 54
Roasted Garlic Asiago Bread · 50
Robust Date Bread · 61
Rosemary Bread · 34

S

Sauerkraut Rye Bread · 64
Savory Onion Bread · 66
Simple Sourdough Starter (No-Yeast
    whole wheat Sourdough Starter) · 68
Spicy Cajun Bread · 36

Strawberry Jam · 101

T

Toasted Pecan Bread · 46
Tomato Sauce · 103
Traditional Italian Bread · 33; 34; 36;
    37; 39; 41; 43; 44; 46; 47; 48; 50; 52;
    53; 54; 56; 58; 60; 61; 62; 64; 66; 68;
    70; 72; 74; 76; 78; 80; 82; 84; 86; 87;
    89; 90; 92; 93; 94; 96; 97; 98; 100

W

Warm Spiced Pumpkin Bread · 58
White Chocolate Cranberry Bread · 84
Whole-Wheat Seed Bread · 43

Y

Yeasted Carrot Bread · 62

Z

Zucchini Pecan Bread · 76

CPSIA information can be obtained
at www.ICGtesting.com
Printed in the USA
BVHW090320020621
608480BV00005B/917

'DANGEROUS WATERS'

THE LIFE OF ADMIRAL WILLIAM BLIGH

Copyright Nigel Barnes 2018

CONTENTS

Introduction

One.   A Smell of the Sea   7

Two.   Toote and Bry   17

Three.   A Taste of Powder   41

Four.   Scudding Before The Foresail   50

Five   A *Tyo* of Otaheite   73

Six.   Sharks   91

Seven   The Ever-Rolling Ocean   104

Eight   'Prosper Therefore Our Undertakings'   126

Nine.   The Rocky Road   146

Ten.   That *Bounty* Bastard   155

Eleven.   A Very Delicate Business   168

Twelve.   Heart of Oak   175

Thirteen.   Blind Eye   184

Fourteen.   A Question of Rum   191

Fifteen.   In Limbo   211

Sixteen.   Finem Respice   221

Footnotes   *231*

Bibliography   *241*

This book is for Aoife, Andy and Dylan

Introduction

Everyone in the English-speaking world surely knows about 'Captain Bligh' and the Mutiny on the *Bounty*. It is the story of a sadistic ship's Captain against whom the crew mutinied under the valorous leadership of Fletcher Christian. The story has been immortalised in book and in several movie adaptations. The figure of William Bligh has become a by-word for cruelty and oppression.

The mutiny did, of course, occur - on 28 April 1789. Fletcher Christian was the ringleader. The facts of the case have been mulled over and repeated ad nauseam, but the usual reason has been put down to Bligh's unacceptable behaviour. However, there may be other factors which have largely been ignored and it is important to consider all angles before denouncing the Captain. What were examples of his sadistic behaviour? How did the dissatisfaction reach its head? What really happened?

The mutiny was only one small part of William Bligh's long and varied career. In that time he held various positions at sea and even acted as a Governor. By the time he was laid to rest he had reached the heights of Rear Admiral and that in itself was a measure of the esteem in which he was held. How much that was deserved is the integral part of this book and covers his life from his early days in Plymouth to his death in London.

Bligh began his career at any early age as Captain's boy; but a ship might not have been the best milieu for a child of tender years. This was the eighteenth century and the Navy was a different concept to today's. Press-gangs prowled about the city street. Serious offences on board ship could result in execution by hanging from the yard-arm, now that keel-hauling had been banned. More minor offences would earn the lash. A long voyage was a major undertaking which ran the risk of disease and attack from hostile tribes. Navigation was performed using the crudest instruments. Geographical knowledge was patchy and, on voyages of discovery, sometimes non-existent. Apart from ambitious naval ratings, ships could be a good place for those wishing to escape, including cut-throats and thieves. Food could run short or be weevil-ridden. Life on the seven seas was not easy.

Work could also be difficult and besides the tedious jobs of scrubbing down the masts, ratings would be expected to climb high into the masts to unfurl canvas in the worst of conditions. As Samuel Johnson wryly observed: 'No man will be a sailor who has contrivance enough to get himself into a jail; for being in a ship is being in a jail, with the chance of being drowned.' The cabin was once described as 'a dark, cramped space frequently awash with sea water and infested with vermin.' A sailor's lot was rarely a happy one.

To some young men – usually born from privilege – the Navy was a career. For them the ship was a floating college and here they would be taught the intricacies of sailing and navigation. These men would graduate from boy to Midshipman and then on to various grades of Lieutenant, eventually aiming at the envied title of Ship's Captain. The general rule was – the more influence you had, the faster you would climb.

As for Bligh, he was an ambitious man and an ambitious man in the 18th century Navy needed patronage. Some men had climbed the ladder despite their humble origins – one such was James Cook – but these exceptions were rare. Bligh himself had no relatives in the upper echelons and so had to carve for himself. The nearest he got to such help was Joseph Banks, son of a Member of Parliament and eminent botanist who had been elected as a member of the Royal Society and who had accompanied Cook on his first voyage of discovery. Apart from that, Bligh had to slowly climb by his own deserts.

Although Bligh was accused of sadism, severity was the most common link between sea Captains. Cook himself was well known for his fiery tongue and use of the lash. The Captain was the figurehead of the ship and responsible for maintaining order and discipline. On a ship whose complement may include men from unsavoury backgrounds, discipline became all-important. Bligh – like all other Captains – did not flinch from meting out punishment, but whether this was excessive remains to be seen.

In writing this book I have used many sources. For Cook's voyages, the main reference has been his own accounts as written down in his published books. As for Bligh, I have used his own log-books for the two breadfruit voyages and his *A Narrative Of The Mutiny, On Board His Majesty's Ship Bounty; And The Subsequent Voyage Of Part Of The Crew, In The Ship's Boat* – as well as other accounts of the voyages. A standard reference for the life of Bligh was Mackaness, George, *The Life of Vice-Admiral William Bligh* and *An Historical and Statistical Account of New South Wales* by John D Lang was invaluable for historical documentation on the Australian era. The ancestry of Bligh was based on public records searches. All other references are catalogued in the Bibliography, which include many works on Bligh to which I am indebted.

Chapter One. A Smell Of The Sea

The animals might not have entered the vessel two by two, but as the hogs, horses, sheep, rabbits, cattle – even a peacock and a peahen from the King's farm – were herded across the gangplank, it must have seemed like Noah's ark all over again. Bags of hay, corn and other fodder followed them down into the hold and the whole menagerie took up valuable space – which was extremely irritating to the Captain. Beasts were valuable in themselves as a source of food and on a voyage as long as this one, nourishment could be hard to come by – particularly fresh meat. The Captain knew all about husbanding provisions – he had had enough experience. But while a number would be used for the worthwhile cause of cultivating a species, many were gifts sent by persons of some political clout and could hardly be refused. A great voyage needed patronage and sometimes you had to bear with their whims. He had no choice but to bear with his floating zoo and make the best of things.

This was to be his third great voyage. No-one had forced his hand. He had been offered a comfortable sinecure at the Royal Hospital, Greenwich, to take a well-earned rest and earn a leisurely living in semi-retirement. But national heroes cannot be ignored and when the third voyage was mooted, he was called in to advise on the choice of officers best suited to a task of this magnitude. It was 9 January 1776 and attended by some of the most august personages in the Admiralty: the First Lord, the Earl of Sandwich, John Montagu; the Comptroller Sir Hugh Pallister and the Secretary Philip Stephens. It was only months after the Captain had returned from one of the most gruelling voyages in history, but the sea was in his blood and he – as well as the rest of the meeting – knew perfectly well who the most suitable candidate for Leader of the Expedition was.

He was in a quandary. Certainly, he had earned his retirement – few people had travelled as far as he and had suffered greater hardships. But the sea was in his heart and was his life-blood – could he truly step back and give it up? What would his life be without his ship? He listened to the discussion around the table and made up his mind. After a short pause, the Captain stood and stated that – if it met the approval of them all – he himself would be willing to once again act as Commander. The cheers rose in the hall, as this is precisely what they all had hoped for – and what the Captain had intended. The committee agreed to provide two ships for the purpose. It was decided that Captain Clerke should command the other vessel, but there was a serious hitch – he was in prison. Still, it was through no fault of his own – he had been committed for his brother's debts – and he would be freed within six months or so. No-one knew that before his time was up – in the unsanitary conditions of the clink – he would contract consumption. Great influence did not affect the chains of justice; Clerke was doomed to languish until his term was out.

The Captain, a Yorkshireman by birth, had clawed his way up the ladder of success the hard way – he entered the Navy in June 1755 and was involved in Canadian offensives against the Fort of Louisberg, the siege of Quebec City and the Battle of the Plains of Abraham. Cartography was a particular love of his and during his many adventures he had charted the entrance to St Lawrence River as well as the coast of Newfoundland. Fame arrived with his First Voyage of Discovery – which lasted from August 1768 until July 1771.[1] He rounded Cape Horn and arrived at Tahiti where he observed the transit of Venus. At the Society Islands he discovered the breadfruit plant, but was not impressed:

The eatable part lies between the skin and the core; it is as white as snow, and somewhat of the consistence of new bread: it must be roasted before it is eaten, being first divided into three or four parts. Its taste is insipid, with a slight sweetness somewhat resembling that of the crumb of wheaten bread mixed with a Jerusalem artichoke. [2]

Little did he know what would be the impact of this seemingly trivial discovery.

Sealed further orders had him searching the South Pacific for signs of the fabled southern continent *Terra Australis*. He mapped New Zealand and was the first European to encounter the East coast of Australia, entering a bay he named Stingray Bay and afterwards Botany Bay after the specimens brought back by Joseph Banks and Daniel Solander. He met his first Aborigine tribe, the Gweagal. After the *Endeavour* was grounded on the Great Barrier Reef, they repaired it on shore, sailed through the Torres Straits and landed on Possession Island. He made for home via Batavia (Jakarta) after rounding the Cape of Good Hope.

When his account of the *Voyage* was published, the Captain was launched to celebrity status. Between 1772 and 1775 he undertook another arduous Voyage, again to search for *Terra Australis*. His ship was the *Resolution*, accompanied by the *Adventure* commanded by Tobias Furneaux. The ships circumnavigated the world at an extreme southerly latitude. Fog separated the two ships and the *Adventure* went to New Zealand but after men were killed by Maori they sailed home. The Captain, now alone, almost succeeded in his mission but turned when close to Antarctica then sailed to Tahiti to resupply. He would never know how close he came to discovering the new continent, but it made little practical difference – it was hardly the land of plenty is was once predicted to be.

At Tahiti, he allowed a native, Omai, to come with him and on his return voyage to New Zealand in 1774, they landed at the Friendly Islands, Easter Island, Norfolk Island, New Caledonia, and Vanuatu. Before returning to England, the Captain made one more sweep through the South Atlantic from Cape Horn and surveyed, mapped and took possession for Britain of South Georgia, which had been explored by Anthony de la Roché in 1675. He also discovered and named Clerke Rocks and the South Sandwich Islands. The ship then turned north to South Africa and from there continued back to England.

These expeditions were the stuff of legend and they were known in every castle and cot of England. Up until that time, the British view of the planet in which they lived had been a depressingly narrow one and rarely went beyond the limits if their town or village. Now the reading public could not get enough of books of discovery where strange lands and tribal customs were brought to them in vivid detail. The world had been proven to be a round one and sailors had even circumnavigated it. Cook became a legend in his own lifetime.

Now came the greatest challenge of all – to find the elusive North-West Passage which had escaped every explorer to date. It was not a new enterprise – as early as 1497 John Cabot had sailed off in the *Matthew* and discovered the coastline of Labrador and Newfoundland, then between 1576 and 1606 Martin Frobisher, John Davis, Henry Hudson and William Baffin all named bays or straits after themselves, but failed to find a way through to the Pacific. Others followed; but surely if anyone could find a way through, it was this hero of two voyages of discovery. Of course, the Admiralty kept the goal top secret, only stating that it was a trip to take Omai home to Tahiti. There was little time for the Captain to sort out his affairs; he had to sit for several portraits and most importantly put the finishing touches to the long-awaited book, *A Second Voyage round the World ... by James Cook, Esq. Commander of His Majesty's Bark The* Resolution.

There were other urgent things to consider, not least, the crew. The choice of First Lieutenant was an easy one. John Gore – who was American, possibly from Virginia - had twice circumnavigated the globe: first, under John Byron when he acted as Master's mate and under Samuel Wallis, when the crew discovered Tahiti. Both voyages were on board the *Dolphin*. He had also had been third in command of the *Endeavour* on his First Expedition, rising to second after the death of Zachary Hicks. On that voyage he also had the dubious honour of being the first man to kill two newly-discovered living things – a man of Maori descent and a kangaroo. Cook would have taken him on his Second Voyage but he was sailing with

Joseph Banks on a private journey to Iceland. For his Second Lieutenant, Cook looked for a man of astronomical skills, as someone with skill at the sextant would be invaluable to him in his surveying work. Having served under several masters – including Cook's friend and patron, Commodore Hugh Palliser – King passed his Lieutenant's exam and was promoted to that rank in 1771. Later he took time off to study science at Paris and Corpus Christi, Oxford, where he met Thomas Hornsby, Savilian Professor of Astronomy, who recommended him to Cook. The Third Lieutenant was Irish-born John Williamson, who was something of a bully; and there was also William Harvey, a level-headed, steady-handed officer who had served on both of the previous voyages. The last of the Lieutenants was James Burney, whose father Charles was a composer and his sister Fanny a novelist. He had joined Cook on the Second Voyage, befriended Omai and acted as his interpreter on their return to England.

Perhaps the biggest surprise was the appointment of a relative unknown for the post of Sailing Master. Many have queried how an inexperienced young man like William Bligh, with few connections, could have landed himself the plum job before even passing his Lieutenant's examination. Ideally, Cook would have been looking for three things from his Master: a knowledge of the South Seas, a talent for cartography and a man of maritime experience. It is generally assumed that Bligh had little of any of these, so to assess his potential we need to go to the very start of his career at sea.

It takes us to a small child of seven years old, who enrolled on the *Monmouth* as a 'Captain's servant'. The *Monmouth* was almost a legend in itself, having a fine history as a battleship:

'There was no ship she ever chased that she did not overtake: there was no enemy she ever fought that she did not capture.' [3]

The ship was first launched in 1667 and while it had three rebuilds, it participated in no less than ten sea battles. Although she would only have five years left when little William walked her gangplank, she had just done service under Captain John Storr and returned to Plymouth after he had relinquished its command. The new commander, Keith Stewart, had just become a Member of Parliament but had been offered a Captaincy on condition he relinquished the post, so he left politics after only a few months and embarked on what would be a successful career back in the Royal Navy.

What filled the boy's head with dreams of a sea life? His father was a Customs Commissioner in the town and the lad must have heard him talking on many occasions to his friends, most of whom would have had naval connections. There were many conversations which must have fuelled his imagination – tales of great voyages and pirates, stories of sea battles and wars as well as the deeds of smugglers whose hidden caves peppered the south-west. The struggle between the smugglers and the Customs and Excise was a long and troubled one, often leading to pitched night-battles when the criminals were caught in the act. William would have heard all the news at the family hearthside.

There was much to hear and most of it revolved around the conflict between England and France. These two old arch-enemies were now arguing over colonial interests, particularly in India and America and dragging their trusted allies along with them. In 1751 Robert Clive took action against French interests in India; and in the year William Bligh was born, armed hostilities broke out between English and French territories in America. Resentment grew between the two nations until France at last decided that invasion was the only alternative. Troops began to mass along the English Channel, awaiting a fleet to carry them across to Britain.

When William was five years of age, the whole country was buzzing with excitement. 1759 was the year of spectacular triumphs, England's *annus mirabilis*. The French armies could be shipped to England by one of two fleets – one docked in Toulon, the other at Brest. The Toulon ships left port during August and cruised past Gibraltar then headed north. Here it was intercepted and defeated by Edward Boscawen. In November the Brest fleet left dock and was confronted by the English commander, Edward Hawke, in Quiberon Bay, were it was all but destroyed. Across the Atlantic, in September, Wolfe spectacularly captured Quebec. The flood of good news made Walpole quip:

'We are forced to ask every morning what victory there has been, for fear of missing one.' [4]

Quite apart from the political cauldron in which England was living, the eighteenth century turned to the sea for adventure and education. If England was a nation of shopkeepers, at least the middle and upper classes were a nation of travellers, and it was the fashionable thing for the cultured classes to take the air around Europe. Such a thing might have been commendable – it had been *de rigueur* since Shakespeare's day – but the sheer extent of the fashion beggared belief, such much so that it was meat and drink to the satirists of the day. The Englishman abroad was an object of curiosity away and mockery at home. There were other travellers who fared better – the explorers who suffered the hardships of the ocean to discover new countries, to explore navigable passages and to extend trade beyond the known world. These heroes were lauded by the press and the public and stood alongside the generals and admirals who carried the union flag throughout the nations.

It was England at the peak of its jingoism – *Rule Britannia* was still a relatively new song and a very popular one at that. [5] It was a time when she was spreading her wings to conquer an Empire which she would rule with a fist of iron. The key to success was ruling the waves and this is what she determined to do.

In his own small way, so did William. After all, his home was Plymouth, of which Celia Fiennes had written:

The streets are good and clean. There are a great many though some are but narrow. They are mostly inhabited by seamen and those which have affairs of the sea.

On the harbour, she said:

The mouth of the river is a very good harbour for ships, the dockyards are about 2 miles from the town. It is one of the best in England, a great many good ships are built there. [6]

Plymouth had a natural advantage here, lying at the bottom of a large bay, and its maritime reputation went before it. The Hawkins family used it as their main port; William for his exploration of the West Indies; his son John for the more dubious trading in slaves; and his grandson Richard who used it as a setting for *Westward Ho!* Francis Drake was Mayor here and played bowls on the Hoe (it is said) before strolling off to mop up the Spanish armada. The smell of the sea affected all of its people and employed most of them. They were swallowed up in the Royal Navy, the merchant ships, in fishing – or in smuggling, the bane of the south-west and, consequently, William's father.

On 1 July 1762, William Bligh was entered in the *Monmouth*'s records as 'Wm Blyth, Captain's servant'. [7] It was nothing unusual for the Captain to have a servant, mostly sons of relatives or friends, although some abused the system by inventing names in what was termed an 'imaginary muster' – punishable by dismissal, at least in theory. Captain Stewart chose William, possibly because he was in some way related to his mother, possibly because his father's friends held some naval sway. The ship's surgeon, John Bond, had married William's half-sister (and his cousin) Catherine and he might also have exerted some influence.

A Captain's boy was not a position for the *hoi polloi* and boys so chosen were intended for the quarter-deck and expected to rise through the officers' ranks. Should the boy's dreams have been enveloped in the sea – as is likely – then a naval future might have seemed just the thing and it would have done no harm to give him a taste of the life in a lowly capacity. On most ships – certainly on the 66-gun *Monmouth* – there were teachers whose task it was to educate the boys and give them a thorough grounding in basic topics as well as those relating to a ship. It is possible that William received such lessons, but not for long – he was discharged in 21 February 1763, only seven months after he had joined. It was enough to give him a glimpse of naval life, although, apart from possible outings into the Channel, the *Monmouth* did not leave dock.

There is now a nine-year gap in William's history and it is a tantalising one. Did he remain on board His Majesty's ships to learn his trade through the schoolmasters there? Or did he join the local school, possibly the Free Grammar School? There is another alternative – he might have joined the forty candidates at the small Naval Academy, open to embryonic naval officers. After his experience on board the *Monmouth,* it might have been an attractive proposition. Whatever happened, William emerged with a sound knowledge of the three Rs, as is evident in his writings and his later expertise in surveying and cartography suggests a thorough grounding in the subjects; whether he had acquired these as part of his schooling or through practical experience is a matter for conjecture.

One story of his childhood has been transmitted. When he was a boy he was helping his father to catch a horse; his father threw a hatchet to stop it but it accidentally struck William on his face. He carried that scar on his cheek from that time on. [8]

Although his career was not yet settled, there was no doubt that it was dictated by the sea. The short period of service had whetted his appetite and he must have watched the brave ships coming and going with something like awe. When he was twelve, a large ship pulled into port, one which was about to embark on a great voyage of adventure around the world. It was called the *Endeavour* and its Captain was James Cook, a name soon to become almost legendary.

After the death of his mother, William re-joined the Royal Navy when he was fifteen, serving on the *HMS Hunter* – a ten-gun sloop - from 27 July 1770. Bligh saw little active service – the *Hunter* spent her time cruising around the Irish Sea, skirting the Isle of Man and appearing at Liverpool and Dublin Bay. [9] Within seven months he had been promoted to Midshipman, an incredible feat unless he had had experience on other ships or his term as Captain's servant had been taken into consideration. He could now proudly wear the uniform of a commissioned officer, with a badge of white cloth with a gold button and twists of white cord on each side of the coat collar. Midshipmen worked 'amidships', between the main and mizzen masts, and were expected to learn navigation and seamanship under a schoolmaster or a member of the crew such as a senior Master's mate. They would keep logs to be inspected by the Captain. Their duties would include taking charge of smaller boats, keeping watch, relaying messages between decks, commanding a sub-division (under supervision) and supervising gun batteries. They were also expected to prepare for their Lieutenant's examinations.[10]

'Mr Bligh' would also witness the strict discipline aboard ship. Captain John Henshaw meted out several floggings of a dozen lashes each, for desertion and on another occasion for striking and insulting an officer. Harsher penalties such as keel-hauling had been outlawed, but the death sentence still held for major crimes such as mutiny. As ABs (able bodied seamen) were culled from various – and often unsavoury – backgrounds, discipline was important to keep the ship running smoothly, and flogging was the most common penalty resorted to by Captains of the day, some more readily than others.

On 22 September 1771 Bligh joined the 32-gun *HMS Crescent*, again as Midshipman. Her Captain, a bull-headed man by the name of John Corner, had been commander of the *Rodney* and was involved in the first Boston revolt following the Townshend Acts, which imposed taxes on American goods. Now he was master of the *Crescent* and was sent on a mission to the West Indies, where the indigenous Caribs were revolting against British expansion on St Vincent. They were led by chieftain Joseph Chatoyer, who did well against the British troops, holding back the military expedition for surveying the windward part of the island. [11] When they preferred to keep their land rather than sell out to the British, the result was a major military assault with the purpose of deporting the troublesome natives from their land.

There was another problem for the *Crescent* to solve and that involved another of Britain's enemies, Spain. Crab Island lay near Porto Rico and recently a schooner, the *Betsy*, had been seized by the Spanish along with her crew. Corner was ordered to deliver a message to the Governor of San Juan demanding the return of both brig and seamen. Although Spain and Britain were not technically at war at that time, it was a mission which demanded tact and diplomacy, of which Corner had little.

Having sailed to Tenerife by 12 October, the ship reached Antigua on 15 November and pulled in for repairs. English Harbour was a much-feared place, cursed as it was with malaria and yellow fever. Having cruised round the West Indies – which must have been an eye-opener for Bligh – they reached San Juan on 27 December. Their reception was as cold as could have been expected. Governor Dan Miguel de Muesas was less than impressed with Britain's claim on Crab Island and soundly berated them for daring to land in his port. [12] The channel being narrow, an anchor hawser snapped and the ship damaged her keel and rudder.

In November 1772 the *Crescent* joined in the offensive against the Caribs, but Corner was to see no part of the action; he died and he was replaced by Captain Charles Thompson. The men secretly rejoiced at the loss of a commander who was such a strict disciplinarian and who meted out floggings under the least pretence; but their happiness was turned to dismay when Thompson ordered a lashing within one day of his tenure. In fact, Thompson was even more dedicated to the cat-o'-nine-tails than Corner, as the men would soon discover. This was not lost on the young

Midshipman who was experiencing his first overseas campaign.

While of Great Sable Island a wind blew the ship inshore but after anchoring her hull was struck and Thompson flew the signal of distress as the natives opened fire, which was returned from the decks.

Thompson decided that the only solution was a full assault of the natives which he planned for the next day. The morning proved that the bad weather had not abated but the Captain gave direction for the attack to go ahead despite the heavy waves which battered the ship. The boats were launched and struck for shore in heavy surf which was a perilous venture; the men faced bombardment from the enemy as well as the raging sea. Tragedy struck before the men even reached the shore; one of the boats overturned, drowning several men. The remainder did disembark, but their ammunition had become wet and useless in many cases and thus their firepower, which would have given them a distinct advantage, was rendered ineffective. Nonetheless the troops charged on, facing the wrath of the natives, but their ruthlessness and efficiency won out in the end; they managed to drive the Caribs from their encampments. It was a victory but at a bitter price.

Not all the marines felt that their actions against the Caribs were fully justified. On October 1772, one officer wrote in *The London Chronicle for the Year 1773*:

This expedition, little as you may think of it, will cost Great Britain above a million sterling besides the lives that will be lost, and the infamy that it will bring upon the national character to butcher a parcel of innocent savages in cold blood. [13]

In 1773 the British, under Sir William Young, conceded the windward side of St Vincent's to the natives. Despite this, even after this first Carib War closed, the *Crescent* spent the next year and a half cruising around the islands. Their task was to prevent communication between the Carib tribes but in June 1774 she sailed for home. This uneasy peace would continue until 1795, after which the Caribs were defeated in a savage and brutal war.

When the *Crescent* had landed back in England, there was to be no rest for young Bligh; on 2 September joined up with the *HMS Ranger* as AB – presumably there were no posts of Midshipman immediately available, although he was raised to that rank a month later. [14] This was possibly because the Captain already knew him – it was none other than Henshaw again. During this time the ship was based in the Isle of Man and while Bligh did not go on another exotic adventure the ship had an important role – the American Revolution had finally broken out and the *Ranger* was ordered to stop and search any vessel suspected of carrying information or goods to America.

Bligh also had another taste of naval discipline. On 7 November 1774, at Douglas, a man was executed on board the *Albion* for desertion. [15] Just before Bligh was paid off, Henshaw retired due to ill health and was replaced by Captain R Wills.

Bligh had one prize on his mind – passing his Lieutenant's examination. It was the qualification he needed to rise up in the ranks and become what he wanted to be beyond anything else – a ship's Captain. Studying for the examination was not easy – there was no fixed syllabus and the questions were at the discretion of the individual Captains who asked them. Those who passed did not automatically become Lieutenants – much depended on who the candidate knew – but there was the chance of promotion to Master which was usually the stepping-stone to the lieutenancy. Bligh sat his examination early in 1776.

Nothing is known of his cartography skills, or his knowledge of hydrography and surveying, but taking his future abilities into account it is clear he had had quite some experience and that had not gone unnoticed. It is quite possible that he had charted the coastlines during his voyage to the Indies; indeed there were little other opportunities for him to chart foreign lands. It would have been an integral part of his job. Whether he had examples of his work is not known, but his efforts must have been of high quality and of high value for others wishing to explore the region. News of this promising young officer-in-training had reached the ears of James Cook and he might well have seen the maps for himself. He was certainly impressed enough to consider him for the role of Master on board the *Discovery*. A good cartographer was just what he was looking for.

Whatever the reason, Cook considered that 'under my direction (he) could be usefully employed in constructing charts, in taking views of the coasts and headlands near which we should pass, and in drawing plans of the bays and harbours in which we should anchor.' [16]

There was one other very important event in Bligh's life which needs to be recorded. While on the Isle of Man, in Douglas, Bligh socialised with a number of local dignitaries, the most important being Richard Betham, an academic who was the Water Bailiff for the Island as well as the Collector of Customs. A graduate of Glasgow University, Betham counted Adam Smith (*The Wealth of Nations*), Joseph Black the chemist and David Hume the philosopher among his friends. The Excise linked Betham with Francis Bligh and might have been the subject of conversation between them, but Bligh's main interest lay in his second daughter Elizabeth. After the dawn of 1776, there was 'an understanding' between them.

By May he had discovered that he had been chosen as Master to sail under Cook, an offer he would have been insane to refuse. On the 2nd of that month he passed his Certificate and was ready for another adventure. He knew that he would be separated from his beloved Elizabeth ('Betsy') for three years but she was determined to wait for him. It might be that Betham had decided to wait until Bligh had proven himself in the Navy before consenting to their union; at any rate he left her behind in Douglas and made his way to take part in his first Voyage of Discovery under a national hero.

Chapter Two. Toote And Bry

'I am a native of St Tudy'.

So William Bligh said to his friend, the Rev Polwhele; but this was not strictly so. True, his ancestral home lay there, a Cornish pile named Tinten Manor House; but by birth Bligh was most likely a Devonian. No matter how much the people of Cornwall have wished to associate (or dissociate) themselves with his birthplace, the baptism is registered at St Andrew's Church, Plymouth where his parents were married in 1753.

That said, his ties with Cornwall are strong. However you wish to spell it - Bligh, Blighe, Blygh, Blyghe, Bleit, Blight or Bly – his forebears were set down as landowners in the Domesday Book and are known to have held estates in Cornwall during the reign of Edward III. In the late fourteenth century a John Blygh of Bodmin was a commissioner for the suppression of monasteries during the reign of Henry IV; and in 1524 a Richard Bligh of Bodmin signed a town petition against the Prior. During the sixteenth century four Blighs took the office of Mayor of Bodmin. It cannot be verified that any of these are related to William; but it would be a fair assumption that the great spider-web of genealogy connects each of them at some point of their family history.

The first direct link appears in 1472, when one Richard Bligh of Cornwall was born and later married Isabel Tankred, from which union, ten generations later, William would derive. Richard, his son John and his grandson Thomas were all born in Cornwall, but things changed when Thomas Bligh married a Devon girl, Joane Newcourt. It might have been that Thomas had moved there to further his fortunes, but whatever the reason, the next three generations of Blighs – John, Richard and James – were all born in the Devon village of Holdsworthy. At this point, near the beginning of the seventeenth century, James moved back to Cornwall, settling in the village of St Mabyn with his wife Loveday Worthevale. Here were born his son Richard and his grandson John.

It was John Bligh – William's great grandfather - who took possession of

Tinten Manor House, the first of Bligh's line to do so. The building was a large farmhouse house in St Tudy, a small village which would take a crow six miles to reach from the town of Bodmin. The parish – and hamlet - were named after Tudy of Landevennec who was a Breton saint of the 5th or 6th century and grew up around an old Celtic cemetery, God's Acre. It boasted a beautiful parish church dating from Norman times and extensively rebuilt in the 15th century.

There was more to Tudy than ancient history. Myth surrounded the parish and at Damelioc stood, it is said, King Arthur's castle, where Gothlios fortified himself against the army of Uther Pendragon. Even before then there were the Merry Maidens, girls who were turned to stone for laughing at St Tudy then dancing and singing on a Sunday. [2] Apart from a mythos which had enveloped the village, there was a practical side – twice a year there was a fair – mostly for cattle – which were held on 20 May and 14 September. Those farmers with the best stock would compete with others in the locality at Bodmin Show.

The manor house which became the Bligh possession - Tinten – was named after the family which flourished in ancient times – Sir Johannes Tynten was a knight under Edward II – but passed under the Duchy of Cornwall in 1540. It may not have been a castle, but the Manor was an impressive building and more than enough to rank him alongside the most successful of the Blighs, who had become naval officers, lawyers, civil servants, clerics and university students. John married one Mary Watts and went on to have five daughters and four sons, the first named after himself and the second called Richard. John Bligh died when his eldest was twenty years of age, but it was Richard who eventually took over Tinten Manor and would marry a widow named Jane Cock, daughter of Reginald Cock of St Breward. They had eight children, John, Reginald, Richard, James, Francis, William, Joseph and Mary. [3]

Francis Bligh, the fifth son, was born 7 March 1721. He was brought up at Tinten, but having completed his education he looked around for a worthwhile profession, finally settling on the Revenue. As a young man, he left Cornwall to find a career in HM Customs in Plymouth. He took a wife in 1753, a widow Jane Pearce whose maiden name was Balsam. Unlike his father and grandfather, he settled on a small family of Martha, William and Mary. He was successful in his career and a well-known figure in town, with his distinctive carriage and its yellow wheels.

Francis Bligh's only son, William, was born at one in the morning on 9 September 1754 but there has been much controversy over where. That much is proven by a note to that effect in Francis' family Bible. The baptism is registered at St Andrew's Church, Plymouth, on 4 October, although some argue that the birth and took place in St. Tudy Church (where there is a family plaque) or in St Nicholas Chapel which was part of

Tinten Manor. The only evidence seems to be Polwhele's statement that Bligh stated he was a native of that village, although William Bligh always put his place of birth as Plymouth in later years. One solution could be that Jane Bligh had the child at St Tudy, then hurried down to Plymouth for the baptism. This assumes that she returned to Cornwall for the delivery; but the facts suggest that William was both born and baptised in Devon. [4]

Nothing is known of William's earliest years, but living in Plymouth he would have seen little of his family's ancestral home, although it is impossible that he was not taken to Tinten on holidays to meet his near relatives and to play among the twelve acres of land there. It must have been a pleasant change to see the woodlands and orchards of the Cornish countryside, in contrast to the town and its maze of narrow laneways. It is true that few areas of Cornwall are outside a day's journey to the sea; but to William the sea was the main part of his life, waxing and waning in the great bay which was his home.

It would have been hard for the dreaming little boy to imagine that one day he would become Master on a great Voyage of Discovery, but at the age of twenty-two the grown-up young man had walked the gangplank of the *Resolution* and become a member of James Cook's crew. He even had his Master's mate, James Harvey, who had been a veteran of both the preceding voyages and whose experience would be a great fillip for the young Master. Although this sounds ridiculous, it must be remembered that Harvey had not passed his Lieutenant's Certificate and could not have expected much else.

On 8 June the Earl of Sandwich and Sir Hugh Palliser paid a visit to the ships, which set sail for the Nore a week later. The *Discovery* stayed there, awaiting her master Captain Clerke who was still detained 'in the Rules of the Bench', while James Burney sailed the *Resolution* on to Plymouth, but during the journey they hit a gale and had to pull in at Portland for repairs. The setback was a minor one and the ship arrived in Plymouth three days before Captain Cook arrived, accompanied by Omai on the 24th.

Cook's sealed orders did not arrive until 8 July so Bligh remained in his home town for the week and although it is not documented, it would be likely that he took the chance to say farewell to his family. The contents of the orders would hardly have surprised Cook, as he had helped in writing them; he was to sail via the Cape of Good Hope and investigate some island spotted by the French at 48° latitude; to land at New Zealand, if necessary; to take Omai home to Tahiti; and then to hunt for any river or inlet that might lead to the North-West Passage. The bounty of £20000 for any merchant ship discovering such a waterway had by now been extended to any ship bearing the British flag. On the 9th the marines arrived under the command of Lieutenant Molesworth Phillips; and on the

10th the crew received pay up until 30th June, while officers received two months' wages in advance. Then on 12 July the *Resolution* began her voyage.

Cook stopped off at Tenerife as planned and here he met Captain Baurdat, with whom he chewed the fat and compared notes. At one point Baurdat compared his timepieces with those of the *Resolution*. A famous trading port, Tenerife was the usual stop-off place for any ship venturing to the West Indies. It was a good place to stock up on supplies. Cook also bought a barrel of wine, and while finding the quality not as good as Madeira, yet the price was tempting - £12 for a cask as compared with £27 for Madeira. 1-18/9 The ship set sail again, but it was soon found that she had a problem - the repairs in Portland had been far from satisfactory and her seams had been badly caulked. As a result, the heat opened them up and water flowed through.

'Hardly a man that could lie dry in his bed; the officers in the gun-room were all driven out of their cabin by the water that came in through the sides.' [5]

There was little to be done immediately – the ship was on the high seas and was forced to await the next port of call. The Cape of Good Hope loomed up on 17 October and the Resolution – after weathering stormy weather – pulled in at Table Bay on the next day. Here Cook had the necessary repairs done on the ship and awaited the arrival of Captain Clerke and the *Discovery*, which anchored on 10 November. A refit was quickly performed and Cook bought supplies, including more livestock, which made the ship look even more like Noah's Ark – as one journalist commented. Now that the zoo was further augmented and the vessel put to rights, all was ready to resume the voyage.

The ships got under way on 3 December but three days later a sudden heavy squall cost the *Resolution* her mizzen topmast; but this was soon replaced. It had not been an encouraging beginning for Cook's ship, but things were to improve. On 12th December the islands discovered by Marion du Fresne and Crozet came into view and as they were not shown on the map, Cook named them Prince Edward's Islands. Soon there came an even worse danger – dense fog – so thick that one could not see more than two ship's lengths away at times. By the 24th it started to clear a little. Cook had not mentioned his opinion of Bligh during this time, but on this day he paid him a compliment which suggests he was far from displeased with his sailing Master:

At six o'clock in the morning, as we were steering to the eastward, the fog clearing away a little, we saw land, bearing South South East, which, upon a nearer approach, we found to be an island of considerable height, and about three leagues in circuit. Soon after, we saw another of

the same magnitude, one league to the Eastward; and between these two, in the direction of South East, some smaller ones. In the direction of South by East ½ East, from the East end of the first island, a third high island was seen ... We did but just weather the island last mentioned. It is a high round rock, which was named Bligh's Cap. Perhaps this is the same that Monsieur de Kerguelen called the Isle of Rendezvous; but I can see nothing that can rendezvous at it, but fowls of the air; for it is certainly inaccessible to every other animal. [6]

The next day they reached the Island of Kerguelen and they anchored to the entrance of Christmas Harbour. At this point the sea was forty-five fathoms deep, but Cook was an experienced Captain and he wanted someone to sound the harbour and ensure it was safe. Throughout the voyage, this fell to Bligh, as in this case, when he found it to be 'safe and commodious'. Soon after, Cook wished to explore Palliser Bay and he sent Bligh to sound the upper part of the harbour, while he himself sailed to the North point. Captain Clerke sent his own Master to survey the channel to the south of the small islands. Bligh returned after Cook with his report:

...He had been four miles up the harbour, and, as he judged, not far from the head of it. He found that its direction was West South West; and that its breadth, a little above the ships, did not exceed a mile; but grew narrower towards the head. The soundings were very irregular, being from thirty-seven to ten fathoms ... He landed on both shores, which he found barren and rocky, without the least signs of tree or shrub, and with very little verdure of any kind. [7]

Anderson, the surgeon, agreed and noted:
'Perhaps no place hitherto discovered in either hemisphere under the same parallel of latitude affords so scanty a field for the naturalist as this barren spot.'

It had been a tough few days and Christmas had been spent at work; so the celebration was held on the 27th. Four days later they set off for New Zealand.

After the recaulking of the ship and the repair of the mast, the fortunes of the sailors seemed to have changed. The crew's excitement at making these new discoveries is left to the imagination. On such as voyage, viewing conditions had to be optimal; ideally they needed clear skies, a calm sea and crystal clear air. But no-one could foresee the elements and very soon they fell foul of the unpredictable weather conditions.

Once again the ships were plagued with fog, this time so dense that Cook reported that they 'ran above 300 leagues in the dark.' We can only imagine the frustration and disappointment of the navigators. Nothing at all could be seen in the near distance and the ships were helpless to unseen dangers such as rocks and passing vessels. The crew peered hopelessly into the blanket of mist, knowing that any lapse in concentration could spell disaster. The chances of spotting new lands and islands had shrunk to zero. For many days the ships ploughed on, half blind, until the fog eventually lifted. But the weather remained poor.

On 19 January a squall took off the fore topmast and the main topgallant mast and they spent all day repairing the former. Having no wood to replace the other, they continued on to Tasmania, as they had no choice but to limp along until they reached a haven. Eventually, they reached Adventure Bay on the 26th. Cook spied a few natives, carved COOK 26TH JAN 1777 on a tree and decided that while the timber was good, it was too heavy. They did what they could and then they sailed on to New Zealand, meeting the infamous 'Southerly Bluster' storms on the way.

Their stay in New Zealand was brief; Cook and the veterans will have remembered their last visit to Queen Charlotte's Sound and the unfortunate squabble with the Maori which led to some of their number being killed and Gore retaliating with gunfire. The natives had not forgotten and when Cook landed they kept away for fear he was seeking reprisals. It did not take long for the inquisitive Maoris to come closer and within a short time the shore was covered in their makeshift huts. Visitors began to arrive and one, named Kahoura, had been the leader of the group who attacked the men previously and Omai advised Cook to execute him. That was the proper tribal etiquete. The Captain decided that diplomacy was the best option and as the attack had not been premeditated, he let the matter rest. Burney thought that the Maoris considered the English as contemptible on this account, but Cook was carrying out his Orders to 'cultivate a friendship' with the natives and to show them 'every kind of civility and regard'. [8] When they left, Omai persuaded two Maoris to sail along with them, a chief's son named Tawei harooa and a boy of ten called Kakoa.

The voyage went on and the weather improved. On 29 March, they approached the Tongas, or 'Friendly Islands'. Cook discovered an island which he called Manganouia and a native came aboard, falling over a goat which he thought of as 'a bird'. It frightened him so much he had to go back to shore. At another island the crew tried to barter for animal fodder, but trade was slow and the natives were scared by the horses and cows and took the goats and sheep for large birds. [9] Omai could converse with them, so he and a party of crewmen went ashore and were treated well. The problems arose when they were unwilling to allow them to return to their boats. Things were looking dangerous, but Omai parried all of their questions and at an appropriate moment exploded a handful of powder in front of them. This frightened them so much that the crew were able to beat a hasty retreat back to the ship. It was a salutary lesson to Cook, who decided that no risks should be taken in future. As they passed Harvey's Island on 6 April, King saw that the womenfolk were bringing arms to shore, so they sailed off. The 'Friendly Islands' had not proven as friendly as Cook originally thought.

The idea that the natives mistook goats and sheep for birds was reproduced in the later narrative, but Bligh was indignant over it.

The people were not so ignorant as to suppose the Sheep & Goats were birds, but was at a loss to describe any other way that was different from their Dogs & Hogs, for among all Indians as well as civilised Nations, flying is the principle that constitutes the bird. [10]

The voyage continued and the crew saw around 150 Tongan islands, most of which were charted and surveyed by Bligh. He was now in his element; this is the reason he was there and he made good use of his time trying to map them. They were an exquisite sight from shipboard but not without danger; shoals were always around waiting to trap the unwary navigator. One night Cook discussed the problem with Bligh before retiring at midnight and leaving him in charge. A wind blew up and forced the ship westwards, perilously close to Pootooa Island but the crew managed to steer it clear. Cook did not blame his Master
:

Such hazardous situations are the unavoidable companions of the man who goes upon a voyage of discovery. [11]

Never in Cook's log or in the published account of the voyage did Cook criticise his Master and they seem to have got along very well. In fact, there are no adverse remarks at all which have come to light, but this does not mean to say that Bligh held all of the officers in great esteem. In fact, he had little but contempt for King and even more so for Lieutenant Philips, whom he describes as a man 'who never was of any real Service the whole Voyage, or did anything but eat & Sleep,' but was 'a great Croney of C King's'. [12] Given Bligh's irascible temper and his habit of bursting into tirades of strong language, it seems strange that he never came into conflict with them. But Bligh was in his first position of any command and while he expected the men to fall in with his wishes it would have been completely against his nature to question an order from a superior officer. He knew that discipline was imperative to the good running of a ship and he answered any orders with alacrity – whatever he thought of those orders or the men giving them.

Bligh, like other crewmen, would have noticed the behaviour and actions of their Captain; and the veterans would have seen that this Cook was a rather different man to the Captain of the other voyages; more stern, more forthright, more strict. While he could have the compassion of a nurse looking after his children, he could also don the mask of the martinet if a sailor broke the rules. There were more floggings on the third voyage than during any of his others; his temper, always fickle, was shorter and his language, always ripe, was coarser. This was nothing unusual in a naval ship – phrases like 'damn your eyes', 'scurvy landlubber' and 'bitch's bastard' or even worse were commonplace and were expected from a ship's officers.

On 28 April, they anchored at Comango, where the natives were happy to trade with Cook and no-one else – but they were plagued by thefts and Cook resorted to the naval tradition of flogging. It had little effect on the natives and Cook found that it 'made no more impression than it would have done upon the mainmast.' At Happi the crew were well received by the chief, Feenough, and given an entertainment of combat; then Feenough gave Cook so many supplies it took four boats to transport them to the ships. The chieftain was invited on board ship to receive a present in his turn. Feenough needed to sail to an island about two days' sailing away and although Cook promised to wait for him, supplies (particularly water) were running short so they sailed to a bay in Leefooga. Once again Cook turned to his Master, Bligh:

We made sail to the ward along the reef of the island, and, having passed several shoals, hauled into a bay that lies between the North end of Hoolwa and the south of Lefooga, and there anchored. We had no sooner cast anchor than Mr Bligh, Master of the Resolution, was sent to sound the bay where we were now stationed; and Captain Cook, accompanied by Lieutenant Gore, landed on the southern part of Lefooga, to look for fresh water and examine the country. On the approach of night, the Captain and Mr Gore returned on board, and Mr Bligh came back from sounding the bay, in which he found from fourteen to twenty fathoms water, with a bottom principally of sand. [13]

There were wells here, but the water was bad and unusable. Here the natives shaved by using two shells and Cook remarked that the crew commonly went ashore to have a native shave; but Bligh disagreed, saying: 'none of our Sailors could bear it'. As they were anchored there, a large canoe arrived carrying a person of some importance – Tattafee Polaho, the King of all the islands. As a gift Polaho presented Cook with 'two good fat hogs, though not so fat as himself, for he was the most corporate, plump fellow we had met with.'

Cook had decided to make a short stay at Tongataboo; it would be good to give the crew a rest and he himself felt tired of being buffeted in the dangerous waters. Here he met an important personage by the name of Mariwaggee, who turned out to be the father of Feenough and the father-in-law of Polaho.

Rest time was important for seamen, and they determined to make the best of their stay at Tongataboo. Soon after their arrival Mariwaggee organised an entertainment – a four or five hours display of singing and dancing. In return, Cook ordered a spectacle of his own – a series of military parades and fireworks displays with intervals of music played on fife, drum and French horns. Bligh watched on with barely concealed contempt:

A most ludicrous performance for the Marine Officer was as incapable of making his Men go through their Exercise as C Cook's Musicians or Musick was ill adapted. [14]

There were more displays and the usual exchange of gifts, but while intent on relaxation Cook knew enough of the islanders to be alert against theft and he posted guards and took every precaution. This not deter the most determined; and on one occasion two turkeys and a kid were taken, so that a guard was placed over Feenough and two chiefs until they were returned. [15] On another occasions a party of officers sailed to an island without permission, but only succeeded in having muskets and ammunition stolen; once again, after some negotiations, the items were brought back. Despite these annoyances, the crew remained on the island for over five weeks, and Cook delayed their departure to see a solar eclipse. This, however, ended up in a farce:

We were all at our telescopes, viz, My Bayly, Mr King, Captain Clerke, Mr Bligh and myself. I lost the observation by not having a dark glass at hand suitable to the clouds that were continually passing over the sun; and Mr Bligh had not got the sun into the field of the telescope; so that the commencement of the eclipse was only observed by the other three gentlemen. [16]

The voyage was further delayed when Cook and his companions were invited to the initiation of Polaho's son, the prince, and the ceremony took place on the island of Moa. Soon after, on the 10th, the ship sailed on, but made a stop at Middleburg to see Cook's old friend Toofa, where they inspected the vegetables Cook had planted on the last voyage and watched a boxing spectacle.

On 8 August Cook discovered the island of Tubuai then, at last, four days later, the ships reached Tahiti (then known as Otaheite), the first of their destinations and the home of Omai. The first to come to the ship and meet him were his brother-in-law and others who had known him; but Omai had spent years in England and they treated him as if he were a foreigner, one of the crew of strangers. Indeed, Omai had spent enough time in England to have learned the British ways and customs, which were obvious to his old friends and relatives. He had enough intelligence to realise that if they would not be won by family ties, then valuables would do the trick, so he took his brother-in-law to his cabin and gave him some red feathers he had acquired at the Friendly Islands. To the natives, these were priceless, as Cook put it:

'They were of such value that not more than might be got from a tomtit, would purchase a hog of 40 or 50 pounds weight.' [17]

Cook was now paying attention to the spirit supply he had and as here coconuts were abundant and they would need the rum when they moved on to colder climes, he suggested that the rum allowance be suspended for the time being. This was not an order, but he asked the crew to decide; they all agreed, as did the sailors on the *Discovery*. The rum was not to be cancelled completely; it would not be issued 'except on Saturday nights, when they had full allowance to drink to their female friends in England, lest amongst the pretty girls of Otaheite, they should be wholly forgotten.' [18] The reputation of the Tahitian ladies went before them.

On shore, things had certainly changed since Cook's last visit – the Spanish had been and built a house there. They had also laid claim to the country and forbade the natives to allow Cook to land on its shores. On a nearby cross was inscribed:

CHRISTUS VINCIT, CAROLUS III. IMPERAT, 1774.

Not to be outdone, Cook had the following carved on the reverse side:

GEORGIUS TERTIUS REX. ANNIS 1767, 69, 73, 74, ET 78.

The direction of the Spanish was easily remedied: the chief simply signed a declaration formally surrendering his province to Cook.

By 23 August the ships had anchored in Matavai Bay, which was to be their home for the next few months. Here their old friend and ruler, Otoo, met them and Cook gave him a linen suit, some tools, a feather helmet from the Friendly Islands and a large bunch of red feathers. The royal family dined on board the *Resolution* and after dinner they called on the island of Oparee (Pari), unloading most of the animals which were the gifts of Lord Bessborough. Cook was extremely relieved to get them off his hands; they had been 'of a very heavy burden; the trouble and vexation that attended the bringing these animals thus far is hardly to be conceived.'

The Tahitian religion was a primitive one which on occasion involved human sacrifice. When a victim was required, a chief would select him and he would be approached and struck on the head with a heavy stone.

When the chieftain Towha asked Cook what he thought of the practice, Cook replied:

'I think such a proceeding is more likely to offend the Deity than to please Him!'

'Do the English ever practise such ceremonies?'

'If the greatest chief in England killed one of his men, he would be hanged.'

Towha left 'with as great a contempt for our customs as we could possibly have for theirs.' [19]

Cook quickly discovered Venus Point, where he had observed the transit of Venus on a previous visit and here he set up two observatories as well as planting a garden with vegetable and fruit seeds. He also freed several cattle, horses and sheep.

During their stay Bligh and Cook noted the customs of the natives, but the islanders also took great interest in the ways of the British. When an equestrian event was performed, they were greatly surprised by the 'man-carrying pigs'; the parade of the marines amused them and the fireworks display both astonished and entertained them. On the other side, the British found the embalming process of a dead body curious, as well as the interments in '*morais*' or burial-mounds, the shaving of a thief's head and the local musical and singing interludes or *haivas*. Bligh also made lasting friendships with the king and several important natives.

The pronunciation of British names was a great difficulty for the Tahitians, and King Otoo called Cook and Bligh 'Toote' and 'Bry'. [20] He was most keen on sending King George a present, but the double canoe which he presented was too large to fit on board the ship.

Cook then wanted to preserve Otoo's likeness for posterity and asked him to sit for their artist John Webber. When Webber had acquired enough preliminary sketches, he told Otoo that he need sit no more, but the chieftain was curious to know what it was all about. He was told that Webber would complete a proper painting of Otoo back in England and it would be kept as 'memorial of his person, his friendship, and the many favours received from him.' Otoo was very taken with the idea and asked for Cook to do the same for him and after some persuasion by Webber and Clerke, he reluctantly agreed. The painting, when completed, was given to Otoo in a box with lock and key and he promised he would preserve it.

Of greatest interest to the British sailors were the Tahitian women. Warm, affectionate and beautiful, these sirens were like magnets to the hot-blooded tars who had been at sea for many months. Furthermore, sex was not so taboo as it was in stiff-lipped England and it is dictated by the inclination of attraction rather than ties of law or marriage. It is hardly surprising that the sailors found Tahiti a mini-Paradise.

Much has been written about the Tahitian women and descriptions over the years range from tempting sirens, naturally affectionate acolytes of Nature and prostitutes. The early visits of Westerners to the isle fired a myth of another Garden of Eden or a Heaven on Earth. Captain Wallis was the first visitor, in June of 1767, and of the women, he said:

'The women are all handsome and some of them extremely beautiful.'

In April 1768 a French expedition arrived under Captain Louis Antoine de Bougainville, who was more explicit:

' The very air which the people breathe, their dances, almost constantly attended with indecent postures, all conspire to call to mind the sweets of love, all engage to give themselves up to them.'

So taken was Bougainville with the women, he named Tahiti 'the new Cytherea', birthplace of the Goddess Venus. Certainly it was the custom of the women to undress before dignified visitors – sometimes completely – and their dances often involved showing the buttocks and moving them lasciviously as well as often baring their breasts. Sex was something which was natural to the South Sea maidens and there was no stigma against having more than one lover before settling on a husband. Whereas these women were red rags to the bulls of the sailors' lust – often having been deprived for over a year – the men were not necessarily dreamboats for the ladies. They would bathe three times a day and wear subtle perfumes, so that a not-too-clean, unshaven, possibly disease-ridden tar was hardly the stuff their dreams were made on. These visits were the ones which introduced the unsuspecting women to venereal disease, Bougainville blaming Wallis and Wallis Bougainville. Whichever were the culprits – almost certainly both – venereal disease was rampant when Cook's became the third expedition to visit the island.

The two accounts of the visits to Tahiti by the first Captains to arrive there caused a storm in the public imagination. Whereas morality and Christianity ruled Western beliefs and cultures, there was already a backlash among the literati and free-thinkers of the day and questions were constantly being posed about women's standing in civilised community as well as a new growing interest in sexuality and pornography. In the public imagination, Tahiti was the sex capital of the world and it is little wonder that sailors rubbed their hands in glee when they discovered that this was one of their destinations. The Captains, aware of the sailors' needs and noting the willingness of the local women, allowed fraternisation without limit.

Were Tahitian women prostitutes? If the definition is to barter sex for profit, then many would fit the description. On Cook's first voyage, a nail – metal being unknown and greatly prized – would be enough for a sailor to buy a girl's favours. The price would rise on subsequent visits, till on the third voyage a large nail or even a spike would be necessary. Also, chieftains would pimp out the maidens, expecting a cut afterwards, and would use them to welcome visitors with their charms and so ensure a friendly reception and not gunfire. On the other hand, Tahitian women were naturally gracious, well-mannered and warm people, to whom sex was a beautiful act given to mankind by the gods to bring them joy. [21]

There were other things to consider apart from the local women. Now that Omai was back home, the problem was where to settle him. The island of Huaheine seemed to be perfect, so they sailed there, although Cook was too sick to disembark. The crew determined to make sure that Omai would have the best possible start – after all, he had been their companion as well as their friend throughout the voyage. A house was built for him, along with a small plantation built on ground which had been obtained from the chief.

Next came a shameful incident, the most unpleasant of the whole voyage. Cook was the first to agree that he had a hot-headed temperament, although his storms did not usually last. There had been a number of thefts, often leading to tiresome negotiations and threats before the ship's property was returned. Now a theft occurred which was much more serious – Mr Bayly's sextant was stolen from his Observatory. Cook was livid and demanded that the chiefs find the instrument and bring it back – but they ignored him. This increased his fury and then – unfortunately for the culprit – the thief was discovered and taken by the ship's crew. He determined to punish him 'with greater severity than I have ever done any one before', although Midshipman Gilbert argued that the punishment was not carried out until he had been arrested again for setting fire to Omai's house and threatening to kill him. Cook had his head shaven as a thief then ordered his ears to be cut off. [22] It was an act of barbarity, and doubtless Bligh made a mental note on the harshness of the sentence and his commander's raging furies.

Cook had intended to remove the thief from the island and locked him up, but he stole his keys from a guard who was asleep and swam back home. The Captain was furious and gave the guard – a marine named Thomas Morris – twelve lashes a day for three days. Omai did not seem unduly worried, but the thought of his friends leaving him was almost more than he could bear. He joined them for a short distance and when the time came to finally say goodbye, he collapsed in tears and sobbed all the way home.

Soon after there were two attempts at desertion, first a marine and soon after a Midshipman and another sailor. This had nothing to do with Omai and probably nothing to do with Cook's savage punishment, although some of the men might have worried about Cook's increasing severities. It was more likely to have been the lure of the island Paradise they were leaving forever: but their Captain had a way of inducing the natives to help bring them back. He kept one of the chief's family as hostage. It was a method Bligh took a mental note of – and it proved effective as the deserters were all caught and returned to the ship. Although they were caught and received thirty-six lashes over three days, Cook described the incident as 'more trouble and vexation than the men were worth'. [23]

The first part of the voyage was over. Now the crew faced the gruelling task of striking north and seeking the elusive Passage. They left for Bolabola on 7 December and sailed on, passing and naming Christmas Island, until they discovered the Sandwich Islands until early in January. The men anchored at Atooi, where they watered and carried on trade with the natives, of whom Cook wrote:

'No people could trade with more honesty than these people, never once attempting to cheat us, either ashore or alongside the ship.'

On 29 January 1778 they arrived at Oneehow and Cook sent Bligh to survey the island.

In the evening I sent the Master in a boat up to the South-East head or point of the island to try if he could land under it. He returned with a favourable report, but it was too late now to send for our party till the next morning; and thus they had another night to improve their intercourse with the natives. [24]

As well as being used as a scout whenever the *Resolution* arrived at new bays, Bligh also used his talents to survey all the islands they came across in the area. These works would be of invaluable aid to future explorers in the area.

Having sighted New Albion, the ships pulled into Hope Bay (Nootka Sound) on 7 March, staying for wood and water. The stay was longer than expected as they found damage to the *Resolution*'s fore and mizzen masts, so repairs had to be made. The natives were friendly enough if adept at thievery; in appearance they were short, stocky and swarthy with flat faces and high cheek bones. One became so attached to the visitors that he gave Cook two beaver-skins at their departures, and the Captain returned the compliment by handing him a broadsword in a hilt. While they were there, Bligh surveyed the bay.

After over a month, on 26 April 1778, the ships resumed their journey but immediately hit a hurricane and the severe gales battered them as the water rose on the decks. Fortunately the pump kept the danger off, but it was a trying time for all on board. Onwards they went, further to the North, and wooded terrain swept to the sea while snow-capped mountains gave warning of the icy conditions ahead of them. On 4 May they saw Mount Elias and near Cape Hinchinbroke some of the natives trying to board the *Discovery*, wielding knives; but when officers appeared with cutlasses they sped off, remarking that the white folk's knives were longer than their own.[25] Their appearance tallied with Crantz's account of the Eskimos.

Repairs were done to the ship's caulking and they sailed again. By 17 May they had anchored in Prince William Sound and, hoping that there might have been a waterway constituting the sought-for passage, three boats were sent to examine the estuary; two under Lieutenant Gore and the third under Bligh. When asked about his exploration, Bligh revealed that 'the arm I was ordered to examine communicates with a part of the sound we have already seen'.[26] Gore and his companions had no further success, so the voyage continued.

On 20 June they saw a volcano spewing thick dense smoke; and on the 26th they were bound by a dense fog, so – as the breakers were pounding the ships – Cook weighed anchor. When the fog lifted, the crew saw that they had had a fortunate escape – unknown to them they had passed through two great rocks and were moored only about three-quarters of a mile from an island. Thankful for their good luck, the ships bore on, ever further to the North, but the ship's surgeon was sick and failing badly. By the 3 August he had passed away, so Cook named a nearby island after him, 'to perpetuate the memory of the deceased, for whom I had a very great regard.'[27]

Six days later the *Resolution* visited Asia, although quite by accident. In fact, they thought they had anchored at the most western tip of America and Burny blamed Heydinger's map, which he found inaccurate and at times 'unintelligible.' The natives were wary of their visitors, whom Cook found to be taller and stouter than their American counterparts.

Heading further North was fraught with difficulty. At a latitude of 70° 33' they found themselves within the ice blink and soon they were in danger of becoming suck fast, as large lumps of ice ground against the hull. It was Bligh's first taste of Arctic expedition and the cold was enough to pass through the warmest of their winter clothing. After sighting Icy Cape, it was obvious that there could be no more voyaging to seek a Passage any further on. Cook decided that enough was enough and they should turn back and seek winter quarters. The choice was to anchor at Petropavlovski ('place of Peter and Paul') where the crew would rest idle throughout the cold winter months, or to sail back to the Sandwich Islands. While anchored at Norton Island and examining his charts, Cook decided on the latter. Meanwhile Norton Sound was examined and King wrote on his exertions and fatigues during the survey,[28] of which Bligh was scornful:

C King might well say it was fatigues he underwent for he never bore any or was he capable – his whole Account if he had been a seaman he would have been ashamed to have related….[29]

The *Resolution* and *Discovery* set their course for Samgoonoodha Harbour, but they met with such heavy weather that they did not arrive until 3 September. A few days later, a native brought Cook a peculiar present – a salmon pie – and also a letter in Russian. Soon after they met up with three Russians, including one Ismailoff, who was the chief trader of the area, in which no less than 400 Russians were living in various settlements. This Ismaeloff was a consummate story-teller, and he entertained his guests with tales of his voyages with Lindo, a sledge expedition to three islands opposite the Kolyma River and a voyage to Japan and China, after which he ended up in France. Cook doubted his word, but he did produce several charts showing the Asiatic coast and several Russian discoveries to the east of Kamtaschatka. Before parting, Ismaeloff gave Cook letters for the Governor of Kamtaschatka and the Commandant of Petropavlovsk; while Cook wrote a letter to the Admiralty along with a chart, which was delivered the following year. [30]

On 26 October the ships sailed off, sighting the Sandwich Islands on 25 November. At Mowee Cook issued the usual order concerning trading and soon the natives came out and bargains were soon struck. For his part, Cook bought a quantity of sugar cane, which he used to ferment 'a wholesome and palatable beer'; but the crew would not touch the stuff, which annoyed Cook so much that he stopped their grog. His anger is still apparent in his log:

Every innovation whatever, tho' ever so much to their advantage, is sure to meet with the highest disapprobation from seamen. Portable soup and sour kraut were at first both condemned by them as stuff not fit for human beings to eat. Few men have introduced into their ships more novelties in the way of victuals and drink than I have done; indeed, few men have had the same opportunity or been driven to the same necessity. It has, however, in a great measure been owing to such little innovations that I have always kept my people, generally speaking, free from that dreadful distemper, the Scurvy. [31]

The *Resolution* sailed on through bad weather on 24 December, but a mix-up in signals resulted in the *Discovery* remaining behind. While waiting for that ship to catch up, Cook passed several islands and traded with some of them. By 5 January the ship neared Owhyhee and they anchored near a large village, soon after which the ship was surrounded by canoes laden with hogs and women. The next day they were close to a bay called Toe-yah-yah, to which Bligh was sent. The bay was well-sheltered with streams to the north-east. Before he could return, a gale had begun and the canoes began to depart and those lagging behind were soon in trouble. Bligh saw a canoe overturned and two men and an old woman were floundering in the waves, so he managed to rescue them all. On his return to the *Resolution* he filed his report.

Mr Bligh reported that he had landed at a village on the north side of the bay, where he was shewn some wells of water that would not by any means answer our purpose; that he proceeded further into the bay; where instead of meeting with good anchorage he found the shores were low, and a flat bed of coral rocks extended along the coast and upwards of a mile from the land, the depth of water on the outside being twenty fathoms. [32]

After the storm had subsided, Cook found himself nearer to the shore, so off went Bligh again to reconnoitre.

'At two cable lengths from the shore I found no soundings with a line of 160 fathoms; and when I landed he found no fresh water, but rain water lying in holes in the rocks and that brackish with the spray of the sea. The surface of the country was wholly composed of large slags and ashes, here and there partly covered with plants.'

This sounded far from promising, so Cook sailed on, being joined at last by Captain Clerke and the *Discovery*. After cruising around the islands for a few days, Cook sent Bligh with a boat from each ship to explore Karakakoa Bay on Owhyhee (Hawaii), but by the time he returned he had difficulty in reaching the ship as it was surrounded by about a thousand canoes filled with produce and livestock. One native had stolen a rudder so Cook fired muskets above the boat, which astonished but did not frighten them. Bligh's report was a satisfactory one – there was good water and good anchorage - so Cook resolved to anchor there. [33]

Among the many visitors who came to the ships were two of some importance – Touahah and Parea, the first of which was a leading priest. Most of the chiefs had brought gifts of food, but Touahah brought a large hog as well as fruits and root vegetables. It was clear that the natives considered Cook as a man of great eminence – perhaps even a god – so they decided to initiate the Captain in a local ceremony of great import. They ascended a large *morai*, which King describes as a structure fourteen feet in height with a large house in the centre, a fence from which cut the platform in two. Nearest the sea were two smaller houses with a covered passage between them; and on the side nearest the land were five poles over twenty feet high, supporting a scaffolding.

At the *morai*, Cook was given two images covered in red cloth and the islanders sang a hymn. After this they walked to a table in front of the scaffolding, laden with fruits on which lay a rotten pig. Touahah (known to the crew as 'Koah') picked up the pig and made a speech after which he dropped the foul carcass and motioned Cook and King to climb onto the scaffold. A red cloth was draped around Cook and then offered him a live pig; the two then came down and Cook joined Touahah in insulting the idols on the table but prostrating before the central one and kissing it. Moving to the other half of the morai, arms held aloft by King and Touahah, he was seated between two idols while his face was rubbed with coconut which had been chewed and softened by Touahah's assistant. Finally King and Cook were hand-fed roasted pork by Touahah and Parea; but Cook remembered how Touahah had handled the rotten hog and could not swallow a mouthful. [34]

Relations between the crew and the islanders could not have been better and gifts of food were constantly being delivered to the ships. An observatory was set up under Lieutenant King on a potato field which had been donated for that purpose. On 25 January the king, Terreeoboo arrived and paid a private visit to the Resolution, where Cook recognised him as the chief they had seen on the island of Mowee. There was a state visit, the chiefs dressed in their finery, at which a helmet was presented to Cook and cloaks of feathers – of enormous value to the islanders – and five more were placed at his feet. Two boat-loads of provisions were brought over by a deputation of priests, attended by the king's nephew Kamehameha I, known by the sailors as Maiha-Maiha. [35]

By the 28th Clerke, who was very ill, found the strength to visit the shore and the king paid him two visits to the Discovery, bringing gifts. The natives were so taken with the visitors that they allowed them to take the morai's fencing – and the idols with the exception of the central one – for firewood. When gunner Whatman died, Terreeoboo even allowed him to be buried in the sacred morai. However, supplies were running short and the natives might have been relieved to hear that the ships were about to sail, although they regretted the departure of their honoured guests. Before they left, Terreeoboo made them a gift and food and livestock which 'far exceeded everything of the kind we had seen', according to King. On 4 February the Resolution and Discovery finally left the Bay.

They were gone for only a week. Two strong gales caused much damage to the ships' rigging and the fore-mast was so badly sprung that repairs were a matter of urgency. Knowing of no other place to do this work, Cook decided to return to Karakakoa Bay.

The first thing the men noticed was an absence of welcoming canoes. [36] Perhaps it was because the islanders had run short of supplies; but at least they could anchor and get on with the repair work. On 12 February, Terreeoboo returned, having been informed that the strangers had come back, and he questioned Cook over their unexpected reappearance; he did not seem happy with the replies he got.

The next day the watering party hired some locals to help rolling the casks, but some of the chiefs drove them away. King sent a marine with side arms, but soon he was told that the natives were arming themselves with stones. The marine calmed matters to some extent and when Cook arrived he gave orders that the marines were empowered to shoot if there was trouble. Just then there was a gunshot from the Discovery and a canoe set off for shore, closely followed by one of the ship's own boats. Cook and his men ran to intercept, but the canoe had landed and the native ran off. It seems that the man had stolen a pair of carpenter's tongs, but the thief was caught, flogged and put in irons until the tongs were returned – which they were.

The tongs now seemed to have taken on some kind of symbolic value. Parea, keen to restore relations, was visiting Clerke when a native grabbed the tongs and headed off in his canoe. Parea, seeing the danger, had taken his own canoe, promising that he would get the tongs back from his countrymen. As the two canoes raced for the shore, the *Discovery* launched its own cutter, under the command of the Master, Edgar, and the Resolution sent out its pinnace. The first canoe reached the shore, but handed the stolen items to Parea before speeding off, Cook and others in hot pursuit.

After handing over the items to Edgar, Parea might have expected the matter was over, but some sailors, uncertain of Parea's part in the affair, would not let him and one struck him down. This was too much for the natives. They had been watching the affair calmly, but when one of their most respected chiefs had been attacked by the newcomers, this was too much. Arming themselves with stones, they began to pelt the sailors and most of them leaped in the sea and swam to some rocks to escape the missiles. Edgar and Vancouver stayed on shore and were at the mercy of the furious islanders. Things would have looked black for them if Parea had not recovered from the blow and seeing the rising tumult, he ordered the men to stop throwing the stones and kept them from breaking up the pinnace. Even Parea could not keep the angry islanders at bay for long, so he advised the men to get back into their boats and sail back to the ships as swiftly as they could. Unfortunately the oars were lost so Parea began to look for them – but as soon as he turned away the stone-throwing began. At last a native found them, one broken and Parea brought Vancouver's cap, too.

When Cook heard the news he was very annoyed.

'I am afraid these people will oblige me to use some violent measures, for they must not be left to imagine that they have gained an advantage over us.' [37]

All the natives on board were ordered to leave and back at the camp, where the mast and sails were being repaired, the sentries were doubled.

The night brought fresh troubles. The *Discovery*'s cutter, which had been moored to the anchor buoy, had been stolen. This was serious and the boat had to be recovered at all costs. Cook ordered that no canoe must be allowed to leave the bay – and to that purpose he sent out the *Resolution*'s cutter and a smaller cutter to guard the waters. Meanwhile Cook decided to take hostages to force the natives to give up their boat and who better than the king Terreeoboo, who was in residence at Kowrowa. While he was gone, King agreed to calm the natives near the camp and assure them that no harm would come to their leader. Cook took Lieutenant Phillips, a sergeant, a corporal and seven marines and they landed at the village; but as they did so they heard the sound of gunfire from the other side of the bay.

Cook received many tokens of respect and asked to see the king; it did not take long for him to be convinced that Terreeoboo knew nothing of the theft. Still, Cook needed is hostage and he asked the king to accompany him to the *Resolution*; Terreeoboo agreed at once as did his two young sons. His mother, however, suspected a trap and started to persuade her husband to stay where he was, along with other chiefs. Phillips, expecting further trouble, ordered his men to line up on some rocks by the shore, some thirty yards away. Cook too realised that they would not be able to kidnap the king without bloodshed, but at that point a messenger ran into the village and told them that a high-ranking chief had been shot by the camp party.

For the islanders, this meant war. They put on their war-mats and armed themselves with heavy stones and iron spikes. One man threatened Cook so he shot him, but he was saved by his mat. This infuriated the natives even more and soon a storm of stones pounded the visitors. A chief tried to stab Phillips, who knocked him down with the butt of his musket. Cook shot a native, but finding it was not the man he intended, he gave orders for Sergeant Gibson to shoot the right one. Chaos reigned as more stones showered them and the marines replied with a volley of gunfire. As they paused to reload, the natives attacked, killing four of them and wounding the other three. Phillips was stabbed in the back but shot his attacker before he could do any further damage.

At this point of crisis, Cook knew that he had no option but to escape. The boats' crews were still firing and stones were still being thrown, so Cook turned and ordered to men to cease shooting and to pull in the boats quickly. It was the chance the islanders were waiting for. As soon as his back was turned he was struck on the head and someone stabbed him in the back – he fell with his face in the water. Cook's body was dragged away and the natives took turns in stabbing his lifeless body. While this was happening, Phillips and the other two wounded marines made for the boats as the boatmen resumed firing. The battered and stunned seamen made their way back to the ships – after all, there were still men at the shore camp and they were now in great peril. What's more, without their foremast the *Resolution* was a crippled ship.

While the published narrative gives a heroic angle to the fray, Bligh was more critical:

The Marines fired & ran which occasioned all that followed, for had they fixed their bayonets & not have run, so frightened as they were, they might have drove all before them. [38]

King mentions an act of gallantry by Philips who, although wounded, saw a man in trouble and having reached the boats, he swam back to save his life. [39] Bligh found the passage ludicrous and on the act of gallantry, Bligh insists that he 'was only near' the wounded man and besides, 'he could swim nearly as well as Philips'.

As soon as King reached the *Resolution* he sent a boat to Captain Clerke for instructions. The ailing Captain was shocked by the news and gave ordered for all preparations to be made for leaving the island and recovering their equipment. At the time, the mast and sails were being guarded by six marines; King and Bligh now went ashore with a strong party. Their orders were to strike the tents and get the mast and sails on board as quickly as possible. If that could be done at all – the natives were now thirsting for war and would do all in their power to prevent it. Seeing the difficulties, King left Bligh in command of the camp and returned to the *Discovery* for further instructions.

The marines were posted on top of the *morai*, where they had an excellent view of proceedings. They had little time to act. Great numbers had been joined by those from Kowrowa, and all were putting on the war-mats. Although given 'the most positive directions to act entirely on the defensive', [40] the crowds were nearing the camp and the situation looked very ugly. As the natives began to throw stones from their enclosures, the situation grew quickly worse, so Bligh ordered his men to fire. They did not notice a few natives crawling behind a cover of rocks to attack the *morai* from its seaward side. As they reached the foot of the mound they were discovered and Bligh's men opened fire, only getting the danger under control when a number of the assailants had been killed. King, on hearing the gunfire, had returned to find matters deteriorating.

More natives had arrived and things looked bleak, until a number of priests arrived and talked to the islanders, calming them down and persuading them to leave off the attack. In this temporary ceasefire the men gathered up all of their equipment, mast and sails and made their way to the onshore boat. One of the priests – Kerriakair – remained with the sailors throughout and even supplied them with food and water.

Throughout the entire drama, Lieutenant Williamson commanded another boat which never moved its position and was a spectator to all that occurred. Later, the censures and complaints against Williamson were so loud that Clerke had to take note of them and took down the deputations of his accusers – of which there were many – in writing. His cowardice enraged the whole crew and he must have realised that he would now be facing a court-martial from which there could be only one verdict.

Unwilling to leave Cook's body in the hands of the natives, King sailed to shore at 4pm, but was met with flying stones until he produced a white flag. Some of the chiefs promised to bring the remains the next day and Touahah explained that they had been taken into the country, so they needed time to retrieve them. Other Indians, however, explained that the bodies had already been cut up according to local tradition and was to be embalmed.

On 15 March Clerke was officially made Captain of the *Resolution,* his place on the *Discovery* being given to Lieutenant Gore. Kerriakair managed to steal some of Cook's body; they had burned his remains and his limbs distributed among the chiefs. He also warned them not to trust Touahah. Watering parties were now accompanied by armed guards and although they did recover parts of Cook's body, much of it was to remain in Karakakoa Bay. On the 20th a contingent of natives, including Terreeoboo's son and an eminent islander, Earpo, brought all of the parts of Cook's body it had been possible to recover. [41] Clerke commented:

'Upon examining the remains of my late honoured and much lamented friend, I found all his bones, excepting those of the back, jaw, and feet – the two latter articles Earpo brought me in the morning - the former, he declared, had been reduced to ashes with the trunk of the body. As Kerriakair had told us, the flesh was taken from all the bones, excepting those of the hands, the skin of which they had cut through in many places, and salted, with the intention, no doubt, of preserving them; Earpo likewise brought with him the two barrels of Captain Cook's gun - the one beat flat with the intention of making a cutting instrument of it; the other a good deal bent and bruised, together with a present of thirteen hogs from Terreaboo.'

The next day, as the sun set, the *Resolution* fired ten minute guns, with the colours half staff up, and the remains of a national hero were committed to the deep.

The ship was repaired and at last the voyage was resumed. On the 12 March they visited Oneehow, Bligh having explored it for a suitable landing-place:

The weather being moderate, the Master was sent to the north-west side of the island to look for a more convenient place for anchoring. He returned in the evening, having found a fine bay with good anchorage;

to the eastward were four small wells of good water, the road to them level and fit for rolling casks. [42]

It is not difficult to imagine the state of despondency of the crews after the tragedy of Karakakoa Bay; but orders were orders and the new Captains had no choice but to continue the voyage where Cook left off. He had determined to resume northern explorations when the season set in, so the ships made their way north. According to Bligh, Clerke gave him specific orders to conduct and navigate the ships.

'You are to explore the Isles as much as you can and from thence carry the ships to Kamtaschatka and thence do your utmost endeavours to discover the North-West passage.'

If this was the case, it would appear that Clerke had as little confidence in his Lieutenants as Bligh did. It would also suggest that Clerke had a very high opinion of Bligh's navigation skills.

After two months of sailing – on 29 April 1779 – they reached Owatska Bay, where they met with Major Behm, the Governor of Bolcheretsk. Luckily, Webber could speak some German and was able to talk with the Russian officers. It seems that Ismaeloff had described the British men as 'littler more than pirates', but after some discussion the Governor showed them every kindness and supplied the ships as best he could. In return, the ships' doctors helped the Russians who had contracted scurvy.

The ships sailed further north on 13 June, following the Asian coast and entering the harsh uninviting Arctic. They endured the freezing temperatures but ice and fog caused them to cross to the American side, with little result. Reaching a latitude of 70° 33', they abandoned their efforts and decided to return to Owatska Bay for refitting. A day before reaching their destination, on 22 August, Captain Clerke finally succumbed to his long illness and died at the age of thirty-eight. He was buried under a tree and the Russian garrison were present for the interment. Before his death, it is thought that he had destroyed all documentation of Williamson's cowardice and so the court-martial never took place. In fact, Williamson was eventually to rise to the rank of Captain.

So the day before they reached the Bay, Captain Clerke was buried under a tree a little to the north of the post of St. Peter and St. Paul; the crews of both ships and the Russian garrison taking part in the funeral ceremony and the Russian priest reading the service at the grave. [43] Clerke had been all three voyages with Cook, and his experience would be sadly missed.

There was necessarily a change-over of ranks; Gore now commanded the *Resolution* while King took over as commander of the *Discovery*, but most of the navigation remained in the hands of Bligh. Leaving Awatska on 9 October they made it as far as Cape Nambu, Japan on the 26th and Bligh charted the islands of Macao and Typa. Severe weather blew them from the coast and they anchored in Macao Roads on 1 December. Here they received supplies from China and the furs they had obtained from the North were in great demand. The men received about £2000 for their skins.

The ships reached the Cape on 11 April 1780 and were well treated by the Governor, Plattenberg, who was dismayed by news of the death of Cook. They left Simon's Bay on the 9 May and by 12 August had spotted the Irish coast, although gales drew them off Galway Bay and to the North. Sailing round the north of Scotland, they pulled into Stromness, from whence King made his way by land to the Admiralty. The ships finally made the Nore on 4 October; they had been gone for four years, and almost three months.

When the *Narrative* finally appeared, Bligh was not pleased, particularly with the charts and maps. He was irritated by the presence of 'Anderson's Island' on the maps, near 'Bearings Streights' and 2°30' to the east of Clerks Island – 'it does not exist'...

I wish also, and if it is not done now I must take another opportunity, to declare that the Sandwich Islands published with Cook's voyage are entirely my survey – the Friendly Islands, the same except the part of Amsterdam seen before by Capt Cook – The survey of the parts we saw of the East part of Asia to the Southward of Behrings Streights, Kamtaschatka and Japan – Karakakooa Bay – Macao and Typa are likewise my productions. Unfortunately by way of describing mountains and making flourishes Roberts has mortified me by his copy of the Sandwich Islds, for in my plan which he copied from, the situations of the remarkable Mountains were accurately determined and shown, but in the present they are lost. The parts of America from our first making the coast to the time of C Cook's death were surveyed by himself and were copied by Mr Roberts.

In a 1784 copy of the book, 'illustrated with Maps and Charts, from the original drawings made by Lieut. Henry Roberts, under the Direction of Captain Cook'. Bligh:
'None of the Maps and Charts in this publication area from the original drawings of Lieut. Henry Roberts; he did no more than copy the original ones from Captain Cook, who besides myself was the only person who surveyed and laid the Coast down, in the Resolution. Every plan and Chart from the time of C Cook's death are exact Copies of my works.'

Chapter Three. A Taste Of Powder

It is rumoured that when not at sea, Bligh was the 'bouncer' at the Cornish Arms public house in St. Tudy, a ridiculous story with no thread of truth.

Bligh had not been in England long when a family tragedy occurred – his father, who had married for the third time in 1777, died on 27 December 1780. He had lived long enough to see his son see some measure of success, but at the end of that year his fifty-six year old body was laid to rest in St Andrew's churchyard, Plymouth. [1]

Bligh's next priority was to visit his beloved Elizabeth so he made his way as soon as possible to the Isle of Man and it must have been a happy reunion. It had to wait; first Bligh had been invited to the West Country and the Orkneys and Elizabeth might have wondered at her fiancé's delay. She did not need to be concerned; Bligh's feelings had not changed and their relationship continued just as if the past four years had never happened. The voyage did have one advantage, as far as Bligh was concerned – it gave his career some varnish and it was something to boast of: he had partaken in a voyage with the world's most eminent explorer and had returned with stirring tales of far-off lands. In Richard Betham's eyes, his almost certain promotion to Lieutenant would have counted for much, as he desired a secure future for his daughter.

Being on holiday – on half pay – he had other ways to earn money. He was involved in work on the narrative of Cook's voyage, for which he would receive about £1000, but not for some time. In 1786, he would write to a friend:

By this Packet I had the pleasure to hear ... that you had been so good as to get my part of the profits of the publication of Cook's voyage.'[2]

Perhaps he did not mind the leisure time so much and after such a long voyage he deserved some rest. During his time at Douglas he not only socialised with Betsy's family, but also the family friends. There were the Heywoods, who lived in the Nunnery; Peter John had been a Deemster and the family was one of the most respected on the island. Heywood's fourth son, Peter, was the eight-year-old apple of his eye and that of his daughter, Nessy. They also met the Christians and the Hallets – Betsy was a bosom friend of Ann Hallet. Fletcher Christian was sixteen years of age and already looking for a career at sea.

Perhaps Bligh's most important acquaintance at this time was Duncan Campbell, a relative of Elizabeth on her mother's side. His father Neil

Duncan had been Principal of the University of Glasgow and Duncan matriculated there in 1739, joining the Royal Navy as Midshipman of the HMS *Dover*. This was not the life for him; Campbell was a man of business and so in 1748 he left the Navy and teamed up with John Stewart to become a merchant firm for the West Indies. His affairs prospered so much that apart from being a leading merchant for Jamaica he also became a prosperous ship-owner and bought plantations in Jamaica for himself. It was his sister, Mary 'Mip Mally' who was to marry Richard Betham and give him a son and three daughters, the second of which was Betsy. A canny entrepreneur, Campbell's eye was quick to spot an opportunity and he was far-sighted enough to see potentials and exploit them, not only in the West Indies but as superintendent of ships transporting convicts. Today, he would be seen as a man quick to exploit the misery of others, be they black slaves or condemned men, but that is not how he would have appeared in the eighteenth century. He was a well-respected man of society who gathered money just as easily as he did honorary titles.

By now, Richard Betham had given his consent for the up-and-coming naval man to marry his daughter. They were married by the Rev Thomas Quayle in the parish church of Onchan, as recorded in the register:

Mr William Bligh and Miss Elizabeth Betham of the town of Douglas, were married in this Church by license this fourth day of February, *anno predicto*, **by me Thos, Quayle, Vicar.**
This marriage was solemnised between us

Wm Bligh
Elizabeth Bligh, late Betham

in presence of:

Alexander McNaught
Charles Calven[3]

The impetus for the marriage may have been the fact that Bligh had been called up for duty again, the Admiralty requesting him to report to the *Belle Poule* – originally a French 32-gun frigate - as ship's Master under Captain Philip Patton. As he was required to be on board on the 15th, this left just eleven days for the couple to enjoy their moments as a married couple.

It was hardly surprising that Britain was gathering her resources. She had alienated herself from virtually every major power in the world. Bligh had seen some of the American discontent in Boston and this soon escalated to the Tea Party and a War of Independence, which was raging at the time. The French and the Spanish were old enemies and now the Dutch were shipping supplies to help in the American war effort. As a result, in December 1780 Britain declared war on them, but this endangered British trading with countries on the Baltic Sea, a key provider of lumbar for the naval ships. There was only one thing to do – protect their shipping in the North Sea and blockade the Dutch coast. It meant stretching the already thinly spread resources, even though the weak Dutch could not launch an effective response.

The *Belle Poule* remained in Portsmouth for a while but on 10 April she sailed alongside the *HMS Berwick*, a 64-gun ship. Bligh was underwhelmed with the state of the *Belle Poule*, finding that her canvas was in a shocking state and would hardly stand up to a strong gale. On the 17th, while they were sailing off Abb's Head, they spied an enemy sail, *La Cologne*, so the *Berwick* gave chase and opened fire while Bligh ordered his men to clear decks for action. *La Cologne* outsped the heavier *Berwick*, but the *Belle Poule* sailed into action and ran alongside, where she pounded the enemy with broadsides until she at last struck her colours. The next day the ships took their prisoners – including Captain Luc Ryan – to the Leith Road. [4] Here they anchored and, hoping to be there some time, Bligh invited his wife to travel up to Edinburgh. She did, but they had little time together – on 7 May the ship sailed off again.

The *Belle Poule* sailed with the *Berwick*, which contained the Commodore Keith Stewart, and the *Proselyte*; the *Termagant* joining them after they had reached the Shetlands. The officers had been offered prize money and were enthusiastic to capture enemy vessels, but although Bligh's ship chased two, nothing came of it. On 17 July they joined the main fleet

The British blockade had led to a collapse of Dutch trade and a political crisis until it was agreed that any whatever cost, the merchant ships had to be launched. In August 1781, Admiral Johan Zoutman led seven ships of the line as well as frigates and smaller vessels to protect a fleet of merchant ships. But a British fleet – including the *Belle Poule* - was waiting for them.

Admiral Hyde Parker was performing the same duty as Zoutman, escorting his own merchant fleet from the Baltic to England, but on the morning of 5 August he spotted the Dutch fleet and determined to give battle. There were personal reasons. Rodney had blasted him for his inaction off the coast of Martinique in 1780 and he was ready to redeem himself in the eyes of those who doubted his courage. He had the ideal opportunity, but poor tools. Due to shortage of ships, many had been commissioned which were not up to scratch, and those that had seen much service were in a poor condition, with many of their guns inoperative. True, Hyde Parker had two new ships, his flagship *Fortitude* and the *Berwick*, both 74-guns, but the other ships of the line and the frigates – including the *Belle Poule* – were in dubious shape. Still, the commander was determined to give battle and dispatched the merchant convoy on to

England.

As the British sailed on towards the enemy, Zoutman realised that a conflict was inevitable. He ordered his own ships to form a line between his merchant ships and the enemy, then awaited the arrival of Parker's vessels. Luckily for the British, they were upwind and so had the advantage of the weather gauge; soon they closed until they were at close quarters. The Dutch Admiral generously allowed the British ships to form, without making any attack. Parker raised the flag for battle just before 8 a.m., and Zoutman did the same, blasting the *Fortitude* with a broadside.

It must have been a thrilling time for Bligh as this was the first battle at sea he had been involved with. He would soon learn that whereas victory was glorious and noble, the fighting was not. Hostilities at sea meant the possibility of dying by cannonball, fire or drowning. Moreover, the plan of battle was little more than a blueprint as manoeuvring was not easy and action was largely dictated by the movements of the enemy. Signals were often missed in the smoke and sometimes the battle consisted of moving to the nearest target and raking it with shot. Badly-hit vessels had decks thronged with the mangled and dying.

Canon-fire echoed across the sea and clouds of smoke rose from the fleets as the Battle of Dogger Bank raged for three hours. It is doubtful whether the *Belle Poule* played a decisive part in the action but it was still Bligh's first taste of powder. At last the merchant ships headed back towards the Texel River and at eleven Parker gave the signal to reform. It had been a bloody battle – the British lost 104 men, with 339 wounded, while the Dutch report gave their casualties as 142 and 403, although other reports suggested their toll to have been higher. [5]

That night, the *Holland* sank, and the *Belle Poule* carried off her flag and presented it to Parker.

The Dutch claimed a victory (as did the British), but if it was then it was dearly bought. No other convoy ventured out for the remainder of the war, except one which flew a Swedish flag and was accompanied by a Swedish frigate. For his part, Hyde Parker was furious with the condition of his fleet and insisted on resigning his post, claiming that he had not been properly equipped for his task.   On 5 September, the *Belle Poule* having been declared unfit for action, Bligh was transferred to the smart *Berwick*, but only as fifth Lieutenant. This was probably due to Keith Stewart's influence, as Bligh would acknowledge. Twenty years before, Bligh had walked aboard the *Monmouth* to be Stewart's boy servant and he was determined to impress his old Captain by his efficiency and abilities.

By 1 January 1782 Bligh was given the *Princess Amelia*, again as fifth Lieutenant under Captain Billy Douglas. [6] She had also fought at Dogger Bank. Two months later he was moved again as the entire crew were reposted to the first class ship of the line the *Cambridge,* this time as sixth

Lieutenant under Captain John Holloway. The lowly ranking must have been a huge disappointment and it was clear that promotion to the upper ranks was going to be a slow process. To make matters worse, Commodore Keith Stewart had moved on and so disappeared one of the few strings he had been able to pull. Soon he was writing a letter to Admiral John Campbell, a relative of Duncan's:

Sir, It was the only satisfaction I had after a long and laborious voyage to be introduced to you through the means of my best friend Mr Campbell, and from the generous reception I met with (whilst all who ought to know me, I am sorry to say, neglected when in their power my promoting) I am induced again to make myself known to you.. From Mr Keith Stewart's partiality to me from my services I have since gained promotion to a Lieutenant, and now seeing the wished for change in the service, and you taking a part in it, have allowed myself to hope I may come under your cognizance. Allow me, Sir, to wish to go in any manner under your command – I have experienced hard service; but shall never complain while sailing under your notice.

Bligh was attempting to use his small influence to climb the ranks aboard Campbell's ship the *Goliath*. In those days, nepotism was the order of the day and being related to a member of the Admiralty was the surest way to achieve quick promotion. Bligh had no connections there apart from Duncan Campbell, who often supplied the Navy with ships from his yards; but even his friend's relationship with the Admiral cut little ice. Bligh was destined to remain with the *Cambridge* for two years and shift for himself.

According to Mackaness, there might have been one sailor on board whose family was known to Bligh. Fletcher Christian's name appears on the *Cambridge*'s muster-books so he must have known the junior Lieutenant even then, at the age of nineteen.[7] Neither of the men made any note of the other at this time and it is probable that Christian was either an AB intended for the quarter-deck, or a Midshipman. Fletcher was the son of Charles Christian of Mairlandclere, Cumberland and of a decent family; he himself was quite tall, well-built with a 'bright pleasing countenance' and an amiable temperament. Later, Bligh would note that he was slightly bow-legged and perspired profusely, especially in his hands which would 'soil everything they touched.' [8]

In April the *Cambridge* was ordered to join Admiral Samuel Barrington's fleet, but the shipyard could not fit her out quickly enough and by the time she was ready – after a delay of two or three weeks –the easterly winds made it impossible for the ship to sail immediately. Bligh, a hot-tempered man at the best of times, fumed over this, especially as Barrington saw action in the Bay of Biscay and chased a convoy laden with supplies for the

East Indies.

'I imagine officers will get two hundred pounds,' he moaned.

The Admiralty dragged Lord Howe from his retirement to take control of the blockading Navy, so he joined the *Victory* on 20 April, the *Cambridge* joining the fleet on 6 May. When June arrived, one of the ships signalled the presence of an enemy fleet to the south-west and the fleet moved off in hot pursuit, Lord Howe signalling 'line of battle ahead'. Decks were cleared for action and the fleet closed in – to discover that the enemy was in fact an English convoy.

This fiasco was followed by a more serious matter. Captain Montgomery had taken over the Captaincy of the *Cambridge* and the fleet were warned about an allied force of French and Spanish ships heading to cut off a convoy from the West Indies. Seeing that the enemy substantially outnumbered his fleet – and wanting at all costs to keep his own ships to the westward of the convoy – Howe sailed his fleet between the Scilly Isles and the coast of Cornwall. After that a gale blew the enemy off course and the convoy sailed without molestation through to the Channel.

On 11 September, Lord Howe was ordered to address the situation in Gibraltar. The Rock had for some time been a key location and important for Britain's trading in the Mediterranean. Opening up the New World had inevitably brought hostilities as the major superpowers claimed and disputed territories. In 1739 Spain and Britain declared war and much of the hostility centred around Gibraltar. In 1761 Spain negotiated an alliance with Charles XV of France, so Britain retaliated by capturing Havana and Manila; these were returned under the 1763 Treaty of Paris in exchange for Florida territory. In 1778 France declared war on Britain and joined forces with Spain to reclaim their lost colonial possessions. Their first act was to reclaim Gibraltar.

The Rock was besieged from both sides – the ground forces consisted of artillery and cavalry, while Antonio Barceló commanded the combined naval forces in Algeciras Bay, with eleven ships and two frigates placed in the Gulf of Cadiz. General Elliott rallied his troops and morale was high, but lack of food began to affect the troops during the winter of 1779. The first relief came in 1780 when Admiral George Rodney defeated a Spanish fleet at the Battle of St Vincent and brought fresh supplies plus 1052 men. A year later Vice Admiral George Darby managed to land with a hundred store ships. On 13 August the enemy launched their grand attack; 35000 Franco-Spanish troops on land, ten 'floating batteries', 18 ships of the line, 40 gun-boats and 20 bomb-vessels. The British retaliated using red-hot shot which peppered the batteries and did enormous damage. The assault had been repulsed but Gibraltar was in dire need of supplies. The Admiralty now turned to Richard Howe.

The fleet, including the *Cambridge*, sailed from Spithead and arrived off

Cape St Vincent on 9 October. There were 34 ships of the line escorting 31 transport ships and no-one expected that this would be an easy task. Providence lent a hand. A gale blew up on the 10th and the French-Spanish fleet was scattered, which allowed Howe to simply sail into Gibraltar unmolested. Along with fresh supplies, Howe delivered the 25th 29th and 97th Regiments of Foot which increased the number of troops to 7000. The enemy did little to prevent the landing and when the fleet sail set for home, they followed and for some time it looked as though they might close for action. They seemed to have little desire to do so and after a few distant shots they allowed Howe and his ships to continue homeward. During the short battle the *Cambridge* lost three men and seven were wounded – plus minor damage to the ship. In Madrid, the fiasco was reported as a complete rout of the enemy instead of an unmitigated disaster. [8] This humiliating defeat broke the back of the opposition and soon afterwards they ceded Gibraltar, more content to retain their possessions in the West Indies.

On 14 November Howe's fleet returned triumphantly to Spithead. A day later Bligh's first daughter, Harriet Maria, was born.   Soon after, Bligh received his share of the prize money - £22 0s 6½d.

The end of 1782 saw the conclusion of the American War of Independence, which was seen as a disaster in Britain. It had one advantage – it reduced the numbers of troops of ships which needed to be deployed and after the success at Gibraltar there was little work for a junior Lieutenant to do. Many sailors – including Bligh – were without work and so on half pay, which in Bligh's case was two shillings a day, not enough to live on. Others, including Fletcher Christian, decided to move into the merchant service, which hat least guaranteed a pay packet and often a good one as compared with Royal Navy rates. Christian had contacts – a relative was Captain Taubman, who used his influence to get him a berth on the *Eurydice* as a Midshipman under Captain Courtney. [9] Seeing no other alternative, Bligh turned to Duncan Campbell, who was positive about the possibilities:

'Perhaps something may cast up by the month of August or September to require your presence here [in London], in which case I will advise you, meantime it may be proper that you apply for leave to go into the merchant service.'

As Bligh's future now seemed to centre around London, it made sense for him to move there – but there was a new baby on board and Betsy was in no position to move; besides, they did not have the wherewithal to afford decent lodgings in the capital. They decided that Betsy would stay in the Isle of Man until circumstances improved; meanwhile Bligh followed Campbell's advice and wrote to the Admiralty for permission to join the merchant service.

The reply was delayed in coming; at that time the Admiralty cogs moved slowly but finally a Mr Stephens gave him clearance to go back to sea. It had taken six weeks and Campbell was wondering if his letter had not been received, but Bligh could now put his mind at rest in a letter dated 18 July 1783:

I am sorry this delay has made you apprehensive of my not receiving your letter, but I assure you, Sir, it was expecting much sooner a letter from Mr Stephens only that prevented my writing ... I am glad to hear you think it likely I may soon be wanted in Town as I am anxious to show you that whatever my services may be, my endeavours in every respect will not be wanting either in exercise or care. – I shall be ready at an hour's notice and nothing can stop me now but a contrary wind, which at this season of the year is not likely to happen...[10]

Campbell was not a man to wait on ceremonies. No sooner had he received this news than he gave Bligh command of one of his newer ships, the *Lynx*. Bligh was very impressed by her sailing abilities and told Campbell so; he replied:

'The account you give of the *Lynx* is very pleasing. I hope she will continue to deserve it.'

Although the Admiralty had given Bligh little in the way of preferment, his reputation had grown as the man who had sailed around the world with Cook and who had taken part in the Battle of Dogger Bank and the Relief of Gibraltar. Even John Campbell, who had ignored his request to join the *Goliath*, made sure that his son John had a berth under Bligh. The young man was determined to make himself 'as perfect in my profession as possible' and become a 'diligent officer and seaman'. John Junior realised he had a difficult task ahead, as the Admiral's son he needed to prove that he was worthy to step into his father's footsteps. Although Bligh was an irascible, passionate man he was also an excellent instructor who would take time out to instruct any young seaman who showed a genuine interest in navigation and especially in surveying. John praised Bligh in this regard and also had much to say in favour of the First Mate Mr Ross. Ross knew – as did Bligh – that the *Lynx*'s Captain had little experience in the world of merchant shipping and helped him in every way he could. Bligh appreciated that and kept Ross at his First Mate for many of his voyages, which also proves that Ross was an efficient sailor.

By 1783 Betsy and Bligh had relocated to London, finding a place at 3 Durham Place, Lambeth. The Captain was earning a decent wage now and soon his family was expanding – Mary was born in 1783 and a year later Anne Campbell Bligh arrived, although she was epileptic and born with a mental handicap. In all, Bligh spent four years in the merchant trade and for some months was Campbell's official agent in Port Lucea, Jamaica. Letters from this time are strictly about business, concerning expenses, complaints, bad debts, cargoes and sugar and rum, the colony's most important exports.

In the West Indies Bligh was familiar with the concept of black slavery and it was something he came across on a daily basis. While considered a normal part of trading and colonial life at that time, it would be interesting to know Bligh's feelings on the subject. He was not devoid of compassion, as shown in a ship's log where he later wrote:

Slaves are a property here [Cape Town] as well as in the West Indies, and the number imported by the French, (to whom that Trade has been confined) from Madagascar, Mosambique, Sumatra & Mallacca have been considerable, but it appears there is in some degree a stop put to this Trade, for the Seller has now only permission to part with as many as can pay for the supplies he absolutely is in need of. To this if the Police would oblige the owners of these Poor Wretches consigned to constant drudgery, to cloath and feed them properly it would be much in their honor and humanity, for it is distressing to see some of them carrying weighty burthens naked, or what is worse in such Rags that one would imagine could not fail to reproach the Owners of a want of decency and compassion in not relieving such a degree of Wretchedness of which they were the Cause, and had every call on their humanity to remove. Several of these poor wretches I have seen pick up the most offensive offals and clean them for their food. [11]

Bligh stayed with the *Lynx* for two years, then transferred to the *Cambrian* and finally to the brand new *Britannia*. Christian had completed his service with the *Eurydice* and was now looking for a West-Indiaman to continue his training. Once again, Captain Taubman was looking out for him and suggested that he sail under Bligh; but Bligh replied and apologised that he already had a full complement of officers on board the *Britannia*. Christian was a determined man and wrote in person:

We midshipmen are gentlemen, we never pull at a rope; I should even be glad to go one voyage in that situation, for there may be occasions when officers may be called upon to do the duties of a common man. [12]

Bligh was impressed by the young man's enthusiasm and might have remembered the willing young man who had served under him on the *Cambridge*. So Fletcher Christian joined the crew of the *Britannia* and although rated as AB, the Captain made sure all the officers realised that this was a man with a future in the service. For his part, Christian spoke well of his new commander, although he notes Bligh's flashes of rage. He described him as 'very passionate' but after some time, he knew how to 'humour him'. In fact, Bligh's anger would rarely last and after a few hours the storm would have passed. Christian's attitude impressed Bligh so much he brought him on the second voyage as Second Mate. However, not everyone agreed with Bligh's approbation. Later, First Mate Ross would write:

I recollect you putting him in the articles as gunner, telling me at the same time you wished him to be thought an officer and desired I would endeavour to make the people look upon him as such. When we got to sea and I saw your partiality for the young man, I gave him every advice and information in my power, though he went about every point of duty with a degree of indifference that to me was truly unpleasant; but you were blind to his faults and had him to dine and sup every other day in the cabin, and treated him like a brother in giving him every information. [13]

By the end of April, unbeknown to Bligh, plans were afoot to send him on a voyage which would become perhaps the most famous voyage in the history of sailing. On 2 May Duncan Campbell wrote to relative Dugald:

I wish him home soon, as thereby he might stand a chance of employment in his own line, but of this more by and bye. [14]

Chapter Four. Scudding Before The Foresail

In 1771 Valentine Morris was appointed Captain-General of the British West Indies. [1] A friend of Joseph Banks, the botanist, the pair had been in correspondence about the breadfruit plant, which Banks had tasted on Cook's first voyage and had suggested it was an excellent foodstuff which could provide the wants of the slaves in the plantations. The idea grew and by April 1772 Morris was pushing for the idea to become a reality. Word soon spread and reached the ears of one of the major planters, Hinton East, who wrote to Banks, stating that the breadfruit was 'of infinite importance to the West Indian Islands, in affording a wholesome and pleasant food to our negroes, which would have the great advantage of being raised with infinitely less labour than the plantain, and not be subject to danger from excessively strong winds.'

By 1786 East was in London for serious discussions and Banks took the matter up with King George III, who was soon convinced and gave orders for an immediate expedition The plan gained the backing of Lord Sydney and Banks was to supervise the project. Little escaped the attention of Duncan Campbell and by 1787 he had offered the Navy the *Lynx* for sale but instead they chose Wellbank, Sharp and Brown's *Bethia* – it was docked in Wapping Old Stairs. Meanwhile Campbell was looking for a suitable Captain for the voyage and had no hesitation in recommending William Bligh.

There was no objection. Bligh had already been to Tahiti on more than one occasion – once in the company of the great James Cook. Moreover, he had been a commissioned officer on more than one of His Majesty's ships and was ripe for further promotion.

Bligh was, at the time, on the high seas, so the offer could not made until his return – in the meantime the *Bethia* was moved from Wapping to Deptford Yard and at the beginning of June was renamed the *Bounty*.

Price of the *Rose*, Revenue Cutter, and the *Bethia* (now the *Bounty*), Armed Vessel, purchased by the Navy Board … £3075 10s 6d.

On 31 July, the *Britannia* arrived at the Downs and Bligh was home on 5 August, to hear the news. The next day he wrote to Banks:

Sir, I arrived yesterday from Jamaica and should have instantly paid my respects to you had not Mr Campbell told me you were not to return from the country until Thursday. I have heard the flattering news of your great goodness to me, intending to honour me with the command of the vessel which you propose to go to the South Seas, for which, after offering you my most grateful thanks, I can only assure you I shall endeavour, and I hope succeed, in deserving such a trust. [2]

There was a down side. The news of having a command in the Royal Navy might have flattered him, but not his status; he might well have expected a Captaincy, but the Admiralty left him at Lieutenant. Campbell himself had tried to influence the top brass, but without success.

'Tho he goes out only as a Lieutenant yet if his conduct is approved it is the sure road to being made a Capt. on his return, this Lord Howe has absolutely promised.'

Bligh was upset at this decision, but this was his first command of an armed forces ship and he determined to make the best of it. He travelled to Deptford to inspect his new ship, a 200-tonne vessel of length 90 feet and maximum beam 24. Its figurehead was that of a woman in a riding habit.

Improvements had to be made to the ship, both with regard to its seaworthiness and its novel purpose – to transport breadfruit plants to the West Indies. As to the first point, Bligh had the *Bounty*'s masts and sails cut down for refitting. The second required more thought. A great cabin was requisitioned for the purpose, lined with lead which had pipes at each corner to collect precious water in tubs. Above were two large skylights and at each side three scuttles for air. A false floor was built with holes to accommodate the flower-pots. David Nelson, the botanist, would sail to look after the plants and he would be assisted by a gardener, William Brown. Banks knew Nelson well; he had been recommended by James Lee of the Vineyard Nurseries, Hammersmith and had sailed with Cook on his last voyage – so Bligh knew him, too.

All of these arrangements necessarily meant a shortage of space for the crew. Bligh's cabin was near the side of the deck, with another nearer the centre to eat in. The Master's cabin was opposite his own and here the key to the arms chest was always kept. The berths of the mates and Midshipmen were to either side of the great cabin and the other seamen had space further forward. This was the best that could be arranged under the unusual circumstances.

Bligh was a conscientious and scrupulous man, so he wanted to understand as much as he could about the project and in particular the breadfruit plant. Banks was delighted to see such an interest and gave him all the papers he had and even so, Bligh asked for some assistance in studying the subject. Banks found Bligh a very deserving man:

'He is to become my pupil by accident. I will make him a botanist by choice.'

As with everything Bligh ever did, he took the matter very seriously and pored over the information he had been given until few botanists knew more about the growing of the breadfruit or its nature than he did. For Bligh it was simply a part of his duty. Incidentally, this marked the beginning of a friendship between Banks and Bligh which would last for a lifetime.

Bligh's next task was selecting his crew and a place on the *Bounty* was much sought after. His friends in the Isle of Man were quick to forward their own sons. He already knew Fletcher Christian, of course, and so his place was assured; he was given the post of Master's Mate. Both had worked together before and their relations were very good. George Stewart, half West Indian, had met Cook and Bligh when they had put in at the Orkney Islands. Doubtless Ann Hallet made the most of her friendship with Betsy and her son John was given a berth as Midshipman. Campbell himself recommended Tom Ellison. There were also the Heywoods and while their son Peter was only fourteen, he was eager to pursue a naval career and his uncle Thomas Pasley, who would become an Admiral, pushed hard for his cause. So did his father-in-law, Richard Betham ('he is an ingenious young Lad and has always been a favourite of mine and indeed everybody here'), so Bligh agreed to give the lad a chance and put him down as Midshipman. Peter was taken with the traditionally naval custom of tattooing and already had a number on his body, including the three-legged Manx symbol on his right leg. The Heywoods had just lost the business from the Duke of Atholl and were not as affluent as they would have been. For his part, Peter was a young romantic and a dreamer; interested in poetry and art, he longed to join a great adventure.

Of the rest of the crew, Lawrence Lebogue, like Christian, had sailed on the *Britannia.*

At the time of sailing, the ship's complement was as follows:

- **Commander:** *William Bligh*

- **Commander's Steward:** *William Musprat*

- **Commander's Cook:** *John Smith*

- **Master:** *John Fryer*

- **Master's Mates:** *Fletcher Christian, William Elphinston*

- **Boatswain:** *William Cole*

- **Boatswain's Mate:** *James Morrison*

- **Gunner:** *William Peckover*

- **Gunner's Mate:** *John Mills*

- **Armourer:** *Joseph Coleman*

- **Master at Arms:** *Charles Churchill*

- **Carpenter:** *William Purcell*

- **Carpenter's Mates:** *Charles Norman, Thomas McIntosh*

- **Surgeon:** *Thomas Huggan*

- **Surgeon's Mate:** *Thomas Denman Ledward*

- **Midshipmen:** *John Hallet, Thomas Hayward, Peter Heywood, Edward Young, George Stewart*

- **Quartermasters:** *Peter Linkletter, John Norton*

- **Quartermaster's Mate:** *George Simpson*

- **Sailmaker:** *Lawrence Lebogue*

- **Cooper:** *Henry Hillbrandt*

- **Clerk and Steward:** *John Samuel*

- **Cook**   : *Thomas Hall*

- **Butcher:** *Robert Lamb*

- **Boy:** *Robert Tinkler*

- **ABs:** *Matthew Thompson, John Sumner, Richard Skinner, Thomas Burkitt, John Millward,Thomas Ellison, Michael Byrne, Matthew Quintal, Alexander Smith, John Williams, Isaac Martin, William McKoy, James Valentine*

- **Botanist:** *David Nelson*

- **Assistant Gardener:** *William Brown*

Bligh could not acquiesce with everybody's requests and he turned down three candidates: John Bligh, his second cousin, as well as Dunbar Douglas, son of the Lord Selkirk and his tutor William Lochead. The Comptroller had given him his Master Fryer and his surgeon Huggan, but Bligh had no objection to Fryer and stated that the surgeon 'had a good character.' There were three foreign nationals: Michael Byrne from Kilkenny, Isaac Martin from America and Henry Hillbrandt from Hanover. As for supplies, Cook's voyages had for some time set a precedent and Bligh was not willing to give any trouble there, although as commander he was also the purser and responsible for the ship's spending. He was also the only commissioned officer, those holding the King's warrant being

Huggan, Fryer, Purcell, Cole and Peckover. Although the *Bounty* was an armed ship, she had no marines.

Carpenter William Purcell was busy even before the voyage began; he and his mates, Norman and McIntosh, built four cages on the forecastle deck to house the livestock. Besides the sheep, pigs and chickens there was the inevitable ship's mascot - a dog.

The voyage had become the talk of the town and it seemed that everyone knew about Bligh's project and wanted to benefit in some way from it; even Arthur Phillips, on his way to set up a penal colony and begin his tenure as Governor of New South Wales, wrote from Rio de Janeiro asking Nepean if some articles (musket balls, paper cartridges, slops for the women and other tools) could be sent along with 'the ship that goes for the bread-fruit.' In the middle of September Sir George Yonge had plans of his own, which he made known to a suspicious Bligh…

I have been honoured with a visit from Sir Geo. Yonge who was particularly inquisitive & anxious about my proceedings & orders. As I never heard you mention S'r. George I have avoided answering any direct questions. What he aims at particularly is my carrying plants to Madras, because he says he has informed Lord Cornwallis he should get a ship to bring them, to which I took the liberty to say I thought the plan not eligible for me to carry them there. He then wished some might be left in Java from whence they might be taken to Madras by any Vessel they would send for them.

Richard Betham was sceptical about the Navy's preparation and wrote to Bligh saying that they did not understand the mercantile business and had gone 'too frugally to work', providing a ship and a crew which were too small for such an undertaking. He too was concerned about Bligh's rank and had been making some enquiries about it:

I always imagined you would be made Master and Commander on your going out, and some Navy officers here persuaded me that you will have a commission for that purpose to be opened with your instructions in a certain latitude at sea – as no Promotion in time of peace are made at land... ' [3]

Betham also had good and bad news about his wife; she had been left a legacy from a Mr Sangster, but she had caught smallpox which would probably prevent her coming down to Portsmouth. This must have been a blow for Bligh, who throughout his life showed his affection and concern for his Betsy. However, it did not prove so serious and she did in fact make the trip. On 4 November the *Bounty* sailed to Spithead but even that short trip was fraught with difficulties. A very strong gale carried the ship way off course and Bligh was driven to the coasts of France, but with some effort he corrected his ship and they at last arrived at port. He also had a chance to get first impressions of some of his crew members; he was little impressed with his surgeon, Huggan, who was a fat man and seemed very indolent. It now seemed advisable to find a suitable surgeon's mate. Fryer seemed 'a good man and gives me every satisfaction' and Bligh was also impressed with Nelson and his assistant. However, he was anxious about the absence of marines. These, he felt, were important for the keeping of discipline and for defence in case tribes were hostile. The death of Cook was still fresh in his mind.

There was only one more worry in his mind – the voyage would entail rounding Cape Horn and the season was already advancing. It was imperative that he set sail as soon as possible, otherwise the infamous Cape would not be passible – yet he was still awaiting his final orders from Lord Hood.

Betsy had recovered somewhat and made her way to Portsmouth, arriving on 14 November and finding lodgings at 16 Cumberland Street. On sailing there, Bligh had brought a wineglass urgently needed by Campbell as a pattern and had treated it with extreme caution, nursing it and keeping it from harm. He was proud to have brought it on shore in one piece, until it was broken by 'one of the confounded maids'.

The days went by and still Bligh anxiously awaited his final orders, watching the fine wind passing by as the season grew late. Lord Hood treated him with the greatest respect and agreed to do anything in his power to help the expedition, but still the Admiralty dragged its heels. At last, on 24 November, the orders came; Bligh was to sail around Cape Horn and sail to the Society Islands, where he would take the breadfruit plants on board. He was then to proceed through the Endeavour Straits to some port on the north of Java, where any injured breadfruit plants might be replaced by other tropical fruit trees. Then he was to sail round the Cape of Good Hope to the West Indies, where half of the plants would go to the Botanical Gardens at St Vincent, the other half to Jamaica. The mission completed, the *Bounty* would then return to Spithead.

The orders arrived on Saturday and as Sunday was lost Bligh feared it would be at Tuesday when his crew would receive their two months' pay; at this time every day lost would make Cape Horn a more difficult prospect. He was also worried about his coal allowance and in the next couple of days wrote to both Banks and Campbell, asking them to use their influence as much as they could. His excuse was that they were required for the forge and plants which was true as far as it went, but he was also anxious to have fires during wet weather, of which he was assured of much judging by the lateness of the season. He argued that Cook and Clerke had five times his allowance and that he had already spent over £42 for what was on board. Nepean had asked for precedents and Bligh had furnished them, but knowing how slowly the Government worked he wanted his friends to apply urgent pressure on his behalf.

On 28 November the crew received their pay and the next day the *Bounty* set sail, but as Bligh feared the winds were contrary and he struggled to move any more than seven leagues, anchoring after they had passed the Needles. There was one good thing; Thomas Denman Ledward, surgeon's mate on *La Nymphe,* was now discharged from duty and was available to join Bligh, although there was no allowance for the post. As Ledward wrote at the time:

She is not allowed any Surgeon's Mate, so that I am to enter as AB, but the Captain is almost certain that I shall get a first Mate's pay, and shall stand a great chance of immediate promotion, and if the Surgeon dies (as he has the character of a drunkard), I shall have a Surgeon's acting order.

Bligh tried again to set sail, but the weather was just as bad and he got nowhere. Already 'his People', as he called the crew, were catching colds and soon frustration gave way to rage, as he stormed to Campbell on 10 December:

If there is any punishment that ought to be inflicted on a set of men for neglect, I am sure it ought on the Admiralty for my three weeks' detention at this place during a fine fair wind which carried all outbound ships clear of the Channel but me, who wanted it most. This has made my task a very arduous one indeed for to get round Cape Horn at the time I shall be there, I know not how to promise myself any success and yet I must do it if the ship will stand it at all or I suppose my character will be at stake. Had Lord Howe sweetened this difficult task by giving me promotion I should have been satisfied, but he has done it with a Lieut. Moorsom of the *Ariel* bound on a surveying Voyage to the East Indies, who was made a Lieut. 5th Jany 1784 whose difficulties are not likely to be any way equal to those I am to encounter.

The hardship I make known I lay under is, that they took me from a state of affluence from your employ with an income five hundred a year to that of Lieut's pay 4/- per day to perform a voyage which few were acquainted with sufficiently to ensure it any degree of success.' [4]

It was difficult to be within a stone's shot of his family and not being able to see them. In the end he decided he would, having first discussed the matter with Lord Hood, who generously winked at the breach of regulations. He wrote to Campbell:

I could not help revisiting my dear little family for I did not expect a change of Wind, and Lord Hood winked at my absence as he did not imagine it would happen any more than myself. My absence is quite a secret from Sir J Banks and everyone except Lord Hood who has (altho a stranger to me) behaved with the greatest kindness and attention.

By 23 December 1787, there could be no more waiting, although Bligh asked for permission to choose the Cape of Good Hope if Cape Horn proved impassable. This was granted.

The season of the year being now so far advanced as to render it probable, that your arrival, with the vessel you command, on the southern coast of America, will be too late for your passing around Cape Horn without much difficulty and hazard; you are, in that case, at liberty (notwithstanding former orders) to proceed in her to Otaheite round the Cape of Good Hope. [5]

Then the *Bounty* went back out to sea, complete with their new surgeon's mate, to face dreadful weather and foul conditions. Winds blasted the ship and on the 24th sleet and squalls pounded her, as Bligh noted in his log:

Squally with Sleet, One of the People in furling the Main Top Gt sail fell Over & was saved by Catching hold of the Main T. Mast Stay by Which he came down not at all hurt. Hard Gales with Sleet Close Reefed the Main & Fore Topsails. Handed the Mizen Topsl. and Mainsail. Got all the Dead lights in and Hatches battened down.

A Very heavy Sea Struck us on the Larboard Quarter & carried away a Sweep and Spritsail Topsail Yard.

Heavy Squalls & Rain with a high Sea which obliges me to Carry much Sail to prevent it breaking over us.[6]

The elements relented on Christmas Day and Bligh ordered beef and plum pudding to be served, along with an allowance of rum. It was a mere respite; for the rest of the journey to Tenerife the squalls became heavier and by 27th the winds were so furious that the waves broke into the hold, damaging much of the bread and several casks of beer were lost. The boats were secured, but there was little to be done about the wind, the *Bounty* scudding under the foresail before the sea. Seeing that the crew had suffered much, he ordered grog in addition to beer 'to make up for their wet miserable situation'. As soon as possible fires were lit and wet clothes were dried by two men from each watch.

By the 29th, the storms had abated enough for the crew to inspect the ship and check on damages. Stock was taken of the ruined ship's biscuits and bread while running repairs were performed. Bligh also opened a barrel of pork and one of beef, to find four pieces short in the first and three in the second. This was a most irritating fact of naval life, that suppliers always short-changed the ships and it was a running joke that a sailor's pound was fifteen ounces and his gallon seven pints.

By 5 January 1784 the *Bounty* had reached Tenerife and as soon as they anchored Bligh sent Christian to the Governor, the Marquis de Brancheforté, to explain that they had come for repairs and to supply the ship. Bligh also wished to salute, provided he was answered in like kind. The Governor answered in the kindest terms, stating that he was welcome to whatever the island had in the way of provisions; but he could not return the salute as he could only do so for persons of equal rank. [7] Soon after the Port Master, Captain Adams, arrived, sending compliments from the Governor.

As it was already January Bligh was in something of a hurry to get his ship in order and to obtain supplies, so on the 7th he gave his instructions to the contractors, Collogan and Sons. When he bargained for goods, he found that prices were very high as crops and vegetables were out of season; but wine was a bargain at ten to fifteen pounds a pipe and Bligh purchased some, as he had promised Banks to do so. As there was a lot of surf and landing was not easy, the supplies were taken on board by means of the boats. Bligh had received permission for Nelson to roam about and check on the plant life; while Bligh was interested in the politics and social structures of Tenerife. Poverty was desperate here, so much so that the government had launched a charitable institution – the Hospicio – to look after those in need. Disease was uncommon, but if a crew brought one – for example the smallpox – it had devastating effects. This is why the Governor was reluctant to allow any ship's crews to wander around Santa Cruz, unless they had been given a clean bill of health.

On 9 January Bligh found time to write a note to Banks and on the next day the *Bounty* sailed off. Bligh now divided the watch into three, giving Christian charge of the third watch. As Bligh explained:

I have always considered this as a desirable regulation when circumstances will admit of it on many accounts; and am persuaded that unbroken rest not only contributes much towards the health of a ship's company but enables them more readily to exert themselves in cases of sudden emergency. [8]

Time was still a precious commodity and as Bligh wished to sail direct to Tahiti with no further stops, he ordered that the men should be put on two-thirds ration of bread, as this is as much as they ate anyhow. He did have a number of fresh pumpkins and he later offered these to the crew at the rate of two pounds of pumpkin for one of bread. There was a problem with the cheese. The cheeses were counted, after bringing them up to the air; but after dinner Bligh found that two were missing. As he could not find the culprit, he ordered the cheese to be stopped from each person until the amount was made up. This led to some muttering and some of the crew complained to the Master about casks of meat being light and the matter of the cheeses. When Fryer told Bligh he realised that he needed to do something to quieten the men: such talk was close to mutiny. He also knew that in times of unrest a Captain must exert his authority or lose it. He gathered them together and in a moment of anger for which he was famous, he cried out:

'Everything relative to the provisions is transacted by my orders, and it is therefore needless to make any complaint for you will get no redress. I am the fittest judge of what is right or wrong. I shall flog the first man severely who should dare attempt to make any complaint in future!'

He then 'dismissed them with severe threats' and the entire affair was forgotten.

Despite this menacing speech, the old lags would have smiled and nodded to each other. Bligh was a sea dog, all right. While the greenhorns might have shuddered at his harangue, the more experienced sailors had heard this all before. Sea Captains were renowned for their bad language and their bombast and they were well used to it. The more seasoned tars had heard worse and endured worse; Bligh might storm but so far his menaces were simply hot air. Bligh had learned his trade from many Captains – including the dreaded Cook – but while they never baulked at using the lash, Bligh was hesitant to do so. Although hot-headed, he preferred to keep his crew in line with the strength of his personality and he was, at heart, a humane commander.

Bligh cared for the welfare of his crew and was solicitous for their well-being. For purity, the water was filtered through dripstones Bligh had bought at Tenerife for that purpose. The commander also gave thought to the mental health of his crew and insisted that there would be time, whenever possible, for recreation; and to that purpose he hired a fiddle-player, Michael Byrne, who was blind in one eye and could see little with the other.

Some time for relaxation and Mirth is absolutely necessary, and I have considered it so much so that after 4 o'Clock, the Evening is laid aside for their Amusement and dancing. I had great difficulty before I left England to get a Man to play the Violin and I preferred at last to take One two thirds Blind than come without one.

Sailing went along without a hitch, but on the 23 January Bligh made a serious discovery – his surgeon Huggan was an alcoholic. The good doctor had made sure he had gone aboard with abundant supplies, and spent most of his time in his cabin in the company of his bottles. The able-bodied seamen also liked their liquor, but they burned it off with everyday work and used alcohol socially; Huggan, on the other hand, was more often than not in a drunken stupor. Bligh was both surprised and irritated by his surgeon's activities:

I now find my Doctor to be a Drunken Sot. He is constantly in liquor, having a private Stock by him which I have assured him shall be taken away if he does not desist from making himself such a Beast. [9]

It was just as well that Bligh employed Ledward at the last moment; for Huggan was hardly to be relied upon. At the start of February, rains came and fires were lit to dry clothes. The ships was cleaned and sprinkled with vinegar.

On 9 February the *Bounty* crossed the equatorial line, when all the old hands demanded the traditional ceremony to take place. Bligh acquiesced and so began the strangest and time-honoured ritual in the Royal Navy.

Deep was the bath, to wash away all ill;
Notched was the razor — of bitter taste the pill.
Most ruffianly the barber looked — his comb was trebly nailed —
And water, dashed from every side, the neophyte assailed. [10]

The origins of the ceremony are lost in time, but possibly dated to Viking times, who might have handed them down to the Anglo-Saxons. The ceremony is performed by shellbacks, or Sons of Neptune – those who have crossed the line before. One is called upon to enact King Neptune, and his Royal Court consists of Her Highness Amphitrite, the First Assistant Davy Jones, the Royal Scribe, the Doctor, the Dentist, the Baby, the Navigator, the Chaplain, the Judge, the Attorney, the barber and others. The uninitiated are scum, or 'pollywogs' and must be prepared for their ordeal. They are washed, covered in some obnoxious substance and shaved with some rusty or inappropriate instrument. Many may be 'ducked', but Bligh would not allow this part – usually tying a man with rope and casting him overboard – as some were almost drowned for the amusement of the crew. But the rest of the pageant was permitted and twenty-seven endured the ritual scraping. It is not known if the new *Bounty* shellbacks obtained a certificate, but one was often given, addressed to '*all Mermaids, Sea Serpents, Whales, Sharks, Porpoises, Dolphins, Skates, Eels, Suckers, Lobsters, Crabs, Pollywogs and other living things of the sea*', stating that '*in latitude 00-00 and longitude X, So-and-So has been found worthy to be numbered as one of our trusty shellbacks, has been gathered to our fold and duly initiated into the solemn mysteries of the ancient order of the deep.*'

The 'razor' used on the *Bounty* was an iron hoop and the officers gave up two bottles of rum and the men one - which Bligh promised to pay for - and he even dished out half a pint of wine to each man to encourage the festivities. Byrne tuned up his fiddle and the evening ended with dancing.

After these celebrations the voyage continued with little incident until their ship met up with the *British Queen of London*, a whaler headed for the Cape of Good Hope on 17 February. [11] This gave Bligh the opportunity to write a report to Banks, which contained the following paragraph:

The Calm as usual was attended with heavy Rains & very sultry weather however by constant drying & Cleaning ship we kept perfectly in health as we are to turn all circumstances to our advantage all our empty water Casks were filled with Rain Water and I have now a very sufficient quantity to carry me to Otaheite without touching any where. I am happy and satisfied in my little Ship and we are now fit to go round half a score of worlds, both Men & Officers tractable and well disposed & chearfulness & content in the countenance of every one. I am sure nothing is even more conducive to health. I have no cause to inflict punishments for I have no offenders and every thing turns out to my most sanguine expectations. Nelson & the gardener are very well, indeed I have not had a sick Person since I left England, and I hope to have the honor to give you like accounts on my return.

The *Bounty* sailed on, travelling into fairer weather and higher temperatures – the thermometer at times topped 85°. At sunrise there was a dense mist which generally cleared away by sunset and the nights were clear. Bligh knew that in the Tropics, a mixture of calmness and rains led to a sultry atmosphere which was a breeding-ground for disease, so to combat this he insisted that the ship was aired and clothes cleaned and dried. To add to their diet they sometimes caught fish and one day they landed a shark as well as five dolphins. The crew now seemed to be content and on Sunday 2 March Bligh led the divine service; he also gave a written order for Christian to act as Lieutenant.

It may be that Bligh felt that he needed a second-in-command to help with the running of the ship. He was, in fact, very much alone and depended on Fryer to control the men in his absence, but Fryer was at best a mediocre Master, quarrelsome and not a man in whom to rely upon. Instead of settling the unrest among the men, he had simply reported the discontent to Bligh and left him no choice but to stamp out the problem. He could not have promoted Fryer even if he wanted to, but Christian was a different matter; he had educated him in navigation and surveying and he realised that he was also a popular officer among the crew. Moreover, he owed his advancement to Master's mate solely to Bligh. If there was anyone on the ship he could depend on, that man was surely Fletcher

Christian. He had proven himself a worthy subordinate on past voyages and on the *Bounty*, there had been not a single adverse word against him mentioned in his log. After his advancement, Christian continued to do all of his duties to the complete satisfaction of Bligh.

This sudden act of generosity might have been one of kindness, but it was not calculated to please the Master of the ship, whose mate had been given preferment ahead of himself. Whether or not it had anything to do with the promotion, from that time forward there seemed to be discontent in the ship. Besides, the ratings were getting the measure of Bligh. So far, he had stormed and raged, but they had seen little in the way of punishment. It encouraged some to push his patience.

Just over a week after Christian's promotion, Matthew Quintal had treated his officer – as reported by Fryer - with insolence and contempt and as such overstepped the mark. He was punished with 24 lashes. In the published narrative, Bligh claims it was also for 'mutinous behaviour'. [12] Of course, the lash was the only naval method of discipline, but it is clear that Bligh was profoundly disappointed that he had to take recourse to such measures.

'Until this afternoon', he wrote in his log, 'I had hopes I could have performed the Voyage without punishment to any One.'

Bligh did not enjoy punishing is crew and would only resort to it when it was necessary. He would threaten, of course, but only carried out the threat if there was no alternative. It is strange, considering the mentors he had, particularly Cook, who lashed a third of his crew during his final voyage. Others were even harsher and the most sadistic would award two hundred lashes or even have a man flogged until he died. Bligh was an intelligent man and watched the excellent commanding qualities of his master, but also saw his faults. This is not to say that Bligh was without fault but cruelty was not one of them. He was fastidious about duty and expected each member of his staff to perform his tasks punctually and efficiently. If they failed to do so, they would receive a lashing – from his tongue. Bligh was hot-headed and his temper raged like a flash storm; he would gesticulate with his hands and give his victim verbal abuse and insult. Then again, he was a naval officer and in that respect differed no more from his peers than anyone else. After the tempest came the calm and Bligh would always act as if nothing had ever happened, as if his bark had been his punishment and once administered the case was closed. Often he would rail at a particular officer, then a couple of hours later ask him to dine with him. It was a mannerism which most members of his crew attested to.

Quintal had left him little choice. He had defied authority and that was not to be borne. The *Bounty*'s crew could commit and offence through ignorance or by error – that was unavoidable – and Bligh would respond with a tongue-lashing. But order had to be maintained and his men had to obey instructions punctiliously. To refuse an order was an act of mutiny and was treated very seriously. If insubordination was allowed to go unchecked, it could pave the way for general unruliness and, in the end, out-and-out mutiny. Bligh had no marines on board and discipline was maintained through the strength of his character. Quintal had flouted authority and this had to be deterred. The flogging was not a harsh decision, it was inevitable and not given lightly.

There was little incident until 23 March, when Bligh sighted the coast of Terra del Fuego and later was almost tempted to pull in at New Year's Harbour. He knew that it had good anchorage and was an excellent place for watering and wood, but the season was running very late and the dreaded Cape Horn was looming up ahead of them, so he decided to strike on for Tahiti. They sailed onward and soon they were through the Straits of Magellan and now faced the terrible passage to the Cape.

Cape Horn was what Bligh had dreaded and the last thing he wanted to do was face its terror out of season. In its rage, the Cape was the most dreadful place for a ship to be and its tempests outdid any that could be faced in the ocean. No Captain wanted to fall foul of its legendary wrath and – at its worst - no vessel could survive the virulence of its wind and pounding waves. That prospect would make the firmest heart quail and although Bligh was no coward he must have feared for the safety of the *Bounty* if he met with adverse conditions. He could only hope that he was not too late and that he could pass the Cape unnoticed by the elements.

It was not to be. As if to welcome them, on 29th a heavy storm hit them. When they entered the Cape, they found themselves in a watery hell. The wind howled and screeched around them and the sea rose up and up, breakers as high as cliffs frowning down upon them and swamping the decks. The sight of the battering waves dismayed Bligh, and he wrote:

I do not Wonder at Lord Ansons Account of the High Sea, for it exceeds any I have seen, and to be here in a laboursome Ship must be an Unhappy Situation. [13]

There was worse to come. The wind was to reach hurricane level and snow storms attacked the ship with all their fury. The days of April brought more wind and such storms as Bligh had never seen; the ship was a toy at the mercy of the booming elements. The seas, now mountains, broke on them at all sides and the pump was at full stretch to keep the water below critical levels. Between the 6th and the 9th they had something of a respite; but the forces of nature were regrouping and on the 10th hit the *Bounty* with all their power. By the 14th they were attacking the ship with all their rage; the *Bounty* found herself high on giant seas only to fall helplessly into the abysses in between. It is only by a miracle that no men were lost at sea although there were times when they were flung about the decks. On 13 April Bligh wrote:

My Gunner who has had charge of a Watch is now laid up, and my Carpenters Mate, and from the Violent motion of the ship the Cook fell and received a severe bruize and broke one of his Ribs, and One Man Dislocated his shoulder. [14]

In such desperate conditions, Bligh did what he could for the comfort of his crew. He insisted on issuing them with a hot breakfast and burned fires continually to keep their clothes dry. He opened up the great cabin for his men to hang up their wet hammocks and even gave a personal sacrifice. [15]

'I now Ordered my Cabbin to be appropriated at Nights to the Use of those poor fellows who had Wet Births, by which means it not only gave more room between Decks, but rendered those happy who had not dry beds to sleep in.'

To keep up their spirits, he regularly ordered a dram of rum to be served to the crew. In his log he gave credit to the steadfastness of 'his People', stating that they bore 'the fatigue with Cheerfulness and health' and that he insisted on his men only wearing dry clothes:

It is from this I date, with some trifling comforts besides, their great share of health.

By April Bligh had noticed that of all his animals, only the hogs had survived. It was already clear in his mind that the attempt to round the Cape was a useless one and could only lead to their destruction. In a fortnight they had battled against insuperable odds and yet had made hardly any ground at all. He had noted that if the ship – or the men – grumbled, that would decide the matter. Now it seemed like a case of suffering for no good reason and at 11 o'clock in the morning he announced to the crew that he intended to give up these tempestuous waters and make for the Cape of Good Hope, a resolution which was met with loud cheers. Bligh gave a speech thanking the crew for all of their stout efforts. He also had a hog killed 'to give them a valuable meal'. He then made an official note in the log of the reason why he had abandoned his attempt – in short, that any further trials would eventually endanger 'the project'.

After their ordeal, Bligh looked to his men and his care is reflected in the following log note:

To enable me to keep my People as healthy as possible, I have not only appropriated my Cabbin to as many as could hang their Hammocks in it, but I also have all the others bedding brought into it every day while I cannot get them upon Deck in the bad Weather, by this means I have the Tween Decks clear and can be properly Aired by Fires as well as the Cabbin. It is to be remembered that all hands are at three Watches, which with the necessary comforts I can give them, such as allways a hot breakfast of wheat with Sugar, Portable Soup in their Pease and a Pint to each man of Sweet Wort a Day, with their allowance of Spirits, (very fine Old Rum) besides keeping them dry as Possible and Clean is all that can be done. I have ommitted to mention that they have as much Sour Krout, Mustard & Vinegar as they can use.

Cape Horn had not forgiven their audacity, but sent storms in their wake which hammered the *Bounty* as she flew from its wrath. They chased her until 8 May, when the crew could finally take stock and repair the damage; the naturally quarrelsome carpenter Purcell had much to grumble about, the boats needing repair as well as parts of the ship. Seeing his crew in better health, Bligh stopped serving the sweet wort although he continued to give them a hot breakfast every day. This was almost unheard-of at the time. As the Captain was also the Purser, he would have to shoulder the cost of overspending, which is why some sailors received very poor rations. To his credit, Bligh never stinted at providing for his crew. He looked after their diet, their well-being – even their entertainment.

By 13th they passed near to the island of Tristan da Cunha, but failed to see it due either to faulty positioning or the overcast weather. By the 22nd Bligh saw Table Mountain marking the Cape of Good Hope, and fearing that Table Bay might be unsafe for anchorage, they pulled into Simon's Bay – the inner part of False Bay – on 24 May.

Bligh was rightly proud of the fact that he had taken the *Bounty* through such distances and extremities of hardship, yet without any serious sickness. Colds he kept at bay by airing the ships and insisting on dry clothing; and the scurvy by means of dried malt, 'sour krout' and portable soup.

'With these Articles properly issued, I am firmly convinced no Scurvy will appear.' [16]

He also stressed the importance of exercise and keeping a happy ship. He remained content that discipline had been virtually non-existent, although he had occasion now to give John Williams six lashes for neglect in heaving the lead.

Bligh saluted the fort, which replied with the same number of guns. Then they inspected the ship and found she needed to be completely recaulked and sails and rigging repaired. While this was going on, Bligh ensured that fresh meat with soft bread and plenty of vegetables were supplied daily to the ship, then he travelled to Cape Town to visit the Governor, van der Graaf. Although anchored some way from Cape Town, van der Graaf arranged everything so that supplies were sent so methodically that the *Bounty* hardly felt any inconvenience from her position in Simon's Bay. Once again, however, Bligh found that inflation had hit the price of supplies and sheep were so expensive that he found it more economic to but mutton at fourpence per pound. [17] After their terrible experiences at Cape Horn, they found that much of their supply was damaged; thirty bags of bread which lay at the bottom of the Bread Room were totally rotten and two barrels of pork were unfit for consumption. With his typical attention to detail, Bligh wrote down all the supplies he had taken aboard:

- **Bread in Biscuit & Soft Bread (9200 lbs)**

- **Flour (7166 lb)**

- **Oil (34 Galls. 5 lb)**

- **Callivances (69 Bushels)**

- **Wine (776¼ Galls.)**

- **Fresh Meat (1656 lbs)**

- *** Raisins (119 lbs)**

- **Gun Powder (3 Barrells - 300 lbs)**

- **Cabbages (256)**

- **Bunches of Greens &ca. (256)**

   Note * The Raisins by neglect was not charged to Government. It must therefore come in the next supply.

On 20 June Bligh wrote to Banks:

I fully thought of sailing the 20th Inst. but the ship requiring much caulking & refitting I find it impracticable, owing to very unfavorable weather before the 26th. Every assistance has been given to Nelson & his

assistant. They have been with Mr. Mason and most of the specimens & some seeds that he has collected will be left with him ... Governor Vander Graaf vastly in favor of the Prince & has paid us a great compliment by his attention to our equipment in the little matters I wanted. The strength of the Cape Town is now considerably encreased by lines of heavy Cannon at the Bay Entrance opposite Pengwin Island, with several Batterys at the head of the Bay, which with some extensive improvements & strength added to the old Fort make it now a respectable place with respect to Force. They have also nearly five thousand Regular Troops.

We are [and] all perfectly well and in good Spirits and have no doubt of a speedy voyage to Otaheite & of our success there. [17]

The *Bounty* left the Cape on 1 July at 4 pm and gave a 13-gun salute, which was returned. Up until 10 July they met with fine weather, but this was to change and the ships faced storms and gales for the next ten days. As from this time on the weather was mixed, the crew was given hot breakfast until they finally sighted the Mewstone on August, marking the south-west cape of Tasmania. They wanted to anchor in Adventure Bay; but it took some time, as contrary winds hampered them; but at noon of 21st August they had found their way to the inner part of the Bay, about two miles from Penguin Island. Bligh went on a recce and found the west side of the beach was the most suitable for wood and water, although the surf meant that anything from the shore would need to be ferried by boat. Bligh knew the place well; it was at that spot that Cook and he had watered on their voyage of discovery and death.

When dawn broke on 22 August Bligh sent Christian with a watering party, while a man stayed behind to wash the clothes. There had been little water here when he had arrived with Cook, but at this season the streams were full of good water, which the party soon gathered in barrels. At this part of the shore the surf was not so bad as in other areas, so the boats could bring in the barrels with the least trouble. Bligh had hoped to replenish his food supplies with fresh food, but the fishing proved very poor, catching only twenty flounders and a few other flatfish. There were wild duck on a lake, but Bligh managed to scare them all away after taking an unsuccessful shot at them. Meanwhile Nelson was exploring the bay for botanical samples. He did find a tree which measured thirty-three feet in girth – and a dead opossum. [18] Bligh spotted 'several eagles, some beautiful blue-plumaged herons, and a great variety of parakeets' as well as 'a few oyster-catchers and gulls' around the beach. [19]

Meanwhile Purcell was causing some problems; his job was that of a carpenter and he resented being told to do anything else. He was an interesting character; he saw everything in black and white and had no time for shades of grey. He was hired as a carpenter – that was his job and nothing else. He was skilful and had a passion for keeping his tools in perfect order. But he was argumentative and forthright, not shrinking from voicing his opinions to anyone – including Bligh. In that regard he could be infuriating and would never compromise, which was to lead to a number of clashes with his Captain. Holding the King's warrant, he was immune from corporal punishment, which he knew well – as did Bligh.

When Bligh arrived he found that Purcell was cutting the billets too long and he reprimanded him over to it, to which the carpenter replied:

'I suppose you are come on shore on purpose to find fault!'

On hearing other similar remarks, he uttered other 'impertinent expressions'. Bligh was furious and had Purcell been a rating he would have felt the taste of the whip or been thrown in irons. Fortunately for Purcell, he was protected from the lash. Bligh was not like other Captains and anyway, there was more than one way of skinning this particular quarrelsome cat. The loss of a strong fit man was a waste of manpower, so he decided to send him back to the ship:

My Carpenter on my expressing my disapprobation of his Conduct with respect to orders he had received from me concerning the mode of working with the Wooding Party behaved in a most insolent and reprehensible manner, I therefore ordered him on board, there to assist in the general duty of the ship, as I could not bear the loss of an able working and healthy Man; otherwise I should have committed him to close confinement until I could have tryed him: the prospect of which appears to be of so long a date made me determine to keep him at his duty, giving him a Chance by his future Conduct to make up in some degree for his behaviour at this place.

Purcell must have felt extremely fortunate that he escaped without further punishment. He seemed to be asking for it. Back on board ship, Fryer had ordered all men and officers to help in bringing the water into the hold, but the obstinate Purcell had refused to do so, even when Bligh appeared. When ordered to help with the loading, Purcell replied:

'I will do anything in my line, sir: but as to that duty I can't comply with it.'

It is highly likely that the reply earned him the lash of Bligh's tongue. He could not allow this man to behave in such a way in front of him and he decided that until he came to his senses his rations would be stopped and anyone supplying him would be harshly dealt with. This 'immediately brought him to his senses.' It is arguable that he might have been too lenient, as such merciful actions could goad others into similar outbursts. Then again, there was really little else Bligh could have done.

Purcell was not one to easily learn a lesson and he seems to have held a grudge against Bligh since that time. When Bligh, the same day, issued elixir of vitriol to prevent the scurvy, Purcell again refused to obey.

'I am well enough, and therefore I do not choose, nor won't take such stuff as this. I do not know what it is.'

The next few days were spent in exploring the terrain, although on 27 August board ship Bligh discovered a minor disaster; a leaky cask had caused 32 gallons of rum to leak out. He put it down to experience. A little later, Bligh was interested when Hayward found a tree with AD 1771 inscribed on it, apparently by Captain Furneaux's earlier expedition. Nelson advised Bligh to plant fruit trees on the east side of the shore, as this seemed best for the purpose, so he proceeded to plant apple-trees, vines, 'plantain-trees, orange and lemon-seed, cherry-stones, plum, peach, and apricot-stones, pumpkins, also two sorts of Indian corn, and apple and pear kernels.' This was for future travellers but also as a gift to the natives, of whom they still had seen nothing. At this time mussels were plentiful and the crew ate so many that a number were sick.

The natives were first spotted on 1 September, their fires being seen on the shores near Cape Frederick Henry. It was Brown, the gardener, who had the first contact with them as he was searching for plants in that area and came across an old man, a woman and a few children. The man was alarmed, but became more friendly when Brown presented him with a knife. Brown noticed some run-down wigwams with kangaroo skins used as matting. The old man at first appeared alarmed, but became familiar on being presented with a knife. He nevertheless sent away the young woman who went very reluctantly. In one of the wigwams he saw nothing but a few kangaroo skins spread on the ground, and a basket made of rushes. When he left the, a few other natives – about twenty – followed him and when he arrived to the shore he was amazed to see the *Bounty* lying just off the shore. Bligh had been determined to find the natives and it was sheer coincidence that they had arrived at that time. The commander noted that they were of medium height, the shoulders and breast scarified and that they were painted with a soot-like substance which made it difficult to discover their true colour. Although Bligh threw gifts to them wrapped in paper (it was impossible to land), they took them nervously and would not be induced to come aboard.

On 4 September, the *Bounty* sailed out of Adventure Bay, Bligh intending to pass New Zealand on its south side: but as the winds were variable they altered their course on the 14th. On the 19th they passed thirteen small islands and spotted some penguins. As Cook had not seen them, Bligh decided to call them the Bounty Isles. [20] As they sailed on, they were followed by some of the sea birds - and some whales.

The *Bounty* sailed on without incident until 9 October, when Samuel the clerk presented the boatswain's and carpenter's expense books to Fryer for him to sign. This Fryer refused to do, possibly because he felt slighted by Bligh in the matter of Christian's preferment. Instead, he asked Bligh to sign a certificate to say that he had done nothing amiss while aboard the *Bounty*. This was enough to light Bligh's fuse and he would not have his officers doing their duty on conditions. He then read the Articles of War to the crew, with particular attention to the rules for signing the books. Fryer, seeing that he was backed into a corner, then signed the books as requested.

The next day brought tragedy; the ailing James Valentine died. [21] His sickness began on Adventure Bay with an 'indisposition' and was bled in his arm; but the arm became inflamed and painful. It would be an interesting question to ask whether Huggan, in his constant state of inebriation, performed this task with any skill. Soon Valentine had taken to his hammock and after a few days his arm seemed to improve; but he then complained of chest problems – a cough and a shortage of breath. Blisters began to appear on his chest and some on his back, four days before his death. Huggan told him that Valentine died from a disease one 'may call an Asthma'. The incident shocked Bligh:

The loss I met with this day by the Death of James Valentine was of equal Surprize and regret. This poor man was one of the most robust People on board, and therefore the surprize and shock was the greater to me. He had no Effects of any Value I therefore directed the few Shirts and Trowsers that belonged to him be given to the two Men who had attended him during his illness with great care and Affection.

The month of October also brought a spate of complaints which Bligh put down as 'rheumatism'. The surgeon had other ideas and put it down to scurvy, something which must have alarmed Bligh; he went on to prescribe draughts of essence of malt. It is hardly surprising if he doubted the doctor's word; he was rarely fully sober and was completely incapable of performing his duty. On 18 October Bligh found that the men Huggan had diagnosed with scurvy had nothing more than prickly heat.

Meanwhile there was more subordination in the ranks – Mills and Brown both refused to participate in the evening dancing; Brown indeed had complained of a complaint which again the doctor diagnosed as scurvy but which was, according to Bligh, a 'rheumatic complaint'. In any case a direct refusal to obey orders was a serious thing and both Mills and Brown had their share of grog stopped, with threats of further punishment should they persist in their refusals. It is not difficult to imagine Bligh's exasperation – the fiddling and dancing had been provided for their amusement and benefit.

Whoever had the correct diagnosis, it is true that none of the men actually had scurvy and the doctor's ability had to come under question. By the 22nd he himself appeared on the sick list along with Thomas McIntosh and John Millward, whom he had diagnosed as having scurvy. Huggan's complaint was 'owing to a constant state of intoxication'. In fact the weather was getting hot and a number of men began to feel faint at midday, which may explain some of their symptoms. Fearing dehydration, Bligh stopped all salt foods and issued portable soup thickened with barley and as much vinegar, mustard and sour krout as they could use. Within a couple of days he could see the improvements; the invalids were fast recovering and the midday faintness was disappearing. They had no swellings and their gums were good, which convinced Bligh that scurvy was not an issue.

Huggan's erratic behaviour was getting out of hand and Bligh saw the only thing to do was to remove all liquor from his room; this was done, but not without a great deal of protestation from the good doctor:

I found to Day the Doctors assistant was deceiving me with respect to the Surgeons Illness. It was now four days since he had seen light and in bed all the time intoxicated, I therefore ordered his Cabbin to be cleaned and searched, and all liquor to be taken from him which was accordingly done, but the operation was not only troublesome but offensive in the highest degree. [22]

As a result, Huggan diagnosed the invalids with scurvy again.

The *Bounty* was nearing its first destination. On 25 October they passed the island of Maitea; going to the north, Bligh found it little more than cliffs, which is why most of the natives settled on the south side. Some seemed to want to trade, but the surf was so high that they went on their way. The next day the ship anchored in Matavai Bay and Bligh looked forward to seeing his old friends – the chief Otoo and the native Omai whom they had delivered home so long ago. He did give strict orders that on no account should anyone mention the death of Captain Cook.

Otoo was not present when they arrived; but that did not stop a host of well-wishers, who thronged to the ship with questions, mostly about Toote, whom, they said, had died; at least, so the last visitors had told them. Bligh evaded questions about Cook, but asked about Otoo. He was in another part of the island, they were told, but messengers had gone to inform him of their presence. The natives seemed overjoyed at seeing them and such was the scene of rejoicing that not a piece of equipment was stolen.

Of the first visitors on board the ship were Otoo's father and brother,

Otow and Oreepyah, accompanied by another chief by the name of Poeeno. While Bligh was giving out presents, a messenger arrived from Otoo bearing a small pig and a plantain tree. After this Poeeno invited them on shore and when they embarked he led them through a walkway shaded by breadfruit tress until they reached his house. Soon Bligh found himself surrounded by well-wishers and the crush was so great that he became affected by the heat; on seeing this the islanders stood back and gave him air. Everywhere were people bringing their blessings and it was like an island carnival. After an hour the womenfolk dressed him in a red cloth and mat, then they each took a hand and led him back to the waterside.

Back on the *Bounty* there was a disturbance. One of the islanders had tried to steal a tin pot and when Otoo's brother Oreepyah found out he was enraged, so much so that the thief barely escaped with his life. Oreepyah then turned on his own countrymen and ordered them all off the ship, telling Bligh to severely flog anyone he found stealing anything from the *Bounty*. Soon after that a representative came on board and Bligh saw that he was carrying Cook's picture, the same that had been painted by Webber and presented to Otoo at their last meeting. They had given it a title – *Toote Earee no Otaheite*, or *Cook, Chief of Tahiti* – and the man told them that Toote had asked Otoo to show it to any English visitors and it would be taken as a sign of their friendship. The frame was in need of repair, although the painting was in good condition and Bligh promised to have it fixed.

The next morning – that of 28 October – Otoo had returned and sent a messenger to request a boat to bring him to the ship. Bligh sent Christian to conduct him on board and soon the two old friends were face to face. They joined noses as a sign of their mutual esteem and affection.

Chapter Five. A *Tyo* of Otaheite

Bligh discovered that his friend's name had changed; he had conferred 'Otoo' as well as *Earee Rahie* on his eldest son, although he was still a minor. Otoo's name was now Tinah, and this is how Bligh knew him from that time forward. Tinah was accompanied by his wife Iddeah, who wore a large hoop of cloth about her, which she took off and handed to Bligh as a gift. The couple also presented him with a large hog and a quantity of breadfruit. In return, Bligh gave Iddeah ear-rings, necklaces and beads, while to Tinah he presented hatchets, small adzes, files, gimblets, saws, looking-glasses, red feathers, and two shirts. Although grateful for her gifts, Iddeah looked upon her husband's and told Bligh she also wanted 'iron', so he handed her a similar present to that of Tinah. [1] At Tinah's request Bligh fired some of the large guns which astonished and amazed the islanders.

Bligh found that Tinah had changed little over the years, still a mountain of a man, six feet four inches tall, of a large build and stout, although a few years older – about thirty-five. His wife Iddeah was also tall and Bligh noticed that she had 'a very animated and intelligent countenance'. She was about twenty-four. It was an act of courtesy to ask them to dinner so that evening they both returned, along with the chieftain Poeeno and several of Tinah's family: his father Otow (who was known as Whappai on their last visit) and two of his brothers, Oreepyah and Whydooah. Tinah was proud of his sons; Whydooah was an able warrior but was addicted to *ava*, the local hooch, so much so that he was thought of as the greatest drunkard in the country. Tinah was fed by his servant, as custom demanded and Bligh was reminded of the man's prodigious appetite:

'I must do him the justice to say he kept his attendant constantly employed.' [2]

He also joined the ladies later – who dined separately, and he had quite forgotten that he had already dined. The chief and Iddeah stayed the rest of the day – Tinah eating roast pork four times – and Bligh allowed him a locker in which to keep his gifts, as European goods were a great treasure and a magnet for audacious thieves.

The next day was a busy one for Bligh. In the morning he returned Tinah's visit, finding them in a hut with Iddeah and three small relatives. As there were lots of children, he handed them beads and soon they were queuing up for the privilege, which proved a great entertainment for young and old alike. Hearing that one of the most important chiefs of the district was with Poeeno, Bligh decided to stop there on his way back to the ship. This chief, a relative of Poeeno, was called Moannah and both men were intrigued when Bligh began to plan a garden for them which would grow into fruit-bearing trees. Moannah joined Bligh for dinner on board the *Bounty*, then he returned to Poeeno's to work a little more on the seeds for the garden. While Bligh was there, a messenger came from Tinah asking him to come to his brother Oreepyah's house.

When he arrived, he realised something important was about to happen; a large crowd had gathered and made way for him to sit by Tinah. Then a large strip of cloth – about six feet wide and forty feet long – was arranged on the ground while Bligh was dressed like a Tahitian chieftain; cloth draped over his shoulders and around his waist. A gift was brought to him – two huge hogs and a supply of breadfruit and coconuts. After this Bligh was asked to walk the length of the cloth and as he did so the crowd shouted out '*Tyo! Ehoah!*' (names meaning 'friend'); and with that the

Ceremony of Friendship ended. [3]

Although an English gentleman and an officer, Bligh had a very philanthropic nature as can easily be noticed in his narrative of the voyage and his personal log. He had a deep interest in the customs, rites, behaviour and language of the natives of Tahiti and while he considered Otoo a lazy and somewhat gluttonous man, there can be little doubt that a strong friendship grew between the two, cementing the earlier relations they had had when Bligh visited with Captain Cook. Of course it was necessary to be on good terms with Otoo 'for the success of the project'; but Bligh was quick to write down the best qualities of the islanders – their genuine amiability and their hospitality. It goes without saying that, as an eighteenth century Lieutenant of the Royal Navy, he had a jingoistic and rather superior concept of his own people; but his natural affection for the Tahitians was genuine. There was only one thing which annoyed and plagued him through his stay – and Tahiti was by no means exceptional – the propensity among many of them to steal whatever they could when no-one was looking. It was natural for them to covet the belongings of the newcomers – particularly the smallest articles of metal, as they had no skill in forging – but the small thefts which took place regularly were a source of some annoyance, both to Bligh and the chiefs who were mortified by the actions of their countrymen.

A good example took place not long after their arrival. Bligh decided to visit a district to the west of Matavai known as Oparre, ostensibly to visit Tinah's son Otoo who was the *Earee Rahie* and lived with the rest of Tinah's children. On the morning of the visit Tinah was afraid to come to the ship and Bligh discovered that he feared Bligh's wrath when he discovered an item had been purloined. That item turned out to be the ship's buoy, presumably stolen for the iron hoops around it. Bligh had intended to sail with Tinah and other chieftains including Oreepyah and Moannah, but Oreepyah did not join them as he was determined to find the thieves and the lost buoy. When they reached their destination, Moannah declined to go ashore, preferring to stay aboard to ensure that none of his people stole anything else.

During the thirty minute voyage, Tinah explained some of the more recent history of Oparre. Five years after their last visit, Oparre was attacked by the islanders of Eimeo who had combined with the forces of Attahooroo, part of Tahiti; there was much bloodshed after which Tinah and his people fled to the mountains. The invaders destroyed much of the villages and took away their cattle; some they ate and others were taken to Eimeo. Bligh found that his friend had spoken the truth; in Oparre the well-built homes were all gone, to be replaced by makeshift huts. It was natural that Tinah should look to the British to help him avenge their humiliation; but Bligh was not sent to involve himself in intertribal warfare. He was in Tahiti for breadfruit trees.

It was a subject which had been worrying him since his arrival. He knew that if Tinah realised the breadfruit trees were of prime importance, then bargaining would be very difficult; so he hit upon a stratagem. He needed to bring the conversation to the gifts which he had given to the chiefs and particularly to himself. Meanwhile, Tinah was disparaging the other islanders.

'Here, you'll be supplied plentifully with everything you want. All here are your friends and friends of King George: if you go to the other islands you will have everything stolen from you.'

'King George had sent out those valuable presents to you on account of your goodwill and from a desire to serve you and your country; and will not you, Tinah, send something to King George in return?'

'Yes, I will send him anything I have.' [4]

At this point Tinah listed all the things at his disposal - then came to the breadfruit trees. That was it – just what the King wanted! Tinah was thrilled that the King would be happy with something so readily available – so the matter was settled.

Otoo, or simply 'Too', the *Earee Rahie*, was a young boy of about six years of age. Tinah and Iddeah had four children: Otoo Terrenah Oroah, a girl; Terreetappanooai, a boy; and Tahamydooah, a girl. Bligh did not get a clear view of the *Earee Rahie*, as his house stood over a river which Bligh was not permitted to cross. Meanwhile Oreepyah had arrived bringing an iron scraper and one of the buoy's hoops. To make him feel better, Bligh told him that he was completely satisfied with the outcome.

News of the arrival of the British sailors from a distant part of the earth travelled fast and it was not long before Bligh would meet other tribes and chieftains. One day he met a party of Arreoys and as soon as they arrived a ceremony was called for at which Bligh played an important role, joining the welcoming committee with baskets of breadfruit and a suckling pig. Unfortunately, Bligh – as a celebrity on the island – was required to join the others in the speechmaking and his lines were prepared for him. His pronunciation being 'not vey exact', as he puts it, the oration was met with laughter from most of the bystanders, although the chieftain watched on with a serious expression, taking everything very seriously. [5] Bligh was interested to learn that the first-borns of this society were usually killed at birth due to overcrowding; in fact, Teppahoo, (the *Earee* of the district of Tettaha) and his wife, Tetteehowdeeah (Otow's sister) had eight children, every one of which was killed at birth. Bligh concluded that this was not an act of choice but some barbaric superstition. Tinah's people were not exempt; if a lower-class woman had a child by a chief, it was immediately put to death.

The taking of the breadfruit trees having been sanctioned by Tinah, preparations were now made for their removal and potting. Tents were erected at the Point of Venus and a group of men, led by Nelson, were responsible for transplanting the young trees. Meanwhile it was important that the crew were diligent and responsible for their duties; the rules of trading were regulated by Peckover and the men on watch were ordered to be on guard, particularly as some of the natives had a penchant for thievery. The chiefs also were aware of this and Moannah for some time kept guard on the ship to prevent pilfering. On a social level Bligh rarely ate alone but more often than not was accompanied by Tahitian leaders such as Tinah, Poeeno and Moannah.

To remain watchful and alert on this tropical paradise – where food and women were welcoming and enticing – was not an easy task for many of the seamen. But any dereliction of duty was looked upon as a great sin by Bligh. Although all hands were on deck in the tempestuous weather at the Cape and for much of the journey to Tahiti, now was a time for relaxation and enjoying the balm of the Society Islands. Their commander, although averse to punishment for punishment's sake, could not let a lapse go by without its consequences, so when Alexander Smith allowed the gudgeon of the cutter to be stolen under his nose, Bligh ordered twelve lashes. There were a number of chiefs on board and their wives pleaded for Smith, which 'marked them to be the most humane and affectionate creatures in the World.' But an order was an order – and poor Smith had to endure what he was sentenced to. Besides, it acted as a good deterrent for native would-be thieves. [6]

There were times when Bligh had a mischievous sense of humour and, realising that the ship's barber had brought a painted head from London, he had the men form a body with cloth and a stick and placed the wooden head on top – then he made it known to the islanders that they had an English woman on board. The quarter-deck was cleared and the 'lady' made her appearance to shouts of great approbation from the natives.

'*Huaheine no Prittannee myty!*' ('Women of Britain are good!') [7]

Many thought it was Bligh's wife and an old woman came forward and laid breadfruit and cloth at her feet; but soon they realised the joke and laughed at it very much– even more when the disgruntled woman took her gifts back! Tinah and the other important personages thoroughly enjoyed the gag and requested Bligh to bring a cargo of British women next time they visited. Later, when Bligh had the figurehead painted as part of tidying up the ship, they repeated their request.

One person Bligh longed to see was his old friend Omai, whom Cook and himself had left in his own house and plantation in Huaheine. After the *Resolution* and *Discovery* had left, there was a conflict between the islanders and some of the people of Ulieta; the natives of Bolabola also took part in the fighting. Being a man of some importance – thanks to the possession of three or four muskets given him by Cook – Omai was consulted and he advised that they should do battle. Although the muskets did not work as well as he hoped, they were sufficient to assure victory. Although he won peace for his island, he was not destined to enjoy it as he died within thirty months of his return to his native land. The two New Zealand boys who were left with him – Tawai Harooah and Kakoa – had also passed away. Omai's adventures in Britain had made Omai someone of great importance in the region and he often spoke of the people of England and their goodwill and kindness towards him.

The potting of the breadfruit plants went ahead speedily, so that by 8 November they had 252, which were kept on shore although the great cabin was ready and prepared for them. [8] Nelson felt that they would root better and could be cared for more successfully here than on board ship. Bligh's interest in the plant had not wavered and he noted that there were eight different species of the breadfruit at Matavai which in the native tongue were: *patteah, erorroo, awannah, mire, oree, powerro, appeeree* and *rowdeeah*. He was also interested in the way the islanders cooked it, which gave it a flavour they could not emulate in the ship's galley; they dug a hole and built a fire surrounded by stones, then buried the dressed fruit and left it for about two hours.

As part of the hospitality, Tinah would often arrange concerts or *haivas* for the British; usually music of drums and flutes with native singing. There were also wrestling bouts which did not resemble a Graeco-Roman tournament – instead the combatants would grab a handful of each other's hair and tussle until they were parted. Another method was to lay one hand on the breast while striking the other with the hollow of the hand which made a loud slapping noise.

'Upon the whole,' Bligh wrote, 'this performance gave me a better opinion of their strength than of their skill or dexterity.'

After one of the exhibitions, some of the chiefs dined on board the *Bounty* and afterwards Tinah asked if his *taowah,* or priest, could join the company. This soon resulted in a theological discussion, the *taowah* being interested to learn of the religion of the British.

'Our Great God is called Oro and we have many others of less consequence. Do you have any God?'

'Yes, of course.'

'Does He have a Son? Who is His wife?'

'He has a Son but no Wife.'

'Who were his Father and Mother then?'

'He never had either Father or Mother.'

This amused the islanders and they laughed a good deal.

'You have a God then who never had Father or Mother and has a Child without a Wife! Did He not lie with a Woman to get him?'

'No...'

'Who was then before your God and where is He? Is He in the Wind or in the Sun?' [9]

Bligh was relieved to escape this perplexing interrogation and settle down to the drinking of wine, something the natives had developed a great taste for. They soon learned that it was a custom for the British to drink to the health of King George, so during dinner they would constantly remind Bligh of the custom by shouting: '*King George Earee no Prittannee!*' and demand that their glasses were filled. Bligh noted:

'Nothing could exceed the mirth and jollity of these people when they met on board.' [10]

Bligh was interested to discover that not all of the cattle had been destroyed or stolen by the Eimeo marauders. There remained a bull and a cow, but he was dismayed to find that they were located at different parts of the island, the bull at Itteah and the cow in Tettaha. This was a ludicrous situation and Bligh decided that the two must be obtained to preserve the species. Unfortunately before he could visit the closest area, Tettaha, he fell ill through exposure to the sun. His sickness dismayed Tinah and his people and he was overwhelmed by their affection and kindness towards him. The chief himself wept at the news and visited Bligh with Iddeah, insisting on giving him a Tahitian massage called *oommee*. His sickness was short-lived and by 14 November he felt well enough to go on a trip to Tettaha, accompanied by Tinah, Oreepyah and Poeeno.

They set off for their destination in the ship's launch and when they reached it, Tinah sent messages to the chief, Teppahoo. When Teppahoo heard that Bligh was interested in the cow he was naturally suspicious and sent his own messenger to ask if he wanted merely to see it or if he meant to take it away. The messenger returned with the reply that they only wanted to view it; so the chief asked the visitors to proceed westward along the shore. When they landed, a crowd soon gathered around them, which soon gave way when Teppahoo himself arrived. He took them about a quarter of a mile and there Bligh was a magnificent heifer. He presented the chief with a gift and with little other ceremony the party made their way back to Matavai. They stopped off at Oparre, and dined aboard the ship, where Tinah and the rest did not fail to remind Bligh of the health of King George. The morning brought a sweltering sun and plenty of hangovers.

On 19 November Bligh determined to meet up with Teppahoo again and found him at the farthest part of the Bay. The people of Tettaha were not on the best of terms with those of Matavai, although not at war; when Tinah had arrived at their land, he had to buy (or rather, Bligh did) any coconut or fish he required. Bligh gave him a present which pleased him very much and the conversation turned to the cow. The chief was not averse to the idea f selling, so long as he benefitted from it; and when Bligh spoke of the items he was prepared to pay, a bargain was struck. Two days later the heifer arrived and Bligh paid Teppahoo a shirt, a hatchet, a spike nail, a knife, a pair of scissors, a gimlet, a file and a small quantity of loaf-sugar. The chieftain felt he had done well in the business and the cow was sent to the rich grass of Oparre. [11]

Since their arrival, many of the sailors had formed friendships with the natives and most had a *tyo*, or friend which is many cases was more like a bond of brotherhood. They also had attachments with the women, who were beautiful and accommodating, bringing venereal disease to the sick-list. Bligh had an ambivalent attitude to the pox; he saw it as a dreadful affliction and talked to a local woman about it, who told him that it was still prevalent among the islands. Yet sailors were sailors and it was hopeless to prevent them from sowing oats when they had the chance; he did not even contemplate the idea, but turned to the drunken surgeon to cure the men. Among the locals, even the higher class women had their own intrigues and one man, Odiddee, told him that it was the worst-kept secret in Matavai that Iddeah herself had a lover who was none other than the servant (*tow-tow*) who fed Tinah at dinner. When Odiddee saw the disbelief in Bligh's face, he asked Iddeah herself to confirm it, but she just laughed and told Odiddee that he was very naughty to tell Bligh about it.

A number of the men had settled on one woman and developed relations with her. But results of venereal disease could be clearly seen among some of the islanders. The doctor diagnosed Tinah's sister, Wow-wo, as having this complaint when he saw her legs and hands covered in ulcerations, but Bligh asked him to do his best for her.

Time soon passed on the tropical paradise and when not attending to the chores on board ship the men passed their time eating and drinking and living with their women. It made their lives bearable, so Bligh did not object. This laxity would come back to haunt him. What sailor, exposed to the delights of a tropical heaven, with women at his call and food readily available, would trade this for a future of drudgery and pain on board His Majesty's ships? The longer they lingered in this idlyllic paradise, the harder it was to bear the harangues and punishments of their Captain. Bligh was blind to the danger; his 'people' had stood by him through Cape Horn and all the perils of the sea voyage so – so long as the tasks were done – he was happy to allow them to enjoy the delights of Tahiti. For himself, his goal was always at the forefront of his mind; but beneath that, he had a personal interest in the ways and customs of the natives.

he was also his country's ambassador and understood the diplomacy which was expected of him. On 24 November Tinah's mother, Oberreeroah, arrived from the island of Tethuroa; she was old and as fat as her son but greeting Bligh with tears of joy. She brought him a hog and fruit. She spoke much about her son and the misfortunes which had beset him when the men of Eimeo arrived. After their conversation, Oberreeroah wanted to go back to shore and Bligh dined with Moannah and Poeeno; they told him that Tinah and Oreepyah had fallen out following some argument between their wives.

Thefts from the ships had stopped, but when December dawned they began again. During the night of the 1st a rudder of one of the boats was stolen from the tents, possibly by some visitors from other tribes. On the 4th bedclothes were stolen from a hammock. There was little the crew could do but be extra vigilant.

The natives had little in the way of tools, so on 5 December Odiddee asked Bligh if he could arrange for a large stone to be carved so that they could sharpen their hatchets on it. It seemed a small task, so Bligh turned to Purcell the carpenter and asked him to attend to it. Purcell replied:

'I will not cut the stone for it will spoil my chisel, and though there is law to take away my clothes there is none to take away my tools!' 12

Although he left no account of his reply, it may safely be assumed that the carpenter got the lashing of Bligh's tongue; as a punishment he confined him to his quarters for a day. His main fault had been his blunt reply, which amounted to insolence; his reasons for the refusal were sound. It did seem that while not at sea, the sailors were freer with their tongues than they might have been. Matthew Thompson, perhaps mimicking Purcell, also refused orders and gave an insolent reply. He was not so lucky as the carpenter and should have realised that Bligh would not put up with this type of behaviour for long. He was given twelve lashes.

6 December brought an unexpected change in the weather. The wind changed direct to the north-west and a gale forced high raging seas into the Bay. The huge waves pounded the ship which rocked and rolled in the lurching sea. It is almost like Cape Horn all over again and Bligh had to batten down every part of the ship. In the middle of this dangerous weather, a small canoe set out from the shore and the sailors doubted it could exist for more than a few moments. It was determined to reach the ship and although that seemed an impossibility it made it under the skilful steerage of Tinah and Iddeah who, terrified for the safety of their friends, had decide to come and see if everything was all right. As soon as they clambered on board they made for Bligh and embraced him. Iddeah braved the sea to return to shore, but Tinah stayed with the ship for the whole tempestuous night.

Nelson's quick thinking saved the breadfruit plants. Despite the howling wind and heavy rains, they cut a passage in the beach at distance from the tents, so that the swollen river could no longer be a danger.

By the next day the wind had moderated and the peril was over. Tinah and Iddeah paid another visit with a hog, breadfruit and coconuts; they told Bligh that everyone was deeply concerned about them and made him promise to come and visit their parents and sister who had been out of their minds with worry. Later Poeeno and his wife also paid a visit and the woman began to strike her head with a shark's tooth so violently that the blood poured. This was often done in times of joy and grief, but Bligh stopped her and her passion seemed to ebb away. Poeeno said that if anything happened to the *Bounty*:

'You shall live with me if the ship is lost, and we will cut down Trees to build another to carry you to Prittannee.'

On 10 December there was an accident which almost proved fatal. The sailors were hauling a launch on shore for repair and were pulling it down over a series of wooden rollers. A ten-year old boy was thrown under one of these rollers and word of the incident was sent to Bligh who asked for Ledward, the surgeon's assistant, to go and see what could be done. The surgeon himself, Huggan, was ill after continuous alcohol abuse. Luckily, the boy was fit and no bones were broken.

At 8 o'clock, Ledward decided to see how Huggan was; he had rarely left his cabin since their arrival and had spent his energy in drinking. The fact that he had been unable to help the wounded boy was enough to alarm the surgeon's mate. He found him worse than usual and in need of air and so took him on deck; then he reported his state to Bligh, who arranged for a cabin to be prepared for him. When Fryer came to take him up, with the help of a few others, he found the doctor completely senseless. He was still alive, but had difficulty in breathing and after some efforts brought up some phlegm. They tried to get him to drink some coconut milk, but to no avail. By nine o'clock he was dead.

Bligh wrote a note in his log:

This unfortunate man died owing to drunkenness and indolence. Exercise was a thing he could not bear an Idea of, or could I ever bring him to take a half dozen of turns on deck at a time in the course of the whole Voyage. Sleeping was the way he spent his time, and he accustomed himself to breath so little fresh air and was so filthy in his person that he became latterly a nuisance. I directed his Cabbin and property to be secured untill I can take an Inventory of his Effects. [13]

When the death reached the ears of the natives, they were not surprised. They knew Huggan – or Teronnoo as they called him – well, and put his death down to 'not working and drinking too much *ava no Prittannee*.' After gaining permission from Tinah's father, Huggan was buried on shore in a grave dug by the natives, lined up east to west. As Tinah told him:

'There the sun rises and there it sets.'

At four in the afternoon the body was buried in the presence of his shipmates and a great number of natives, all of whom behaved with the greatest respect. Afterwards some of the chiefs asked what Bligh intended to do about the dead man's cabin; when a man died he was carried to the Tupapow and when night came the death chamber was surrounded by spirits; no less than two men should enter the room at one time. A single man would be devoured by the invisible presences.

Thomas Ledward was promoted to ship's surgeon, something he had foreseen before he had embarked on the *Bounty*. Huggan's effects were auctioned in a public sale, apart from thirty-three shirts for which the bidding only reached half their value.

There was good news for Tinah on 14 December – the doctor's attentions to his sister Wow-wo has been efficacious and she was almost free from her ulcerations. His joy was turned to dismay when he learned that Bligh was planning to leave his shores very soon and his visit was coming to a close. He had not decided whether to visit the island of Tinah's old enemies, Eimeo, or to sail to the harbour of Toahroah near Oparre. Needless to say, the islanders were distressed at the idea of visiting Eimeo and did all in their power to persuade him against it. Their entreaties swayed him and so he asked Fryer to go and sound the water. When he heard a favourable report, he announced that he had determined to choose Toahroah and on hearing this Tinah and the islanders rejoiced. So the crew brought 774 pots of plants on board and on Christmas Day they moved on to the new harbour.

Bligh sent the launch with the tents before them and ordered that it should meet the ship at the harbour entrance to demarcate the safest part of the channel. When they got close to the launch they anchored, but it was not a moment too soon – the front of the ship ran aground which was completely unexpected as the ship had sailed without a hitch up till that point. The crew sent anchors out astern but in the chaos a cable caught a rock and it took a lot of work to free it again. At last they moored the ship successfully with the east point of the harbour a quarter of a mile away. Three times Tinah sent present of a pig and a plantain leaf – the first for the God of Prittannee, the second for King George and the third for Bligh.

The crew did not seem to settle wholeheartedly to naval life again – and who could be surprised? It was not easy to get back to routine and on 27 December William Musprat received twelve lashes for neglect of duty. As they had spent Christmas wrestling with the grounded ship, Bligh decided to celebrate the festival on the 28th and gave orders for double the grog allowance. All the chiefs dined with Bligh on the shore. As a matter of form – and to impress the natives – Bligh exercised the great guns and small arms, the men being divided in two divisions. The islanders were shocked and delighted at the performance, but were also very afraid and were no less happy when the exercise was finished. They had not realised the full extent of their British friends' capabilities.

The crew's lethargy continued and carelessness seemed to be spreading among the men, much to Bligh's annoyance. The butcher, Robert Lamb, allowed his cleaver to be stolen, which was a valuable tool and could also be a formidable weapon. [14] He was punished with a dozen lashes, although Tinah said he would do his best to locate the article. The whipping took place before the chiefs, which gave Bligh the opportunity to warn them that this would be the fate of any native caught in the act of pilfering. Bligh realised that the chances of retrieving the cleaver were minimal, so was all the more surprised when Tinah returned on 1 January 1781 with the item in his hand. Apparently the thief had taken it to Attahooroo and gave it up with the greatest reluctance. This Bligh could well believe and tried to reward Tinah with gifts, but Tinah would have none of it as the cleaver should never have been purloined by one of his people in the first place.

A more serious incident occurred at four o'clock on the morning of the 5th of the month. The small cutter was missing, as were three crew members – Charles Churchill, William Musprat and John Millward, who had been on sentinel duty from midnight to 2 am. [15] For the Royal Navy, desertion was a crime punishable by execution and so Bligh took the matter gravely. His first act was to inform the chiefs on shore and he soon learned that the cutter had moored at Matavai and that the three men had sailed off in a sailing canoe for the island of Tethorua. Having retrieved the cutter, Bligh enlisted the help of his native friends, so Oreepyah and Moannah set off for Tethorua to seek them out. They had taken eight muskets and rounds of ammunition, but Oreepyah was worried in case they had pocket pistols and Bligh assured him that they did not.

At the time of the desertion Peter Hayward had been on watch – or rather, sleeping. As a punishment he was disrated, turned before the mast and clapped in irons. In is usual hot-headed way, Bligh fumed in his log:

Such neglectfull and worthless petty Officers I believe never was in a ship as are in this. No Orders for a few hours together are obeyed by them, and their conduct in general is so bad, that no confidence or trust can be reposed in them. In short they have drove me to every thing but Corporeal punishment and that must follow if they do not improve. [16]

The weather favoured the deserters and Oreepyah could not get far because of the squally conditions. Poeeno was very worried because they had got away in one of Matavai's canoes; but Bligh soon assured him that he had no problems with him or his people. Meanwhile Bligh had been considering the bull at Itteah and through Tinah had sent many messages to the chief. At last Poeeno agreed to act as go-between and make very fine offers for the purchase of the animal.

Soon after, in the company of Iddeah, Bligh met his first '*mahoo*'. He was an effeminate man with all the signs of femininity, so much so that he consorted with the womenfolk and was thought of almost as one of them. As the Tahitians were sexually free, they had no problem with this and Bligh was even told that the menfolk often used him for sexual gratification. Of course this was a crime at that time and Bligh was shocked at the revelation; but he wanted to know more about the young man and his way of life. Bligh's account simply reflects the mores and views of his time:

Here the Young Man took his Hahow or Mantle off which he had about him to show me the connection. He had the appearance of a Woman his yard & Testicles being so drawn in under him, having the art from custom of keeping them in this position, those who are connected with him have their beastly pleasures gratifyed between his thighs, but are no farther sodomites as they all positively deny the Crime. On examining his privacies I found them both very small and the Testicles remarkably so, being not larger than a boys of 5 or 6 years old, and very soft as if in a state of decay or a total incapacity of being larger, so that in either case he appeared to me effectually a Eunuch as if his stones were away. The Women treat him as one of their sex, and he observes every restriction that they do, and is equally respected and esteemed.

It is strange that in so prolific a country as this, Men should be led into such sensual and beastly acts of gratification, but perhaps no place in the World are they so common or so extraordinary as in this Island. Even the mouths of the Women are not exempt from the pollution, and many other as uncommon ways have they of gratifying their beastly inclinations.

Soon Bligh had something else to fume over. Probably the most important consideration on board a ship is the care of the equipment, without which the ship could not function or even sail. On the morning of 17 January the sail room was being cleaned out and the sails were to be taken on shore to be aired. To Bligh's horror, he found them mildewed and rotten. Once again he stormed in his log.

If I had any Officers to supercede the Master and Boatswain, or was capable of doing without them considering them as common seamen, they should no longer occupy their respective Stations. Scarce any neglect of duty can equal the criminality of this, for it appears that altho the Sails have been taken out twice since I have been in the Island,

which I thought fully sufficient and I had trusted to their reports, yet these New Sails never were brought out, or is it certain whether they have been out since we left England, yet notwithstanding as often as the Sails were taken to air by my Orders they were reported to me to be in good Order. To remedy the defects I attended and saw the Sails put into the Sea and hung up on shore to dry to be ready for repairing. [17]

On the 18th there was news to calm Bligh's anger. Poeeno had been successful in his negotiations and the bull was waiting for a boat to pick it up. The next day it arrived and on the 21st a representative from Itteah, Oweevee, spoke with Bligh about the sale. He was a man who could talk with the Eatua and now demanded that the bull be taken from Tinah. Bligh argued that this was ludicrous; why should this man sell a beast the Eatua had ordered him to keep? But Oweevee replied that the Eatua had ordered the sale in the first place. Having already paid the price for the animal – using everything he had to barter with – Bligh claimed the bull as his own and directed that Tinah and Poeeno should care for it until his return.

The following day Bligh had news of the deserters. Teppahoo sent a message to say that they had passed him by and arrived at Tettaha, five miles further on. The cutter was prepared and Bligh sailed with Odiddee, landing some distance from Teppahoo's house. Securing the boat they began to walk; it was a windy night and so dark that after a few minutes they lost sight of the boat. Some natives joined them, obviously looking to rob them, but soon vanished when Bligh produced a pistol. When they reached the dwelling, Teppahoo and his wife made them welcome, then told them that the deserters were holed up in a house close by. However, news travels fast in Tahiti, so the three men already new of Bligh's arrival as he was creeping up to the house with some of the local natives.

There was to be no fighting. Oreepyah and Moannah had already been there but had not been able to take them, possibly being frightened off by the sight of their muskets. But the three had decided that resistance would not help their cause; they could not fight the arms of the *Bounty* and all the local natives together. [18] They wanted to make their way back to the ship themselves to avoid the ignominy of being captured; but it was impossible to escape through the net of islanders who were on the lookout for them. Their arms were confiscated and Teppahoo took charge of the criminals for the night; they returned to the ship the next day. The prisoners were put in irons as Bligh deliberated over their punishment.

The obvious thing to do was to let the Admiralty decide their fate – which might well have been hanging from a yardarm. Bligh was reluctant to do this, but they had to be made an example of. Other Captains had given inhuman punishment for less crimes – five hundred or even a thousand lashes – which was the equivalent of death by torture. Bligh's most excessive punishment so far had been a mere two dozen, but this crime deserved much more. In the end he decided upon four dozen lashes for Musprat and Millward and two dozen for Churchill. He was not a cruel man and he understood that even this would be much for a man to bear; so he decided to give them half of the punishment immediately and then wait until they had recovered somewhat before meting out the rest. On the 24th he read the Articles of War and the three received their first whippings. Afterwards, they wrote a letter thanking Bligh – after all, they had expected no less than death and they hoped perhaps it might mitigate their ordeal – but Bligh had given his decision and the rest of the punishment was given on 4 February.

Their letter ran:

SIR, We should think ourselves wholly inexhaustibility, if we omitted taking this earliest opportunity of returning our thanks for your goodness in delivering us from a trial by Court-Martial, the fatal consequences of which are obvious; and although we cannot possibly lay any claim to so great a favour, yet we humbly beg you will be pleased to remit any further punishment, and we trust our future conduct will fully demonstrate our deep sense of your clemency, and our stedfast resolution to behave better hereafter. We are Sir, Your most obedient, most humble servants, C. CHURCHILL, WM. MUSPRAT, JOHN MILLWARD. [19]

Among the spectators at the flogging was at least one native man - Tinah's younger brother, Wyetooa. He was furious over the fact that his *tyo* – Hayward – had been imprisoned and if Bligh had meant to flog him too, Wyteooa was ready to kill him with the club he held in his hand.

Bligh might have been more lenient than many a sea Captain, but more punishment needed to be given, this time to Isaac Martin, who had struck a native. The orders were very clear, that none of the crew should ill use an islander and this was in direct breach of his most express commands. He was awarded twenty-four lashes, but this was reduced to nineteen after the chiefs had intervened. He had hit the native after he had accused him of stealing an iron hoop, for which he had no evidence.

Teppahoo had come to Oparre to live for a while and was a constant guest of Bligh's along with Tinah. Teppahoo had been complaining of hoarseness and a sore throat and Ledward, after examining him, concluded that he had cancerous growths in the roof of his mouth. Tinah was concerned over Teppahoo's health; should he die, Tettaha would be ruled by his brother who was Tinah's enemy. After discussing this, they dined and then Tinah suggested that Bligh took himself and Iddeah to England with him. The stories they had heard from Bligh and his companions opened up unknown vistas before them, of lands they not never heard of and longed to see. Wander-lust had grown insidiously into their hearts and Tinah wanted to see the great King George and how the other side of the world lived. His land, which had seemed like an Empire, seemed very small now. Bligh promised to ask permission to return with a bigger ship, capable off lodging him and his wife in the manner they deserved.

The warm relationship between Bligh and the natives was almost disrupted when, during the night of the 5th, the ship's cable was cut down to a single thread, which could have endangered the ship. [20] Bligh was livid and let Tinah know about it. Typically Bligh ranted although Tinah and Iddeah did their best to calm him, explaining that such an act was more likely to be an act of animosity against themselves than him. Although Bligh – as usual – eventually calmed down, news of his great wrath reached the ears of old Otow who left Oparre and Teppahoo returned to his home, although the rains were particularly bad. In fact, Teppahoo had to return in any case – there was to be a great *haiva* which required his presence. Tinah vowed that he would do everything in his power to track down the culprit, but when he returned the next day he had no news. Bligh received the news with a coldness which distressed Tinah and had Iddeah in tears. Eventually Bligh could no longer keep up a pretence of displeasure, but urged them to try harder to find the offenders. This Tinah did and the parties were reconciled.

What Bligh did not know was it was Heywood's *tyo* Wyetooa who and had cut the cable in revenge. He would rather have seen the ship founder than have his friend in chains any longer.

On 11 February a party of strolling *haiva* people arrived and offered to perform for Tinah and Bligh, who of course accepted their hospitality. The performance began with two girls, the youngest only a child; they gave a short dance to the accompaniment of wood drums beaten with sticks. After they had finished, they gave Bligh a 'gift' – they let their dresses fall about them before moving off. Next came four young men, who gave a performance which both delighted the islanders and disgusted Bligh:

They suddenly took off what clothing they had about their Hips and appeared quite Naked. One of the men was prepared for his part, for the whole business now became the power and capability of distorting the Penis and Testicles, making at the same time wanton and lascivious motions. The Person who was ready to begin had his Penis swelled and distorted out into an erection by having a severe twine ligature close up to the Os Pubis applied so tight that the Penis was apparently almost cut through. The Second brought his stones to the head of his Penis and with a small cloth bandage he wrapt them round and round up towards

the Belly, stretching them at the same time very violently untill they were near a foot in length which the bandage kept them erect at, the two stones and head of the Penis being like three small Balls at the extremity. The Third person was more horrible than the other two, for with both hands seizing the extremity of the Scrotum he pulled it out with such force, that the penis went in totally out of sight and the Scrotum became shockingly distended. In this manner they danced about the Ring for a few minutes when I desired them to desist and the Heivah ended, it however afforded much laughter among the spectators. [21]

Another *haiva* followed on 13 February. This was to be a grand occasion and many representatives of foreign tribes arrived for the entertainment. Girls danced and a gift was presented to Bligh – some cloths and a breast-plate. After this, the men began to wrestle – and this is where things turned violent. Many of these men were of rival tribes and they took this opportunity to vent their resentment. The sport quickly turned into a riot and Otoo asked Bligh if he could help put an end to the fray. Bligh ordered his men to line up in battle formation and two shots were fired from the ship – this was enough to restore order. [22]

On 2 March there was another theft – this time a water cask, part of a compass and Peckover's bedding. When Tinah heard the news it is not difficult to guess his reaction. He avoided the ship, although Bligh spotted him with Oreepyah at a distant house; then they marched off on the track of the thief. It easy to imagine Tinah's mortification in the wake of the cable-cutting incident; so in less than an hour he returned with a party of people, the thief and the cask and the compass. The bedding was still missing, but Bligh complimented Tinah on his efforts and explained that friends should be trusting and protect each other. The two embraced and the crowd called out '*Tyo myty!*' ('Good friend!') [23] Afterwards the offender – who was not a local – was given a severe flogging of one hundred lashes. This was incredibly severe and was meant as a strong deterrent to the islanders.

Tinah had often asked Bligh for firearms and his fear that his country would be attacked after they had gone was very real. After issuing some guns, they taught Tinah and his party how to use them and Iddeah turned out to be very proficient; Odiddee turned out to be an expert marksman.

The native who was punished was still held prisoner and Bligh had written orders that their security should be in the hands of the mate of the watch. On the night of the 7th that duty belonged to Stewart, but the native had not only managed to break free from his irons, he also dived overboard and escaped before anyone could stop him. Once again Bligh had occasion to let off steam in his log:

I have such a neglectfull set about me that I believe nothing but condign punishment can alter their conduct. Verbal orders in the course of a month were so forgot that they would impudently assert no such thing or directions were given, and I have been at last under the necessity to trouble my self with writing what by decent young officers would be complied with as the common Rules of the Service. [24]

On 23 March, Hayward was at last released from his bondage, much to Wyetooa's relief. On the 27th, botanist Nelson announced that the breadfruit plants could be transported after the rainy season – in four weeks.

It was almost time for the *Bounty* to leave the shores of Tahiti. Additional supplies were taken on board, although the sale of hogs had been banned in Tettaha. Teppahoo explained that they had very few left and they needed time to breed and replenish the stock. There was to be a similar prohibition in Matavai and Oparre, but that was delayed until the ship sailed as a token of friendship. Tinah busied himself having two *parais* (mourning-dresses) made for King George and prayed that the king would forever remain his friend and never forget him. When he handed them over to Bligh there was an emotional scene and Tinah burst into tears.

It was not the only tearful parting. Many of the men had forged strong relationships with local women and leaving them was sometimes hard. McIntosh had a local 'wife' called 'Mary', who was pregnant by him although she might not have known that at the time. Christian's mate was 'Mainmast', his affectionate name for the long willow-like chief's daughter who was known as Mauatua. Like the other men, he rechristened her with an English name – Isabella. A few years older than Christian, she became his constant companion and witnesses would later recall that they were always in each other's company. To leave Mauatua was a dreadful wrench for Fletcher Christian.

By 31 March all the plants were placed on board – 774 pots, 39 tubs and 24 containing mostly breadfruit plants – 1015 of them. Bligh then handed out the last of his presents, these to his best friends, particularly Teppahoo. Some, such as Odiddee, begged to sail with him but that could not be.

3 April was to be their last night, and Tinah came on board with his wife and family. There was no customary laughter and dancing on the beach – all was a silent mourning. As they left the bay of Toahroah Tinah and Iddeah begged Bligh to anchor at Matavai Bay and stay just one more night, but he had to refuse. Their gifts were placed in the boat and Tinah was given firearms and ammunition; then sadly the couple boarded the boat, leaving them with affectionate cries.

'May the *Eatua* protect you, for ever and ever!' [25]

Chapter Six. Sharks

So the *Bounty* took her last farewell of her friends in Tahiti. Tinah wanted them to salute with their great guns, but that might have damaged the plants, so they gave three rousing cheers instead, which were returned.

The ship steered close to Huaheine, where they had left Omai all those years ago. A number of canoes sailed up to the ship, one containing an old friend of Omai's and some brought hogs and yams, which Bligh bought.

The ship sailed on, heading towards the Friendly Islands but on the 9th they spotted a water-spout travelling at bout ten miles per hour which passed close by their stern. On the 11th they saw nine low keys, all covered in trees. Some canoes came to the ship as they passed the most southerly key and told them that the largest of the islands was known as Wytootackee. Bligh gave them a boar and a sow and some yams as well as knives, adzes, nails and a mirror. Here Bligh had more trouble with his crew and gave Sumner twelve lashes for neglect of duty. He also had words with Christian, and in the words of Fryer Christian replied:

'Sir, your abuse is so bad that I cannot do my duty with any pleasure.'

A change had come over Fletcher Christian. He was not the amiable, pleasant young man he had been before his arrival at Tahiti. Now, as the ship sailed on to new shores, he was morose and almost suicidal. He had a plan – to build a raft and escape the *Bounty*, even getting his friends to rally round and find planks he could lash together to form a makeshift raft. His close friend Peter Hayward was particularly worried about him. There were times when he was found sobbing, big tears rolling down his face and was desperate, desperate enough to do something stupid. Nothing would appease him – he had to escape the ship and quickly.

This behaviour was not of someone who was simply disgruntled with his lot. As his brother later stated, he was no milksop and could endure hardship as well as the rest of the crew. He had no animus against Bligh who had always treated him with respect and he knew how to calm his raging storms. There is nothing in Bligh's log book to show he had the least criticism of Christian personally. Even if he had, he would not weep like a schoolboy or think of throwing himself into a shark-infested sea with a few planks of wood to carry him to nowhere. But for five months he had had a woman. There is no doubt that many of the others felt a sense of loss at leaving their mates, but 'Isabella' was special to Christian and while he was in Tahiti they were never parted. His actions were surely those of someone utterly lovelorn, someone who did not wish to live without his lover. What could he do? He was a sailor and Bligh would never have given him permission to stay behind. That would rank as desertion. To sail back in a patchwork raft was born of sheer desperation. There was no way back and that, it seems, was preying on his mind so much that he had to give vent to his grief. It even affected his duty as his mind was not on his job.

Despite Christian's anguish, the voyage went on. On 18 April the *Bounty* passed Savage Island and on the 24th Caow was seen from the masthead. They anchored at Annamooka (Nomuka) and a canoe arrived from the island of Mango, containing their chief Latoomy-Lane who dined with Bligh. Other canoes began to arrive with yams and coconuts but none of the natives came aboard without seeking permission to do so. By now larger boats were coming in from other islands and in one Bligh found an old man he recognised, Tepa, who told him that Polaho, Feenough, and Tubow, were alive and at Tongataboo. He sent word that Bligh was here and in the meantime showed them around the ship. [1]

On 26 April they went onshore for watering and Nelson searched for some breadfruit plants as a few had died since they left Tahiti. Bligh visited the west side of the bay and found the garden Cook had planted which was flourishing with twenty fine pineapple plants. The watering was done at the same place that Cook found, a quarter of a mile inland; and the wooding was completed within a day. There was also a flourishing trade for hogs and yams going on by the side of the ship.

Nomuka was not Tahiti and Bligh remembered well the tragedy at Hawaii. He was determined to take no chances and gave Christian specific instructions to keep his men away from the natives. He provided the men with muskets, but to avoid misunderstandings he told them to leave them on the boat when they landed on shore and only to use them from there. Christian's mind was not on the job and he allowed the islanders to surround them, so that they managed to lose an axe and an adze. Meanwhile they insulted Nelson and stole his spade from him. Tepa did manage to recover the spade, but it is not difficult to imagine Bligh's reaction when Christian brought the news back to the *Bounty*.

The men cleared themselves of the neglect as they could not comply with every part of their duty and keep their tools in their hands, and they, therefore, merited no punishment. As to the officers I have no resource, or do I ever feel myself safe in the few instances I trust to them.

Next day did not improve Bligh's temper: a grapnel had been stolen and Bligh was determined to get it back. It was useless to remonstrate with the crowd; it was now huge and canoes sailed in all the time. They needed a chief of sufficient authority to reason with these people; but there were none about. Bligh ordered the watering party aboard. By noon the *Bounty* would receive no visitors, not even the chieftains when they returned, but by then Bligh allowed Latoomy-Lange and Kunocappo to embark. As soon as they had done so, Bligh warned them that they would remain as prisoners until the grapnel was returned. After a while canoes came to inform them that the grapnel had been taken to another island and could not be retrieved until the next day.

Bligh kept to his word and detained the chiefs till sunset. At this point they both began to get hysterical, beating themselves on the face and sobbing. Bligh decided that a grapnel was not worth such commotion, so he told them they were free to go and before they did he presented them with gifts of a hatchet, a saw, knives and nails. Their desperation turned to joy and they left on friendly terms. [2]

Throughout 27 April the *Bounty* remained near the island of Kotto but no canoes came to visit. There was a large supply of coconuts between the guns of the quarter-deck and Bligh noticed that they had visibly decreased in number. Then he asked each officer how many coconuts they had brought and at last came to Christian, who prided himself on humouring his Captain. His reply was not the way to soothe Bligh.

'I do not know Sir, but I hope you don't think me so mean as to be guilty of stealing yours'.

This piece of unexpected insolence made Bligh fly into one of his fleeting storms.

'Yes you damn'd hound I do! You must have stolen them from me or you could give a better account of them! God damn you, you scoundrels, you are all thieves alike, and combine with the men to rob me!'

Still furious, he told Samuel to cut the yam ration and stormed off. As soon as his passion subsided he (typically) invited Christian to dinner. Christian refused, pleading sickness and Bligh was concerned for his welfare.

In the evening Bligh gave directions for the ship to sail westward and set the watches – Fryer had the first, Peckover the second and Christian the morning. Before Bligh left, Fryer commented:

'Sir, we have got a fine breeze and a Moon coming on, which will be fortunate for us when we come to the Coast of New Holland.'

Bligh replied, 'Yes, Mr. Fryer, so it will.' [3]

After Fryer, Peckover took the graveyard shift and was in turn relieved by Fletcher Christian at four a.m. Christian therefore found himself in charge of the ship in the early hours and for some days had been considering what he should do. It was useless to try to persuade Bligh to leave 'the project' and take him back to Tahiti and the ill-advised attempt to throw himself on a raft had come to nothing. There were too many people about and he knew that those who knew of his plan were determined to dissuade him. Mutiny had not crossed his mind up to that point. He talked with those he could trust and those who had a grievance against the commander and a conspiracy was planned.

It began like any other morning watch. Even in the early hours, there was work to be done; the ship had to prepared for the next day, and Christian ordered the decks to be cleared for washing. Charles Norman and Henry Hildebrandt, the Cooper, went off to coil up the ropes while Burkitt went to prepare the forecastle. It was possibly Stewart's pointed remark, 'the men are ripe for anything', which triggered the idea in his mind. When the early watch began, Churchill went over to Christian and talked to him for a short while, after which Christian told Hayward to keep watch while he went down to tie his hammock. Just then Norman caught sight of a shark basking in the waters and called:

'There's a shark on the larboard quarter!'[4]

Hayward walked over and saw it asked everyone to be quiet. Hallet joined him and quickly asked if someone could fetch a fish hook. When he had been handed one, he called to Burkitt:

'Do you see the shark, Burkitt?'

'No sir,' he replied, 'I have not seen it forward.'

At that moment Norman saw it again on the larboard side.

All attention was now on the inquisitive sea visitor, apart from Burkitt who had been sent to the mainstay to prepare some fowls. Christian had returned and he asked Coleman to get him a musket to shoot the fish with

The shark disappeared from sight and talk came round to the preparations for the morning. Hayward saw that a number of people were now up and about and wondered why.

'What are you about, are you going to exercise already?'

Churchill answered: 'Yes, I don't know the Captain's reason for it, he has ordered exercise at day light.'

It was at this point that the men on watch saw that the men were armed, some with muskets, others with bayonets - Christian, Churchill, Sumner, Quintal, McKoy, Williams, Martin, Hillbrandt and Smith. Christian held out a musket for Burkitt.

'Here, Burkitt, lay hold of this!'

'What must I do with it?'

'Damn your blood, lay hold of it and go aft!'

No-one knew what the conspirators were planning but they feared for the worst. Sumner and Quintal were sent down the fore hatch to act as sentinels to guard the sleeping men. The rest made their way towards the Captain's cabin, while Christian shook a cutlass at Hayward, saying:

'Damn your blood, Hayward, *mamoo*! (silence!)'

Other men now appeared on the decks and Ellison quitted the helm to arm himself with a bayonet; Young, Millward, Musprat, Williams, Skinner and Brown were armed also, while Heywood, Stewart and Morrison remained unarmed on the booms.

Christian reached the door of the cabin and along with Charles Churchill, John Mills and Thomas Burkitt, he crept in and woke him. They threatened him with instant death if he uttered a word – but Bligh was a courageous man and he shouted at the top of his voice for help.

'Murder! Help!' [5]

They were obviously having problems in controlling the reluctant prisoner. Churchill called out:

'Hand down a seizing to tie the Captain's hands!'

The crew stood still in shock, so Churchill bawled:

'You infernal buggers, hand down a seizing or I'll come up and play hell with you all!'

Mills cut a piece off one of the lead lines which hung on the mizzen mast and going to the starboard side, handed it down. Meanwhile, despite threats, Bligh was shouting loud enough to wake the dead. Christian took the cord and bound Bligh's hands behind his back.

Soon after, Bligh was brought up upon the quarter deck with his hands bound behind him, surrounded by the mutineers. Bligh himself was confused and nonplussed, asking why they had resorted to such violence; the men told him to hold his tongue. Poor Bligh was dressed only in his shirt, some of which had been caught up in the cord around his hands, so Burkitt asked Smith to fetch the Captain's clothes.

'Jack, go fetch the Captain's clothes! It's a shame to see him stand naked!'

Fryer, Peckover, Ledward, Elphinstone and Nelson were kept locked below, the hatchway being guarded. Christian himself was armed with a cutlass; the others had muskets and bayonets which had been filched from the arms chest. Bligh asked him what he was planning to do.

'We're going to do you no harm, only to put you on shore.'

Seeing no rescue, Bligh decided to appeal to Christian's common sense.

'Consider what you are about, Mr Christian! For God's sake drop it and there shall be no more come of it.'

'It's too late, Captain Bligh.'

'No, Mr. Christian, it's not too late yet, I'll forfeit my honour if ever I speak of it; I'll give you my bond that there shall never be any more come of it.'

'You know, I have been in hell this fortnight past and I am determined to suffer it no longer.'

Certainly Christian looked like a man who had been in hell; his appearance 'greatly amazed and terrified' Ellison:

'He looked like a madman, his long hair was loose, is shirt collar open.'

Bligh tried to persuade him, but his answer was:

'*Mamoo*, sir. *Mamoo!*'

If Bligh's cries had been enough to wake the dead, they certainly awoke the sleeping crew. Down the hatchway, Quintal called for Purcell the carpenter and his call awoke both Purcell and Cole. Quintal said:

'Mr. Purcell, you and Mr. Coleman go on deck and do as you think proper. We have mutinied and taken the ship, and Mr. Christian has the command. The Captain is confined. All resistance will be in vain - if you attempt it you are a dead man.'

Cole turned to the carpenter.

'For God's sake, I hope you know nothing of this.'

'No I don't.'

The two dressed and Cole asked Lebogue, who was lying in his cabin, what he intended to do. Lebogue was as confused as everyone else and said he would do whatever Cole did. The two dressed and went up the hatchway, where they saw Thompson standing guard. On deck, they saw Bligh and were able to see the situation for themselves; then they went down the fore hatchway and wakened Morrison, Millward, and McIntosh, who all lay in the same tier. All denied any knowledge of the mutiny and as they dressed Churchill shouted for Millward, telling him that he had a musket for him.

The tumult also wakened Peckover who heard the fixing of bayonets; he leaped out of bed and dressed, then met Nelson at the doorway, who told him the news.

'We're a long way from land,' Peckover replied.

The pair decided to go up and see what could be done, but we accosted by Sumner and Quintal.

'Mr. Peckover, you must come up, we have mutinied and taken the ship, and Mr. Christian has got the command.'

Cole was ordered to hoist out the small cutter, with the threat:

'If you don't do it instantly, take care of yourself!'

Cole and Purcell begged Christian to reconsider, Cole crying:

'Drop it, for God's sake!'

Hayward said: 'Consider, Mr. Christian, What a dangerous step you have taken!'

Bligh, who had not given up persuading Christian, asked: 'Can there be no other method taken?'

Churchill replied for him.

'No! This is the best and only method.'

Cole asked Millward to lend a hand in clearing the boat but some of the men complained that it was too small and besides it had a hole in it, so Christian ordered Cole to take the large cutter instead. Cole replied that it was also too small and 'I hope you'll give us the longboat too.'

Samuel had gone off to gather some things for Bligh and on the way he saw Peckover and Nelson, telling them that he was going away in the small cutter with Bligh and asked what Peckover felt he would need. Peckover replied:

'If I was in his place, I should take but very few things.'

Samuel went off and in Bligh's cabin, he busied himself in grabbing all the important documents he could find, while impatient mutineers stood behind him. He took a good handful but when he tried to take the timekeeper and a box containing Bligh's surveys and drawings, he was stopped.

'Damn your eyes you are well off to get what you have!'   6

Meanwhile Ellison had gone to Lebogue to ask what he intended to do. Suspecting that he was one of the mutineers, Lebogue answered:

'Go to hell and don't bother me!'

Fryer had his own tale to tell of the Mutiny and while it may be reasonably truthful, there is no doubt that he was painting a somewhat fanciful portrait of himself. He was asked to give an account of that morning, which he did. He had been awoken by the tumult but found Sumner and Quintal on guard with him, saying:

'You are a prisoner, Sir.'

When Fryer began to argue, they said:

'Hold your tongue or you are a dead man, but if you remain quiet there is no person on board that will hurt a hair of your head.'

Raising himself on his locker, Fryer then saw Bligh being led up the ladder by Christian, his hands tied. Then Churchill entered the room and took his two pistols, saying:

'I'll take care of these, Mr Fryer!'

The Master also swore that he had no ammunition in any case; he argued that Mills had taken the cartridge box out of the cabin to give it to another who wanted it to store musket cartridges. He claimed that Bligh had ordered them to be filled with powder only, to be in readiness. This contradicts Bligh's version.

'What are you going to do with the Captain?' he then asked.

'Damn his eyes,' replied Sumner, 'put him into the boat, and let the bugger see if he can live upon three fourths of a pound of yams a day.'

'Into the boat? For God's sake why?'

'Sir, hold your tongue! Mr. Christian is Captain of the Ship and recollect that Mr. Bligh has brought all this upon himself.'

'Consider, my lads, what you are about...'

John Sumner replied, 'Sir, we know very well what we are about.'

'I am afraid not, or you would not persist in your intentions; let me persuade you to lay down your arms and I will insure that nothing shall hurt you, for what you have done.'

'No, sir, hold your tongue, it is too late now.'

'What boat are they going to put Captain Bligh into?'

'The small cutter.'

'Good God! The small cutter's bottom is almost out, being eaten with the worms.'

'Damn his eyes, the boat is too good for him.' [7]

Cole saw that – considering the state of the boat – this was an act of murder and he and others tried to persuade Christian to let them have the launch. After a while he relented and sent the carpenters and armourer to fit out the launch. It had already been decided that Hayward, Hallet, and Samuel would also be cast adrift, but Purcell was determined to go with Bligh:

'I have done nothing that I am ashamed or afraid of, I want to see my native country.'

Purcell then noticed Heywood leaning against the boom, cutlass in hand.

'In the name of God, Peter, what do you do with that?'

Heywood dropped it, but so had a number of others as they went forward to help hoisting out the launch. Purcell then got to work, having sent McIntosh and Norman to get some necessary equipment:

The Boat being hoisted out, I went down to my Cabin in order to procure such Things as I thought would be useful. I desired McIntosh and Norman to fill a Bucket of Nails of different sizes, and hand a crosscut and whip Saw out of the Storeroom, which they did. I then got my Cloaths Chest, put a Looking Glass and several other Articles into it, got it upon Deck and into the Launch. We then got up several Boats' Sails, a lower Studding Sail, Twine, Remnants of Canvas, and several other Articles. I then went and asked Mr. Christian for my Tool Chest, Whip, and Cross cut saw, which after much Altercation he granted, after Churchill the Master at Arms had opposed it, and had taken such Things as he thought proper out of it.

When Fryer was allowed don deck he tried to persuade Christian to change his mind.

'Mr. Christian, consider what you are about.'

'Hold your tongue, sir, I have been in hell for weeks past … Captain Bligh has brought all this on himself.'

'Mr. Bligh and you not agreeing was no reason for your taking the ship!'

'Hold your tongue, sir!

'Mr. Christian, you and I have been on friendly terms during the voyage, therefore give me leave to speak; let Mr. Bligh go down to his cabin and I make no doubt but that we shall all be friends again in a very short time.'

'Hold your tongue, sir, it is too late!'

The men marched Samuel to the deck, where the boat was out and ready. Midshipmen Hallet and Hayward were ordered to get into it, followed by Samuel, who still held on to the precious papers. Bligh asked what was the meaning of this and tried to persuade those nearest to him to stop this, but he was answered with:

'Hold your tongue, Sir, or you are dead this instant!'

There had been a faint flicker in hope in Bligh's mind. The Master had were two loaded guns in his cabin; they used to be kept in a binnacle for the watch, but they were placed in Fryer's cabin in case they were stolen. The Captain did not realise that he had no ammunition.

Fryer than whispered in Bligh's ear: 'Keep your spirits up, if I stay on board I might be enabled soon to follow you.

Bligh replied: 'By all means stay, Mr. Fryer.'

Then Bligh whispered to him urgently:

'Knock him down! Martin is good....'

Fryer tried to get around Christian to speak to Martin but Christian put a bayonet to his breast, saying:

'Sir, if you advance an inch further, I will run you through!

At this moment Christian dragged the Master back and ordered him back to his cabin. In the meantime Martin fed him with shaddock, seeing that his mouth was parched and exchanged glances to show that he was on his side.

Unfortunately this was seen by some other mutineers, who took Martin away from their captive. After this Martin tried to board the boat himself, but he was dragged back by the crew.

As Sumner and Quintal took him down, Fryer saw Morrison at the hatchway. This is what happened next, according to Fryer.

'Morrison, I hope you have no hand in this business?'

'No sir, I do not know a word about it.'

'If that's the case, be on your guard; there may be an opportunity of recovering ourselves.'

Morrison answered: 'Go down to your cabin, sir, it is too late.'

Millward then joined Sumner and Quintal; Fryer winked at Morrison and motioned him to knock Sumner down. Instead, he cocked his gun and pointed it at him, saying:

'Mr. Fryer be quiet, no one will hurt you.'

'Millward, your Piece is cocked, you had better uncock it, as you may shoot some person.'

It was Sumner who replied. 'There is no one who wishes to shoot you. No, that was our agreement; not to commit murder.'

Fryer now asked to go to the cockpit, where he joined Peckover, and Nelson. Nelson was the first to speak.

'Mr. Fryer, what have we brought on ourselves?'

Peckover asked: 'What is best to be done, Mr. Fryer?'

Fryer related his conversation with Bligh. 'If we were ordered into the boat -say that you will stay on board, and I flatter myself that we shall recover the ship in a short time.'

Peckover moaned: 'If we stay we shall be all deemed pirates.'

'No,' replied Fryer, 'I will answer for you and everyone that would join with me.'

At that moment Hillbrandt left the breadroom and must have told Christian what he heard, because Fryer was now told to go to his cabin. The sentinels told him that they had decided to give the launch, not for Bligh but for the men with him.

'Who is going in the boat with Captain Bligh?

'We don't know but we believe it is a great many.'   8

Back on deck, some of the men insisted that Bligh would be give no more in the way of equipment, stating:

'I'll be damned if he does not find his way home, if he gets anything with him.'

As the launch was hoisted out, Cole caught sight of Byrne, crouching in the cutter. Byrne wished to join Bligh, but being blind he found his way to the wrong boat. He himself recalled:

I do not know whether I may be able to ascertain the exact Words that were spoken on the Occasion; but some said, "We must not part with our Fiddler," and Charles Churchill threatened to send me to the Shades, if I attempted to quit the Cutter, into which I had gone, for the Purpose of attending Lieut. Bligh.

Later, when he saw Hayward in the launch, he heard him call:

'I'm sorry I could get leave to come with you!'

Christian now ordered Smith to bring a bottle of rum and gave every one of his men a glassful; meanwhile Norman, McIntosh, Coleman, and Morrison got the masts, oars, sails, twine, lines, rope, canvas and other necessaries for the launch.

At first it was decided that Bligh should be sent off with Samuel, Hayward and Hallet, the last two weeping and asking what they had done to deserve so harsh a fate. When the launch was out, Martin laid down his musket and went into the boat, determined to share his Captain's fate – but Purcell had him marked down as a mutineer and said:

'If ever we get to England, I'll endeavour to hang you myself!'

Quintal and Churchill overheard that and seeing Martin in the launch, they trained their guns on him and he was ordered back out again. The officers who were still below were ordered out and they were put in the boat while there was some discussions over the carpenter; Purcell was adamant that he wanted to go and so they kept his mates and the armourer. Many of the mutineers – and Bligh – were less than happy to be parted with Purcell, one remarking:

'Damn my eyes he will have a vessel built in a month!' 9

It was clear that Christian was afraid that some of the men would listen to Bligh, so he asked for a bayonet then, grasping the cord which tied his hands, threatened to kill him instantly if he did not hold his tongue. There was a shout of 'shoot the bugger!' but no-one dared to kill him, even though he dared them to it. [10] Certainly Bligh was becoming troublesome and no attempt to shut him up appeared to work. It seemed that Christian was putting on an act rather than being the swaggering mutineer which he made out to be; but it was imperative that all men who were to sail with Bligh should be boarded as soon as possible so that he could get rid of his uncooperative prisoner. He was no monster; he did allow the men to take provisions; the boatswain and other sailors were allowed to take twine, canvas, lines, sails, cordage, an eight and twenty-gallon cask of water, while Samuel managed to get 150 pounds of bread, with a small quantity of rum and wine.

Norton, one of the Quarter Masters, asked for a Jacket and Skinner said:

'You bugger, if I had my will I would blow your brains out!'

There were by now so many bodies on board the launch that she was deep in the water. Bligh said:

'You can't all go in the Boat, my lads; don't overload her, some of you must stay in the Ship.'

Peckover, Nelson and Fryer came back to the deck. There were a number of men who were distressed at being left on the ship and one, Coleman, turned to the gunner.

'Remember, Mr. Peckover, if ever you do arrive in England, I had no hand in this.'

Bligh then asked Christian to allow Fryer and some other stay and Christian replied:

'The Men may stay, but the Master must go with you. Mr. Fryer, go into the Boat.'

'I will stay with you, if you will give me leave.'

'No, sir, go directly into the boat.'

Bligh said: 'Mr. Fryer, stay in the ship.'

'No, by God, sir," Christian said, 'go into the Boat or I will run you through!'

Fryer asked for his brother-in-law, young Tinkler, to be allowed to come with him and after some arguing they allowed it – and a trunk, but no more. Then Fryer got onto the launch.

It was time for Christian to lead Bligh onto the boat.

'Come, Captain Bligh, your officers and men are now in the boat and you must go with them. If you attempt to make the least resistance you will instantly be put to death.'

Bligh turned to him.

'Is this treatment was a proper return for the many instances you have received of my friendship?'

The question hit the mark and Christian looked very disturbed and sad. 'That, Captain Bligh that is the thing. I am in hell, I am in hell!' [11]

Most of the mutineers found the novel situation exciting and Bligh noticed young Heywood brandishing his cutlass with the rest. This was the young man he had treated with some affection, whom he had taken on the voyage because of the friendship between his family and the Bethams. To Bligh, Christian and Heywood were like two Brutuses and he would never forget or forgive either of them. At one point Bligh said something to Heywood, but he laughed in answer, turned round, and walked away.

To the dreamer Heywood, this was the stuff romance was made of. He had lived some months in a Shangri-La, writing and basking in the beauty of Otaheite, making love to the dusky inviting maidens and letting his imagination wander. The mutiny stirred his fancy and he wanted to be a part in this great new adventure. He was still a young man, impressionable and eager to taste excitement. He was more than willing to betray the man who had been a family friend and done so much to further his interests.

As Bligh made his last protestations and entered the boat, he knew that he could do nothing. He asked for his commission and his sextant and Christian handed the commission to him as well as a sextant of his own, saying:

'There, Captain Bligh, this is sufficient for every purpose and you know the sextant to be a good one.'

Bligh now requested arms for protection, but the mutineers simply jeered, Churchill stating that he'd be damned if they'd give him any. He did, however, allow four cutlasses were eventually thrown into the boat, along with some pork and some clothes.

'There, Captain Bligh! You don't need firearms - you're going among your friends!'[12]

Most of the rebels were entertained by the plight of Bligh and his men and laughed at them floundering deep in the water.

Bligh gave the men who had wanted to sail with him a message.

'Never fear, my lads, I'll do you justice if ever I reach England!'

On the launch, besides Bligh, there was John Fryer, Thomas Ledward, David Nelson, William Peckover, William Cole, William Purcell, William Elphinston, Thomas Hayward, John Hallet, John Norton, Peter Linkletter, Lawrence Lebogue, John Smith, Thomas Hall, George Simpson, Robert Tinkler, Robert Lamb and Mr. Samuel. A number of people had collected on the taffrail to watch proceedings. Brown shouted abuse at Bligh and Millward cried:

'Go and see if you can live upon a quarter of a pound of yams a day!''

As they were cut loose, Bligh heard the cries from the *Bounty*: 'Huzzah for Otaheite!' along with 'Shoot the buggers!' [13]

The mutineers were jubilant, but now guilt seized Fletcher Christian. He had done what he had to do to return to Isabella, but his conscience pricked him to remorse. One witness heard him say:

'I would readily sacrifice my own life if the persons on the launch were all safe on the ship again.'

As the stranded men sat in their boat, Bligh pondered over the cause of the mutiny. It had come as a complete bombshell to him, but he thought along the right lines when he concluded that the men reckoned Tahiti a more attractive place to live than England, with its abundance of food and sun and without the necessity of hard labour. He also felt it might have had something to do with 'female connections'. It was not the motive which baffled Bligh, but the secrecy, the close-lipped secrecy of it all!

The secrecy of this mutiny is beyond all conception. Thirteen of the party who were with me had always lived forward among the seamen; yet neither they nor the messmates of Christian, Stewart, Heywood, and Young, had ever observed any circumstance that made them in the least suspect what was going on. To such a close-planned act of villainy, my mind being entirely free from any suspicion, it is not wonderful that I fell a sacrifice. Perhaps if there had been marines on board a sentinel at my cabin-door might have prevented it; for I slept with the door always open that the officer of the watch might have access to me on all occasions, the possibility of such a conspiracy being ever the farthest from my thoughts. Had their mutiny been occasioned by any grievances, either real or imaginary, I must have discovered symptoms of their discontent, which would have put me on my guard: but the case was far otherwise.

At least there was one consolation, good old Samuel had saved his books and even his log, which was proof that he had been completely innocent of any wrong-doing:

To Mr. Samuel I am indebted for securing my journals and commission with some material ship papers. Without these I had nothing to certify what I had done, and my honour and character might have been suspected without my possessing a proper document to have defended them.

Little did William Bligh realise what Fate had in store for him.

Chapter Seven. The Ever-Rolling Ocean

Bligh was still a Lieutenant and the men on the boat were still sailors so Bligh felt it his responsibility to take control. It was his obligation; abandoned they may be, but they were still in the Navy. Supplies were first on the agenda, so he decided to sail to Tofoa and then Tongataboo. These were the closest islands and they already had built some kind of relationship with the natives there. A wind picked up at four o'clock and they set sail, but it was dark by the time they reached Tofoa and the shore was so steep that they had no choice but to spend the night in the boat. To cheer the crew, Bligh issued half a pint of grog to each man. The next day Samuel and some others explored this part of the island but found it barren and only returned with a small quantity of water. At noon Bligh gave them a morsel of bread and some wine, then sailed to another cliff above which hung some coconut trees. A few men climbed up and they managed to gather twenty coconuts and these were the only supply they gained on the first day there.

The next day – 30 April – they fared little better. They put to sea but the weather forced them back, so Bligh decided to explore this region along with Samuel, Nelson and others. They had to climb a precipice using vines which natives had put there for that purpose and having reached the top they began their exploration. They did find some plantain trees and some deserted huts but they only managed to salvage three small bunches of the fruit. A deep gully then led towards a volcano which was burning and the ash-covered bleak terrain offered nothing in the way of food. They made their return, but looking down from the precipice Bligh felt dizzy and had to be helped by the others. The rest of the crew had been looking for fish or seafood, but there was nothing to be had. They ate an ounce of pork each along with two plantains and a glass of wine. At 2 pm another party set out on a different route, but had no success. The men moved to a nearby cave that night, where they lit a fire and took turns sleeping on shore or on the boat; Bligh insisted on a watch in case of attack.

Next day brought the first sighting of the natives. A party of Bligh's men saw well-ordered plantations and happened upon two men, a woman and a child. The menfolk came to the cove and brought two coconut shells of water. Bligh befriended the islanders and made it known that he needed breadfruit, plantains and water; soon other natives arrived and the crew bought a small supply using buttons and beads. Bligh was unsure as to what to tell the natives about their ship, but the crew decided that they would explain that the ship had sunk and they were the only survivors. Natives came and went, from land or canoe; and by day's end they had managed to gather another day's food supply. Bligh decided to stay one more night, buy more provisions in the morning and then set sail for Tongataboo.

The next morning the crew's spirits had revived. The situation was much better than it was; they had some provisions and would receive more, enough to take them to an island where they had allies and friends. Some of the men went on a foraging expedition and after they had gone, the natives began to reappear, many more than the day before. Two canoes also landed, one of which contained an elderly chieftain by the name of Maccaackavow. Soon after the party returned in the company of another chief called Eefow and introductions were made, Bligh giving them the best he could offer – an old shirt and a knife each. Both of them had either seen or heard of Bligh at Annamooka and asked after Captains Cook and Clerke. They also met with Nageete, whom they remembered as being there. After some talk, Eefow agreed to accompany him to Tongataboo to meet up with Feenough and Polaho. Things could not have been better.

At one point, thinking themselves unseen, some islanders tried to haul the boat on shore, so Bligh brandished his cutlass at them and asked Eefow to tell them to stop, which they did. The men continued to bargain for breadfruit and they bought some spears as well, as they were not well armed and during the haggling the rest of the forging party returned with about none gallons of water. Even so, Bligh was a worried man; it was by now clear that they had no firearms which was always a good deterrent and the natives were increasing in number, lining the beach. Then they began to knock stones together, which Bligh recognised as a sign for attack. At noon they dined on coconut and breadfruit, giving the chiefs some and chatting to them; but they constantly asked Bligh to sit down and Bligh realised that if he did they would possibly seize him.

Bligh's priority was to get the provisions on the boat, which they did by wading through the surf. He also noticed that the islanders had no intention of leaving as they had done the previous night. Instead they lit fires on the beach and chose places to stay; all the times groups were consulting each other. The sun was beginning to set so every man on shore gathered up his things to take to the boat. When they saw this, the chiefs asked if he was going to stay with them all night. Bligh replied:

'No, I never sleep out of my boat; but in the morning we will again trade with you, and I shall remain till the weather is moderate that we may go, as we have agreed, to see Polaho at Tongataboo.'

Maccaackavow rose and replied for all of them.

'You will not sleep on shore? Then we will kill you.' [1]

The natives looked on the strangers and began knocking stones together again. Bligh needed a hostage, so he grabbed Nageete by the hand and led him down the beach, while the rest looked on in terror. He remembered how Nageete had wanted Bligh to stay and parley with Eefow, but in reality he was provoking them to the attack. Now as he stood with Nageete, he told Purcell to remain with them until the others had got on the boat; if the attack went forward, he intended to kill the native for his treachery. At the critical moment, Nagette slipped from his grasp and ran back to his people. There was nothing for Bligh and Purcell to do but run for it.

John Norton saw them reaching the boat and also saw about two hundred angry natives surging towards them, stones in hand. He jumped from the boat and ran to push its stern off. When everyone else was on board they shouted after Norton, telling him to leave it and return to the boat as soon as he could. It was too late. The natives hit him with their stones and killed him outright. At the same time the islanders took hold of the stern rope and began to pull the boat back to shore. Luckily Bligh had a knife in his pocket and cut it and hauled off to the grapnel, while the natives continued to pummel Norton's lifeless body. Others piled stones into their canoes and set to sea.

As they tried to haul the grapnel they had more bad luck; it was stuck fast. Fortunately, the effort of hauling broke the fluke and the men took to their oars. It was by now too late to escape the attack and a shower of stones battered the crew as they tried their best to row clear. But the launch was hampered by the weight of the seamen and the native canoes outran them. They had no way of fighting back apart from recovering the stones which had fallen into the boat and firing them back, but the islanders were expert at this type of warfare. Things looked bleak when Bligh had an idea which gave them a slim chance. He threw old clothes out of the boat, hoping that the natives' natural curiosity and thirst for possessions would encourage them to stop. [2] Canoe after canoe slowed to pick up the unexpected loot and before dark they had given up the chase. Perhaps they felt that Bligh had bought their freedom.

Understandably, the men were all shaken and decided against visiting Tongataboo. In these parts friendship seemed to have been bought at the point of a gun and no-one felt the need to test that theory. There was only one sure way to get to civilisation safely, but it pushed the boundaries of desperation. Before telling the crew, Bligh took a check of supplies. Then he made his speech to the men.

There was one hope of relief and one only – an island called Timor, at which there was a Dutch settlement, although he did not know exactly where on the island it lay. It was possible they could get some supplies at New Holland, but that was far from being certain. The problem was that Timor lay about 3600 miles away. They could get there using the paltry provisions they had, but it meant living on an ounce of bread and a quarter of a pint of water each day – and that would soon go off. The crew all agreed to the plan and Bligh made them solemnly promise not to deviate from the agreement. They then set off on their hopeless voyage across often uncharted seas.

From the first it seemed that the elements were against them. On 3 May a violent storm broke out and water began to collect in the launch, threatening their precious bread – which was virtually all they had. They commandeered Purcell's chest and tool box and stowed the bread in there, then they threw out all unnecessary clothing which lightened the boat and allowed them to bail out the water much more easily.

Bligh planned to sail west-north-west to find better weather and also the Fiji islands; both Captain Cook and the natives of Annamooka thought they lay in that direction. By the middle of the next day small islands appeared and by three o'clock Bligh had counted eight of them. All of them seemed fertile and the largest was about 24 miles in circumference; but having no arms, the launch did not even try to land at any of them. By six o'clock they discovered another three. In the first few days Bligh used up the fresh fruit such as broken breadfruit and coconuts, saving the bread (which was going rotten) for later. In harsh weather he would allow a spoonful of rum. But for a few days at least it had moderated.

On 6 May more islands came into view – at least ten, the largest being about 24 miles in circuit. As they passed through they almost came to grief on a coral reef, but managed to navigate it. They experienced great hardships at night due to their cramped condition, as Bligh noted:

As our lodgings were very miserable and confined for want of room I endeavoured to remedy the latter defect by putting ourselves at watch and watch; so that one half always sat up while the other lay down on the boat's bottom or upon a chest, with nothing to cover us but the heavens. Our limbs were dreadfully cramped for we could not stretch them out, and the nights were so cold, and we so constantly wet, that after a few hours sleep we could scarce move. [3]

The launch continued its voyage through the Fiji Islands. They impressed by their variety; some just lumps of rock while others had highlands and lowlands, sometimes covered in trees. Bligh being Bligh was fascinated by them and for posterity he made drawings so that future navigators might be able to locate them. In any other circumstances these findings would have been the cause of great excitement; but their desperate situation blunted the edge of their enthusiasm.

The islands were not devoid of life. Occasionally a canoe or two would row out towards them, but the crew were afraid of their intentions and always rowed on and away from potential danger. On the afternoon of the 7th they cleaned out the boat and found some pistol-balls. Knowing that twenty-five of these balls weighed exactly one pound, Bligh made a pair of scales using coconut shells and used one of these balls of the measure for the bread allowance. This was issued three times a day. [4]

On the 9th a storm hit the launch with severe thunder and lightning, drenching everyone and leaving them feeling totally miserable. There was one benefit – they managed to catch up twenty gallons of water. The crew found themselves baling the boat all night. They were sustained by the smallest morsels of food, as Bligh wrote:

In the morning a quarter of a pint of coconut milk and some of the decayed bread was served for breakfast, and for dinner I divided the meat of four coconuts with the remainder of the rotten bread, which was only eatable by such distressed people.

The rains continued and illnesses began with some complaining of pain in the bowels; hardly surprising, bearing in mind the putrid bread they had to eat. In fact, it would rain almost constantly for the next two weeks. On the 14th Bligh spotted six more islands and plotted their positions as accurately as he could, another appeared the next day. They enticed the men with their promise of food but no-one had the courage to meet up with hostile natives despite their state of near starvation. As least, the deluge of rain meant that nobody was threatened with dying from thirst. Hunger was another thing – it was a permanent phantom haunting every waking hour. These storms broke the resolution of the sailors and by the 17th they were begging for an extra allowance; but Bligh was adamant that if they wished to be saved they had to persevere. He found that the rum had an excellent restorative effect, although it did little to alleviate the hunger pangs.

After another three days the weather and hunger had taken its toll and Bligh saw his men looking half dead:

Our appearances were horrible, and I could look no way but I caught the eye of someone in distress... the little sleep we got was in the midst of water, and we constantly awoke with severe cramps and pains in our bones. [5]

It was to get much worse. Deluges fell from the sky and besides being faint from starvation the crew had to spend their time constantly baling water. By the 23rd, Bligh seriously feared that some of 'his people' would not see another day. He issued two teaspoons of rum to each man.   It was too little. The men were reaching the end of their endurance.

The next day, the sun at last broke out. The sickest man was smiling and they all stripped to dry out their clothes. However, Bligh had some bad news. He had been checking on the stock and planning the rest of the voyage, hoping to reach Timor in about four weeks. But what if they were forced to sail on to Java? Their food would certainly have run out by then and so they had to eke it out to last for another two weeks. This meant rationing the food even more and the only way that could be done was to eliminate the supper bread allowance and serve it twice a day only. It was not enough to survive on. Bligh dreaded breaking this news, but the crew were in better spirits and accepted it 'cheerfully'. [6]

Next day they caught a noddy – a sea bird of the tern family – and killed it, after which they split it into portions. Then they issued the parts by the fairest means they could think of – they played 'Who shall have this?' One man turned his back to the rest and a portion was pointed out; then the men shouted 'Who shall have this?' and the player called out a name. [7] This continued until the whole bird was shared out. The bird's blood was shared between the three men who were suffering the most from lack of food.

While the men welcomed the end of the rains, the sun brought problems of its own and some began to feel the first effects of sunstroke. They did continue to catch the odd booby (a bird related to the gannet) along with flying-fish and cuttlefish which helped to supplement their meagre diet. Hope arose on the morning of the 28th with the sound of breakers which signified New Holland, a place at which Bligh hoped to find refreshment after finding a way through the reefs. Another some difficulty, on the next day they found a break in the reef and found themselves near an island in smooth waters. Here Bligh made some observations and seeing that the island at a distance of fifteen miles bore to the west of the channel and so marked it, he called it Direction. [8] They then sailed within the reef to the islands it enclosed. The first was little more than a pile of rock, but the other had a fine sandy cove in which it was easy to moor. Still fearful of natives, they discovered some fireplaces but they were very old and Bligh considered it a safe place to rest. He inspected the boat and found that one of the gudgeons of the rudder was missing, so they replaced it with a large staple. This could have had disastrous consequences on the high sea, so it was fortunate the loss was discovered on the island.

A foraging party returned to say there were plentiful oysters. By good fortune there was a copper pot in the boat, so soon they were boiling up a stew with oysters and pork and a little bread, which tasted like a royal banquet. [9]

Exploration revealed that the island was only about three miles in circumference consisting of rocks covered in trees, which were small because the soil was sandy and sparse. There was good water to be had, for which the crew dug a well near the shore. There were also a number of berry trees, but Bligh cautioned them against eating, as they might have been poisonous – but they proved to be wholesome and after a while all of the men were helping themselves to fruit which resembled gooseberries grapes and sloe, although they tasted somewhat different. Needless to say, they tasted delicious to the poor hungry sailors. Soon everyone felt refreshed and as a token of their restoration Bligh named it Restoration Island. [10]

They stayed all day on the 29th and enjoyed another stew and by the 30th Bligh was pleased to see all of the men looking much better. Only one thing spoiled the visit – Bligh discovered that someone had been pilfering the pork. No-one admitted to it, so Bligh decided to put it out of temptation's way – as there were only two pounds left, he decided to share it out for dinner, which they had with the allowance of bread. Some men picked oysters and Bligh told them to be quick as he meant to sail that day. They put everything on the boat and then prepared to leave. Not too soon; as they did so twenty or so natives appeared on the opposite shore, armed with spears, and beckoning them to come to them; many more appeared on the hilltops. They were naked and seemed to be black.

The launch sailed past two islands to the north of Restoration Island heading towards Fair Cape. The next day Bligh was surprised to find that the country had completely changed in appearance – it was low and sandy with little greenery. To the north-east they saw many small islands and some looked very attractive, covered in trees and promising good fishing – although they caught nothing. Passing these islands they noticed a number of natives running towards the shore waving green branches as a sign of peace; more were approaching a little further off. Bligh motioned to them to approach but they did not dare, although they were armed with spears. They looked like the inhabitants of Restoration Island – naked, black with short bushy hair. [11]

There was an island four miles away and Bligh ordered the launch to stop there. He then ordered two parties to look for supplies and the other to stay aboard the boat. This was the first moment there was almost a mutiny; some of those being sent out resented the fact that others could stay and sit in the boat and said they would rather do without dinner than go and search for it. It was the moment for Purcell, always quarrelsome, to make his own objection, stating that he was as good a man as Bligh. His command in question and needing to quell another mutiny, Bligh decided to take desperate measures. Grabbing a cutlass, he ordered Purcell to take another and defend himself. Not a courageous man. Purcell cried out that Bligh intended to kill him and was prepared to accept orders. [12]

Having put Purcell in his place, Bligh climbed to the highest point to reconnoitre. He saw a small key to the north-west by north but it was much further from the mainland than the island at which they were and the remains of a canoe in a sandy cove persuaded him that the natives could attack by night if they remained. This island was only a small rock about two miles in circuit. He returned to the launch and the foraging parties had only found a small quantity of oysters and clams, so they felt it was pointless to remain any longer. That afternoon they fed on a stew of oysters and clams with dolicho beans and, after naming their resting-place Sunday Island, they set sail again. Unfortunately the key seen by Bligh had no access so they had to spend the night on board the boat.

On the dawning of 1 June they moored the boat at the entrance to a lagoon on the northernmost of four small keys and as usual sent foraging parties. They found little but a few clams and some dolichos, which were not relished by the men. At noon Nelson returned with the men who had explored the easternmost key, but Nelson was in a bad way and had to be supported by two men. He had been caught by the sun and insisted in working nonetheless. The men all ate their stew made from the clams and oysters from Sunday Island, but Nelson could eat none, so Bligh nursed him by hand-feeding bread soaked in wine.

Although there was little to recommend the place, it did seem that natives visited it as there was evidence of their presence. Nonetheless Bligh directed that everyone needed rest and they slept through the afternoon, having lit fires. As evening approached Bligh warned them not to make the fires too large in case they were noticed by unfriendly eyes. Samuel and Peckover supervised this and as darkness came Bligh wandered to the end of the island to see if any fire could be clearly visible. As he looked back all of a sudden the entire island was enveloped in red light and so he ran back to see what was going on. The culprit was Fryer, who, insisting on having a fire to himself, allowed it to spread to the neighbouring grass. Bligh was livid.

Thus the relief which I expected from a little sleep was totally lost and I anxiously waited for the flowing of the tide that we might proceed to sea. [13]

After eight, Samuel and Peckover went to hunt for turtle; three others also went in search of food. Hayward and Elphinstone were put on watch while the others, mostly sick, rested. At midnight the bird party came back with a dozen noddies, but could have caught a lot more if Robert Lamb had not separated and disturbed them all. Later, Lamb was to confess that he had eaten nine raw birds at that time. Bligh was furious, more angry than even in his usual hot rages; he physically beat Lamb for his actions. [14] His mood did not improve when Samuel and Peckover returned to inform him that there was not a turtle to be seen. Bligh fumed at the incompetence of his crew – only twelve noddies because of Lamb's stupidity and then the turtles had been scared off by Fryer's fire!

The launch left at dawn. That morning the sea was rough and they saw two sandy keys and by noon they had spotted six more, most of which had small trees and brushwood. The mainland was full of sandhills and straight ahead they saw a flat-topped hill which Bligh named Pudding Pan Hill; further north were two more which Bligh called the Paps. Nelson by now had made a recovery and Bligh gave him a glass of wine to keep up his strength. By this time Peckover's watch had stopped, so they had no means of gauging time. That night they moored by an island close to an inlet to the mainland and although Bligh sent out a party they returned with nothing. Natives had feasted there recently, as evidenced by turtle bones and shells. Bligh called the place Turtle Island.

On went the launch across the limitless ocean. On 3 June they saw a number of small islands, finding the highest to have a mountainous top with four rocks to its south-east, which Bligh called The Brothers. A little further there was a bay in the mainland containing several other islands, which Bligh named The Bay of Islands. To the north were more islands, the most northerly of which contained a very high round hill, which Bligh named Wednesday Island. Further north was another reef. As they sailed to the western point of the mainland there were numerous sandbanks so Bligh named it Shoal Cape. At about four they saw a small island bearing west which was no more than a rock full of boobies, so Bligh named it Booby Island. After these discoveries they found themselves back in open ocean.

The days passed and the men grew weaker. Bligh passed his time with observations – on 4 June he saw a yellow and black ringed sea snake – but their paltry allowance of rotten bread was not enough to sustain life, even when supplemented by the odd booby which the men occasionally caught. Need forced one of the men to steal some of the clams they had in store, but no-one admitted to the theft. By 7 June everyone was complaining and Bligh dished out the remaining clams – an ounce each. Ledward and Lebogue was sinking fast and Bligh gave them a few sips of the wine, of which little remained. The next day brought some relief – they caught a dolphin – of which they ate two ounces each, the same being saved for the next day's dinner. It did little to help Bligh, who was violently sick afterwards. Bligh described their plight in his log on the morning of 10 June:

In the morning after a very comfortless night there was a visible alteration for the worse in many of the people which gave me great apprehensions. An extreme weakness, swelled legs, hollow and ghastly countenances, a more than common inclination to sleep, with an apparent debility of understanding, seemed to me the melancholy presages of an approaching dissolution. The surgeon and Lebogue, in particular, were most miserable objects. I occasionally gave them a few teaspoonfuls of wine out of the little that remained, which greatly

assisted them. The hopes of being able to accomplish the voyage was our principal support. The boatswain very innocently told me that he really thought I looked worse than anyone in the boat. The simplicity with which he uttered such an opinion amused me and I returned him a better compliment. [16]

On 12 June, they spied Timor and were almost at the end of the most heroic open-boat voyages ever sailed by man. They had covered 3618 miles with supplies given them from the *Bounty*, which was then thought enough for them to reach the nearest island. They had lost Norton – but to have brought his men through so many hazards and so much suffering is a feat which any man could be proud of.

Still, Bligh did not know exactly where the Dutch settlement was – only that it was somewhere to the south-west of Timor. They bore off to the south-west half west, being three miles from shore – and for dinner they shared a booby and the usual allowance of bread and water. They passed a low shore coated with palm trees and after twenty-five miles they moored, having their allowance of bread and water. It must have been frustrating to realise that they were close to succour and yet had to eat their measly rations until it could be made sure.

They continued their search for civilisation on the 13th, passing the island of Roti. They stopped at a sandy bay where native smoke fires could be seen and Purcell and Fryer asked for permission to explore, but no-one else agreeing to join them they stayed where they were. They continued to steer along the shore where they saw a beautiful country marked out into parks and lawns. This looking more promising, so the boatswain and gunner were sent to look around and soon they returned with five natives, saying that they had met two families who told them that the Governor lived in a place called Coupang, some distance to the north-east. One of the natives came on board and agreed to guide them there.

The launch sailed all night and after passing an island called Pulo Samow they heard the firing of two cannon. Civilisation was tantalisingly close. They passed two square-rigged vessels and a cutter at anchor then the crew rowed until almost dawn. Then they came to grapnel at a small town and fort which the native told them was Coupang. Not wanting to come ashore without leave, Bligh hoisted a small jack as a signal of distress.

After sunrise a soldier hailed them to land and already a crowd of natives were at the shore. An English sailor told them that the Governor was ill, so that the next best person to see was his commander, Captain Spikerman. Having been led to the Captain, Bligh told him of their plight and requested that his people should be cared for without delay. Spikerman agreed to receive them in his house and Bligh went to the launch to fetch the crew. Here they found tea and bread and butter awaiting them.

Their hosts looked upon the sailors with little less than horror. They were scarcely more than skeletons, their bodies covered in sores and dressed in rags, a human portrait of the agony of famine. Never had they seen a crowd so close to death, hanging on to life by the thread of hope. To make the pathetic picture complete, the crew now knew they were at last safe and tears of gratitude poured down their faces.

Bligh had an appointment to see the ailing Governor, William Adrian van Este, who was a humane and sympathetic man. He was prepared to give his crew lodgings at either the hospital or on board Spikerman's ship; but for himself he would give a house of his own. After the interview Bligh returned to his men to find that they had been given every attention. They had been given gifts of new clothes and the doctor – Max - had tended to their complaints and sores.

Bligh's house was all ready for him, complete with servants. It was very grand and had a hall with a room at each end and a loft above; it was encircled by a piazza with an apartment in one corner. After all their sufferings together, Bligh decided that they would not be parted and asked if all the men could be lodged in the house with him. The Governor agreed, so Bligh took a room of his own and allotted the other room to the Master, the surgeon, the gunner and Nelson. The other officers were given the loft while the men had the apartment. To help with the furnishing, van Este sent bedding, chairs, tables and benches. The survivors of the *Bounty* mutiny would stick together. [16]

The Governor told Bligh to ask for anything of which he was in need, but he was dying so Bligh spent much of his time transacting business with his son-in-law, Timotheus Wanjon, who was second-in-command. Wanjon was as sympathetic and helpful as the Governor himself and at noon a sumptuous dinner was served to the crew. After Bligh had seen his men eat to their heart's content, he joined Wanjon for his own meal. Strangely enough, although starved, Bligh felt no strong urge to eat or drink. It was probably the anti-climax after so much suffering.

Bligh took the opportunity to write to his wife:

My Dear, Dear Betsy,

I am now, for the most part, in a part of the world I never expected, it is however a place that has afforded me relief and saved my life, and I have the happiness to assure you that I am now in perfect health....

Know then my own Dear Betsy, that I have lost the *Bounty* ... on the 28 April at day light in the morning Christian having the morning watch. He with several others came into my Cabin while I was a Sleep, and

seizing me, holding naked Bayonets at my Breast, tied my Hands behind my back, and threatened instant destruction if I uttered a word. I however call'd loudly for assistance, but the conspiracy was so well laid that the Officers Cabbin Doors were guarded by Centinels, so Nelson, Peckover, Samuels or the Master could not come to me. I was now dragged on Deck in my Shirt & closely guarded – I demanded of Christian the case of such a violent act, & severely degraded for his Villainy but he could only answer – "not a word sir or you are Dead." I dared him to the act & endeavoured to rally some one to a sense of their duty but to no effect....

The Secrisy of this Mutiny is beyond all conception so that I can not discover that any who are with me had the least knowledge of it. It is unbeknown to me why I must beguile such force. Even Mr. Tom Ellison took such a liking to Otaheite that he also turned Pirate, so that I have been run down by my own Dogs...

My misfortune I trust will be properly considered by all the World – It was a circumstance I could not foresee – I had not sufficient Officers & had they granted me Marines most likely the affair would never have happened – I had not a Spirited & brave fellow about me & the Mutineers treated them as such. My conduct has been free of blame, & I showed everyone that, tied as I was, I defied every Villain to hurt me...

I know how shocked you will be at this affair but I request of you My Dear Betsy to think nothing of it all is now past & we will again looked forward to future happyness. Nothing but true consciousness as an Officer that I have done well could support me....Give my blessings to my Dear Harriet, my Dear Mary, my Dear Betsy & to my Dear little stranger[10] & tell them I shall soon be home...To You my Love I give all that an affectionate Husband can give –

Love, Respect & all that is or ever will be in the power of your ever affectionate Friend and Husband Wm Bligh. [17]

The 'dear little stranger' was actually twins, Frances and Jane, who were born on 11 May 1788.

Hardly had the men began to recover when the carpenter Purcell again created problems for Bligh. He had little enough to repay van Este's kindness, but on hearing that he had little if any chalk about the place, Bligh ordered the carpenter to give him some from his tool chest. Purcell refused, saying he had no right to it and this began a row after which Bligh eventually took some. By now Bligh had had enough of Purcell and ordered him on board the Commodore's ship with leave to come ashore only every Sunday.

There were two important matters which Bligh needed to discuss with van Este. Firstly, the events on board the *Bounty*; he gave a full written deposition and asked for a requisition that an order be sent to all Dutch settlements to stop the ship if she ever landed there. Bligh appended a detailed description and names of all the mutineers. He also wrote a dispatch to the Admiralty. Second, Bligh asked permission for Nelson to be allowed to explore the region in search of plants. Van Este readily agreed, telling him that there was a wonderful variety of plant-life at Timor, some of great medicinal value. Unfortunately, Nelson's exploration would never come to pass. He had caught a fever and on 20 July he passed away. The next day his body was carried by twelve soldiers in black, walking behind the minister; next came Bligh and Wanjon; then ten gentlemen of the town and the officers of the ships in the harbour; and after them Bligh's crew. [18]

The rest of the crew recovered quickly and soon were in good shape. That had been Bligh's first priority; the second was the voyage home. He knew that he needed to reach Batavia before the October fleet sailed for Europe so he had little time to make his preparations. He gave notice that he was looking for a vessel to take his crew to Batavia, but the offers were very expensive so Bligh decided to buy a schooner for 1000 rix dollars. He named it HM Schooner *Resource*; it was thirty-four feet long but had no armament to protect them against piracy. Wanjon helped him out and provided four brass swivels, fourteen stands of small arms and ammunition. [19]

While at Timor Bligh had the chance to meet the natives' king who lived four miles away in a place known as Backennassy. There had been a civil war between the king and one of his nephews lasting from 1786 to 1788 until a treaty was made. The king lived in a house with three apartments surrounded by a piazza which seemed very dirty. He received Bligh very civilly and fed him with tea, rice cakes, roasted Indian corn, and dried buffalo flesh, with some *arrack*. Bligh was given a gift from the king, a round metal plate stamped with a star and he promised to return with a present of *arrack*. The natives were very fond of their liquor. [20]

By 20 August the *Resource* was ready to sail. Van Este gave him some fine plants and Wanjon gave him some seeds for Kew Gardens and mountain rice which was forwarded to the West Indies. Having taken an affectionate farewell of all those people who had helped them, they left for the next leg of their voyage.

The voyage passed with little incident. On the 22nd they passed the island of Flores and after three days had passed Toorns Island. Five days later Bligh was obliged to choose between the Straits of Mangaryn or those of Sapi and he chose the latter; but strong currents obliged him to return to Mangaryn. On 3 September he passed the island of Lombok and after four more days they were off Cape Sandana, the north-east part of Java. On the 10th they anchored off Passourwang, a Dutch settlement on the coast of Java, but the river entrance was muddy and there was the stench of dead hogs who had come to grief there. After about a mile they arrived at the fort and were welcomed by the commandant, Adrian de Rye, who gave him a bullock and other provisions. They also took a pilot to guide them to Sourabaya.

On the way to Batavia Bligh stopped off at two other forts. At Sourabaya they were entertained by the Governor Barkay and his brother, the commandant of the troops, de Bose. They were advised to stay for three days and then travel in the company of the other vessels who were leaving on the 17th, as piracy was rife in those waters. While there Bligh visited some natives who entertained them with a concert of music; the instruments were gongs, drums, and a fiddle with two strings. It was not advised to travel into the interior as it was infested with ferocious tigers.

When the time came to leave, an unpleasant incident happened which must have deeply shocked Bligh. The whole business seemed to begin with the arrival of provisions for the Resource which took place whilst Bligh was saying his farewells to Barkay and de Bose. When the slaves arrived with the stores, the men were drinking at a local house so the slaves left them there. Later, the crew found that they had to transport the goods onto the boat themselves and to hire help they were forced to lay out a penny. This expense, together with the effects of alcohol, made a mountain out of this particular molehill and they began to grumble that they had been badly used. Meanwhile they received orders from Bligh that they were to sail the boat out down the river and that he would join them later. This caused more complaint and although Hayward tried to get the men to comply, they steadfastly refused to do so. When the Captain sailed towards them and saw that his order had been disobeyed, he wondered at the cause and so arrived to find out what was going on.

He was told that two people below decks – Elphinstone and Hallet – were refusing to work and Bligh found them drunk as skunks. It was clear that the rest of the men were far from sober, too. Bligh turned to his Master, Fryer, in a rage.

'What is the cause of your carrying on your duty in such a manner? Why aren't those officers on deck?'

'I don't know.'

'Are they drunk? Or ill? What's the matter with them?'

'Am I a doctor? Ask *him* what's the matter with them!'

'What is the meaning of this insolence?'

'It is no insolence. You not only use me ill, but every man in this vessel! And every man will say the same thing!'

Purcell now became the spokesman and repeated what Fryer had said.

'Yes by God! We're used damned ill and we have no right to be used so!'

Bligh had heard enough. He locked the Master and the carpenter below decks and referred the matter for an inquiry to be held by Barkay himself. By the time the inquiry took place, all the men had sobered up and were ashamed of what had taken place. Everyone gave similar responses to the questions put to them; here is Hallet's questioning:

'Have you received your provisions and everything that is allowed you?'

'Yes except that since the third of September 1789, I have not received all my *arack*, but the Captain told the clerk I should have double when I got to Batavia.'

'Why then did you say to an English sailor now in the service of Holland in this place, that it would not go well with your Captain when he returned to England, he having ill-treated every person under his command, for which reason he would be 'tied to the mouth of a canon and fired into the air'?'

'I do not know that I said any such thing, and if I did utter such an expression, I was drunk when I did it, and I most humbly ask your forgiveness for it, and beg that I may have leave to return to England with you.'

'Do you not think the Captain has done his duty in every respect to your knowledge?'

'Yes.'

'Is he brutal or severe as to give you cause of complaint?'

'No.'

'Has he not to your knowledge taken every pains to preserve his ship's company?'

'Yes.'

Having salvaged his honour, Bligh's thoughts turned to his Master. He had been given the responsibility of being in charge at that time and the outcome had been a total dereliction of duty. For Fryer, this had been a disaster and he realised very quickly that his transgression had been unpardonable. There was only one thing he could do – appeal to Bligh for forgiveness. He wrote a note:

I wish to make everything agreeable as far as lies in my power, that nothing might happen when we come home. As I have done everything in my power, as far as I know, to do my duty, and would still wish to do it, therefore, if matters can be made up, I beg you will forward it.

'As I have done everything to do my duty'? Bligh must have shaken his head when he read those words; in the event, he sent a dismissive response:

Having been informed by the Commandant of this place that you want to see me, I must inform you that being on the point of going on board and having many things to do, I cannot possibly comply with your request. If you have anything to communicate, you must write to me on the busyness, and as you will go in a vessel that will also be under my orders, you can at all times represent your situation.

Fryer was growing desperate. It was clear that Bligh had no intention of taking him along; his fate would be as a prisoner on another vessel. He once again appealed to Bligh:

I have received yours saying that you cannot possibly find time to speak to me, I most humbly beg of you to grant me that favour if possible it can be done – I likewise beg of you to take me with you, if you confine me in irons. I will make any concession that you think proper.

Bligh was not vindictive, but this matter was a very serious one. He had suffered as much as anyone on the launch, but had at last brought his crew to safety. Was this his reward for saving their lives? Their ingratitude was beyond belief. On the other hand, they had all suffered together and he was loath to persecute them after all they'd been through. Then again, they had neglected their duty and for Bligh that was unpardonable. It was by sticking to his duty that he had brought everyone safe to Coupang. Now that his fury had abated, Bligh had to make a difficult choice. As Captain, he was bound to bring the deserters to justice at the earliest opportunity. As a man who had suffered privations with his fellow man, he understood the failing of his crew and could hardly blame them for taking the opportunity to relax and drink after all they had been through. But the things they had said about him under the influence! Above all, the blatant dereliction of duty! The disobedience! Did he have the right to act as his own judge and jury? Could he pardon them?

To his credit, he did. He would never again mention the incident at Sourabaya.

Bligh made fresh plans for his departure. On the appointed day Bligh set off in the company of the other boats and made a tricky passage through the Straits of Medura. The river at Samarang was as unpleasant as that of Passourwang, with dead animals decaying in the mud. A carriage took him to the Governor's house where he received permission to resupply and to fix the mainmast which had sprung. While this took place, Bligh took the opportunity to view the second most important Dutch settlement in Java and he found a good school, a hospital and a theatre. He also made friends with a surgeon called Abegg, who gave him advice and medicines for free.

On 26 September the *Resource* sailed on, reaching Batavia after five days. Their first experience was the strictness of the officials; they had to stop at a house and give all the information about themselves; then a carriage took Bligh to see the *sandabar*, Engelhard, with whom all visitors had to declare their business in Batavia. The *sandabar* accompanied Bligh to pay a visit to the Governor-General and Bligh had an account of the mutiny on board the *Bounty* which van Este had had translated into Dutch for this purpose. Bligh had three requests – that he might sell his schooner; that they might be allowed to leave on a sail bound for Europe; and that his men be cared for. Bligh and his crew were then directed to a large hotel, at which all strangers were compelled to stay and which Bligh found hot and stifling, as well as dusty and unhealthy. He had a violent headache all night. [21]

The next morning Bligh was obliged to sit at a council meeting with the *sandabar* and he was told that all of his requests would be complied with. By the time Bligh got back to the hotel a fever had taken hold and he sent to the *sandabar*, who in turn sent the surgeon of the town hospital to visit him. Within a day the fever had gone down but the headache persisted, so Bligh asked the Governor if it would be possible for him to rent a house in the country. Instead, the Governor directed that he should live in the house of Sparking, the surgeon-general. Bligh was not the only person to be ill and Bligh asked if Thomas Hall could be looked after in the hospital, which was again granted.

At Sparling's house, the change of air did Bligh a lot of good and he was even able to accept an invitation to attend one of the governor-general's country seats, where he met many fine ladies and gentlemen, some of whom invited him to recuperate at their country houses. Despite the ministrations of the surgeon, Bligh's illness got steadily worse until Spalding advised him that he must get out of Batavia. The governor-general warned him that the ships were already crowded and there was no possibility of his crew all sailing on the same ship; but a bark was sailing on the 16th and Bligh requested that he could join her with as many of his men as possible. In reply he learned that only himself and two others could be accommodated but passages for the others would be found at the earliest possible time. Bligh had no option but to acquiesce.

On 10 October the *Resource* was put up for auction at a starting figure of 2000 rix dollars. No-one was interested. To Bligh's great disappointed she was eventually sold to an Englishman, Captain John Eddie, for a mere 295. [22] The launch was also sold, even though Bligh was reluctant to part with it. On top of that, Bligh then found out that he was liable to pay tax on the sale, something he resisted due to the loss he had suffered on it. To make matters even worse, Bligh found out that Thomas Hall had died in the

The Battle of Camperdown

Otoo, later Tinah, by Webber

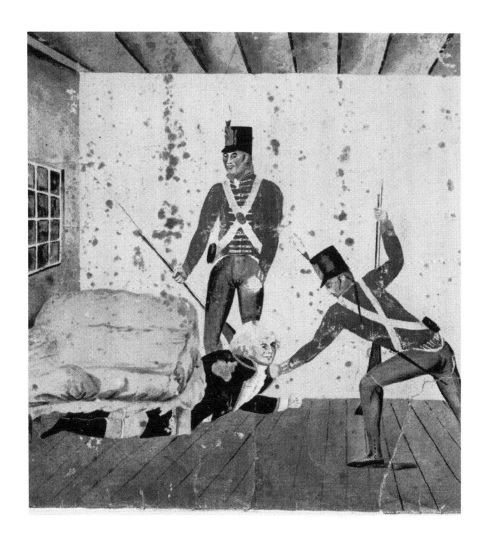

Propaganda drawing of the arrest of Bligh in New South Wales, depicting him as a coward.

William Bligh

hospital of his complaint.

There were a few things to settle before Bligh sailed. First, officers complained that on buying goods they had been presented with extortionate bills from the merchants, so Bligh asked the *sabandar* to intervene and he made appropriate reductions. Next, the crew had to be examined before a notary and give account of the mutiny on board the *Bounty*. Without this, Batavia could not legally issue orders to detain the ship at Dutch settlements. The men left their affidavits. More hurtful to Bligh was the problem of the plants – 'jacks, *nancas, karambolas, namnams, jambo*, and three thriving breadfruit plants'. He was forced to leave all his work at Batavia. [23]

On 13 October he wrote to Banks:

Had I been accidentally appointed to the Command, the loss of the Ship would give me no material concern, but when I reflect that it was through you Sir who undertook to assert I was fully capable, and the Eyes of every one regarding the progress of the Voyage, and perhaps more with envy, than with delight; I cannot say but if[it] affects me considerably. To those however who may be disposed to blame let them see I had in fact completed my undertaking. What Man's situation could be so peculiarly flattering as mine 12 Hours before the loss of the Ship. Every thing was in the most perfect order and we were well stored with every necessary both for service & health, by early attention to those particulars I acted against the power of chance in case I could not get through Endeavour Straights, as well as against any accident that might befall me in them, and to add to this, I had most successfully got my Plants in a most flourishing & fine order, so that upon the whole the Voyage was ¾ over, and the remaining part no way doubtfull. Every person was in the most perfect health, to establish which I had taken the greatest pains, and bore a most anxious care through the whole course of the Voyage. [24]

Bligh now settled accounts with the *sabandar* and left the food account to be closed by Fryer when he left; he also authorised him to pay one month's wages to the crew. There was one problem with his proposed trip to England; he discovered that by order of the Dutch East India Company, no person travelling on a ship would be allowed to leave until it reached its intended port. Bligh's sip was bound for Holland and by now it was too late to get an order from the Governor-General to countermand the order. So, on the 16th, he embarked on the Dutch packet *Vlydte* along with Samuel and Smith and at seven o'clock the ship left harbour. As Bligh himself wrote: 'In the passage to the Cape of Good Hope there occurred nothing worth remark.' [24] He was however critical of the Dutch method of navigation, in that they corrected course after veering away every 2½°. On

16 December, they anchored in Table Bay, Cape of Good Hope.

Governor van der Graaf received Bligh with kindness and readily agreed to countermand the Dutch East India Company's orders. He then wrote an order asking the Captain of the *Vlydte* to allow Bligh and his companions to disembark at the English Channel and gave Bligh a copy, as well as letters of introduction to important people in Holland, should he have to sail there. While at the Cape Bligh also wrote letters to Governor Philip at Port Jackson and Lord Cornwallis in India, giving a description of events and a note of all the mutineers.

On 2 January 1790 the *Vlydte* left the Cape. On the 15th they passed St Helena, on the 21st Ascension Island, on 10 February Cape de Verde and on 13 March they sighted Portland Bill. On the 14th they left the ship and reached Portsmouth by way of an Isle of Wight boat.

Nineteen were cast adrift on the launch after the Mutiny of the *Bounty*. Norton died at Tofua, Nelson at Timor, Hall at Batavia. Elphinstone and Linkletter also died at Batavia before they could embark on a ship home; and Lamb died on board ship. Ledward was not seen again, so his fortunes are uncertain. In any case only one died on the launch voyage and the seven others after they had reached civilisation. Twelve of the crew were able to make it home to England and all of them owed their lives to the courage and firmness of William Bligh.

Chapter Eight. 'Prosper Therefore Our Undertakings'

From March to October Bligh recuperated and spent time with his beloved family, whom he had not seen for more than three years. He also wrote the story of his trials and the first part was published by the end of the year under the title *A Narrative of the Mutiny on Board His Majesty's Ship* Bounty, *and the Subsequent Voyage of Part of the Crew in the Ship's Boat, from Tofoa, one of the Friendly Islands, to Timor, a Dutch Settlement in the East Indies.* By this time the name of Bligh was almost a household word and he was hailed as almost as eminent a hero as Captain Cook.

The loss of the *Bounty* was an expensive business for Bligh, who had lost much of his own property. He therefore made a claim to the Lords Commissioners, including an itemised list of his losses, which included a small library of books, clothing, bedding, crockery, cutlery and alcohol, bringing a grand total of £283 1s 6d. He also wrote to the Victualling

Board claiming for lost foodstuffs including the hogs he had cured at Tahiti. In the end, Bligh received nothing and had to shoulder his losses.

The Admiralty had read Bligh's account of the mutiny and had already made preparations to capture the renegades. To mutiny on one of His Majesty's ships was not something which could be borne as it served as a dangerous precedent for other crews. The *Pandora*, a 24-gun frigate, was commissioned for this employment and they gave the job of Captain to Edward Edwards, a brutal disciplinarian who had already experienced a mutiny himself while in charge of the *Narcissus*. He was ordered to take over the 160-man crew of the *Pandora* on 10 August.

The loss of one of His Majesty's ships was a serious matter and a court-martial into the affair was mandatory. This took place on board the *HMS Prince William* and was presided over by Admiral Samuel Barrington. It was a short affair. First of all the court addressed Bligh:

'Have you any objection or complaint to make against any of your Officers and Ship's Company now present respecting the Seizure of His Majesty's Armed Vessel, the *Bounty* under your Command?'

'I have no other than the charges I have made against the Carpenter.'

The court then turned to the officers and men.

'Have you any objection or complaint to make against Lieutenant Bligh?'

'None.'

The Court was cleared and was of opinion that the said armed vessel, the *Bounty* was violently and forcibly taken from the said Lieutenant William Bligh by the said Fletcher Christian and certain other Mutineers, and did adjudge the said Lieutenant William Bligh, and such of the Officers and Ships Company as were returned to England and then present to be honourably acquitted. [1]

Because Bligh had made allegations against the carpenter, Purcell was arraigned on charges of disrespect, insolence and disobedience of orders. In his charge, Bligh mentioned his behaviour with the wooding party in Adventure Bay, his refusal to drink the elixir of vitriol, his refusal to make a grinding-stone for Tinah, his insolence at Sunday Island when they almost came to a duel, the affair of the chalk at Timor and his general disrespectful behaviour. After interrogating Simpson, Samuel, Hayward and Fryer, the court found the charges in part proved and reprimanded him accordingly.

Bligh was now the talk of England and was invited to meet the King. The Admiralty was also quick to recognise his merits and instantly promoted him – on 14 November - to Commander, giving him command of the sloop *Falcon*, a 14-gun ship. A month later, as a mark of respect, they waived the necessity of three years' service as Captain to promote him again to Post Captain and gave him the *Medea*. However on 15 April 1791 there was no more work, so he was put on half-pay.

In the meantime Joseph Banks had been petitioning for another voyage to transplant breadfruit trees. On 29 December 1790 Lord Auckland wrote to Banks telling him that the second attempt had been approved. The ship that was chosen was the *Providence*, a new West Indiaman, and a small brig, the *Assistant*, was to be her consort. Bligh was chosen to Captain the *Providence* while Lieutenant Nathaniel Portlock was given command of the *Assistant* and her crew of 27 men. Bligh knew Portlock, who had served as Master's Mate on board the *Discovery* and after Cook's death had transferred to the *Resolution* to serve under Bligh. As for officers, Godolphin Bond was probably a relative of Bligh's, while George Tobin was related by his mother to Lord Nelson's wife and so had strings pulled for him. Matthew Flinders, who would later become the great explorer, was advised to seek a birth under Bligh by his friend Captain Thomas Pasley; he had been serving under him on board the *Bellerophon*. There was also a strong military presence, with Lieutenant Pearce commanding a sergeant, two corporals, a drummer and no less than fifteen marines. Bligh was taking no chances this time. The list of officers was as follows:

- **Captain:** *William Bligh*

- **Captain's Clerk:** *Edward Hatful*

- **First Lieutenant:** *Francis Godolphin Bond*

- **Second Lieutenant:** *James Guthrie*

- **Third Lieutenant:** *George Tobin*

- **Lieutenant of Marines**   : *Thomas Pearce*

- **Master: William Nicholls**

- **Master's Mates:** *Thomas Gillespie, John Impey, Thomas Walker*

- **Quartermaster:** *John Letby*

- **Surgeon:** *Edward Harwood*

- **Surgeon's First Mate:** *Rob Bridgeway*

- **Surgeon's Second Mate:** *Douglas White*

- **Boatswain:** *Edward James*

- **Gunner:** *John England*

- **Carpenter:** *John Flow*

- **Midshipmen:** *George Holwell, George Milsha, John Busby, Bob Ogelvie, William Hinde, Matthew Flinders, John Head, William Askew*

- **Botanists:** *James Wiles, Christopher Smith*

The *Providence* and the *Assistant* set sail from Spithead on 3 August and after a week it seemed that Bligh was in for a repeat of his previous voyage; a violent storm burst on the 12th but it soon abated and they had fine weather until gales and heavy rain set in a week later. Bligh used his old custom of keeping fires so that the crew could have dry clothing. He also reinstated the three watch system, although the Master was not expected to participate so as to 'be ready for all calls'. Seas ran high between the 23rd and 26th on which day they met the whaler *Redbridge*, whose Master John Kelly was very ill. Bligh sent his surgeon over to prescribe for him.

On 27 August they sighted Tenerife and anchored there. Bligh sent an officer to meet with the Governor, but found he was absent. They needed to stock up with water, beef and wine, but while they were there Bligh's malaria resurfaced as a severe fever and he was so weak that Portlock had to take command while Bond went over to the *Assistant*. They set sail again on 2 September, but Bligh was so ill that they pulled in at Porto Praya, Santiago, where the surgeon urged him to send ashore for some fruit. They only found a few oranges, so Tobin and Pearce went ashore to find a house in which he could recuperate; instead they discovered that the fever was raging all over the place. It would be better if they sailed on, but Bligh took the opportunity to send a letter to his wife, dictated to Harwood:

I am anchored here to day to procure a little fruit, and shall leave it by midnight, as I find it an unhealthy time of the year. I am now taking the bark and feel considerably stronger; so that hope before we reach the

Cape to be perfectly re-established in my health; from thence shall give you a full account how I have proceeded – I am confident it is ordained for us once more to meet, you may therefore cherish your dear little girls in that happy hope. My blessing to them all and with that affectionate esteem and regard you have every known from me, I remain, y^r sincere & affect^e husband, William Bligh. God bless you, my dear love and my little angels.[2]

Bligh was in fact feeling worse and none the better for viewing the port: 'a more miserable and burnt up and inhospitable place I never beheld.' By the 15th, 'when the air was remarkably cool for our situation,' Bligh felt slightly better, although often 'distracted with head ache'. [3] The slightest noise was painful for him and he asked that there be no noise on board ship; he logged his immense gratitude to the crew for obeying his wishes. When they crossed the line on 3 October he was greatly improved and able to perform divine service on the 9th. On the 30th, there was some trouble aboard; John Letby refused to carry out orders from the Master's mate John Impey and when Barber the boatswain's mate was told to order him back to his duty, Letby struck him and knocked him down. This was a serious charge and Bligh punished him with more lashes than he had ever given a sailor at one time – thirty. [4]

On 6 November the ships anchored in Table Bay and Bligh went to call on his old friend, Governor van Este, but he was away in Europe and his place had been taken by the Lieutenant-Governor Rhenius. The officers began to get supplies for the ships and do running repairs while Bligh tried to recuperate a little more. To do so he went on an excursion to the attractive village of Stellinbosch, situated on a plain twenty-five miles from Cape Town, which was watered by a 'charming river' against a backdrop of hills and mountains. He noted that the farmers on the hillsides grew 'corn, grapes, peaches, apricots, almonds, and abundance of vegetables.' Bligh stayed for a week as the guest of the local minister called Borchaud, whom he described as a 'sensible, worthy man', but after his stay a 'distracted headache' sent him back to Cape Town.

On 16 December a ship arrived flying signals of distress, so boats from ships, including the *Providence*, helped to tow her into port. She contained survivors from the wreck of the *Sirius*, which had come to grief after sailing from Port Jackson. The Governor of New South Wales, Phillip, hired the Dutch ship *Waaksamheyd* to take Captain Hunter and the crew back to England and this was the ship which lay in trouble at Table Bay. This may seem to have little to do with Captain Bligh, but many small incidents would eventually link together to form the tapestry of his later life.

On 20 December Bligh sent Portlock a copy of his general orders with directions as to how the *Assistant* should proceed:

Sir, I have enclosed a copy of my general orders which you will take care of and be guided by in case you are separated from me. I shall not go to the southward of 40° South on our way to Adventure Bay (which you are to consider as the first place of rendezvous) until I get a meridian with the west side of New Holland, unless the wind obliges me to do so. I will wait for you in Adventure Bay ten days. Should a separation be the cause of my being there before you I will leave a bottle with a letter in it on Penguin Island covered with stones on the part nearest the main, and cut some memorandum on a tree near the River's mouth towards the sea. Should you get there before me stay the same time and do the like. From Van Diemen's Land I shall proceed to Otaheite (by the South of New Zealand) where our rendezvous is to be at Matavai Bay on the north side of the island. Should my misfortune prevent my joining you there you are to do the best for His Majesty's Service, and as you think yourself capable to comply with the orders from my Lords Commissioners of the Admiralty. I am, etc., Wm. Bligh. [5]

The ships left Table Bay on 23 December with a fifteen-gun salute which was returned. On Christmas Day the crew were served with a mutton 'sea pie'. Bligh had intended to stop at the island of St Paul, but the foggy weather threatened risk and delays. On 8 February Tasmania was sighted and little did Midshipman Matthew Flinders know that at a later date, in the company of Dr Bass, he would be the first man to circumnavigate this island. Bligh knew this part of the world well, having been here twice before, so having sighted the Mewstone he steered towards Adventure Bay. Here he had found the best place for wooding and watering and he saw no reason to look elsewhere. They wooded on the west end of the bay and watered from the stream which they had discovered on board the *Resolution*.

As before, they found old native huts, containing the remains of shellfish; one had the remains of an animal and others had woven baskets and stones for making fire. The botanists made several excursions – around Bruni Island, Nelson's Hill and Penguin Island – where they picked up some important specimens. Meanwhile Bligh panted some fruit trees planted near the east end of the beach; the plants he had left on his last voyage had not survived apart from a sorry-looking apple tree. They did see a number of kangaroos, but they were timid and hid well among the long wire grass. There were still wild duck on the lake but this time Bligh's clumsy firing did not scare them away and a number were shot for food. They also found a platypus, which was new to Bligh:

It was seventeen inches long, and has a small flat head connected so close to the shoulders that it can scarce be said to have a neck. It has no mouth like any other animal, but a kind of a duck bill, two inches long, which opens at the extremity and will not admit anything above the size of a pistol ball. It has four legs, and on each foot are very sharp claws; it has no tail but a rump not unlike a penguin's, on which are quills of rusty brown. [6]

Eventually and inevitably the crew met with the natives. On 19 February, on the low land surrounding Frederick Henry Bay, some of the men encountered twenty-two men and women. The natives were particularly keen to have hats, but the weather was too wet for the men to spare any. All the men had beards and were stocky and of medium height. [7]

During his wanderings around Adventure Bay Bligh came across the tree on which Cook had cut 1777, so Bligh carved 1792.

By the 20th the work was completed and the ships were ready to sail, but one of the *Assistant*'s crew – a man named Bennet – was absent. It was a nuisance, but Bligh was concerned for the man's safety and that night he ordered a light to be kept on all night on the ships' mastheads to show him the way back. Afterwards, Bennet was to admit that he had meant to desert. The next morning, search parties were sent out to look for him and he was finally discovered by Lieutenant Pearce and one of the botanists, who escorted him back to the ships. They set sail on the 23rd, but while off Cape Frederick Henry the *Assistant* carried away her foreyard so they returned to Adventure Bay for repairs.

Two months after Bligh left Tasmania it was visited by the French Captain D-Entrecasteaux, who is credited with many discoveries. These are deserved, but few people realise that Bligh himself made many discoveries for which he received no acknowledgement. He and his men were the first to explore Bruni Island. He first stated that Isthmus Bay was divided from Adventure Bay by a neck of land. Bligh was the first to see the northern part of the waters which were named D'Entrecasteaux Strait (thinking he had reached Tasman's Frederick Henry Bay); he was the first to chart Table Mountain or any part of the Strait. Admittedly, Bligh described parts of the mainland as islands. Under Bligh's orders, Bond went out in a cutter and found another bay between Bruni Island and Tasman's Peninsula, which Bligh named Providence Bay.

The ships sailed east-south-east across the Tasman Sea and reached the southern shores of New Zealand. Thick mist set in and Bligh thought he saw a small island or quay, which might have been the Snares, fog-banks lying in the tack made by ships. On 5 March the ships passed the Bounty Islands and Bligh was naturally curious to see them again, but the fog did not lift. On the 16th the sea was lit by a marvellous phosphorescence which spread behind them for at least half a mile: 'the water had the appearance as if thousands of small lamps were lighted thereon, and it looked beautiful beyond description.' This amazing phenomenon occurred again three nights later. [8]

By the 21st they sailed within a short distance of the Pitcairn Islands and if Bligh had known who was living there at that time he would certainly have made a detour. On 5 April, as they neared Tahiti, land was sighted in the form of a low lagoon island, later called Bligh's Lagoon Island. By this time they were close to Matavai, so during a short stop at Maitea Island, Bligh issued orders for the crew's behaviour while at Tahiti:

1. No officer or seaman is to speak of the loss of the *Bounty*, or tell that Captain Cook was killed by Indians.

2. No officer or seaman is to mention that we have come on purpose for the breadfruit plant.

3. Every one is to study the goodwill of the natives and not to recover by violence any article that has been stolen.

4. All care is to be taken that no arms or implements are stolen.

5. No man is to offer for sale any part of the King's Stores.

6. A proper person will be appointed to regulate trade and to barter.

7. The mate of the watch will be answerable for all neglects of the sentinel

8. No canoe is to come on board after 8 o'clock.

9. Everything is to be handed out of the boats at sundown.

10. The awnings are to be set at sunrise and furled at sunset (except the after one).

11 . The officer of the watch is not on any pretence whatever to get into conversation with the Indians.

12. All boats to be moored alongside.

13. No curiosities are to be kept between decks.

14. No person is to take fire-arms (without permission) on shore.

Any transgression of these rules will be punished with the utmost severity. [9]

While at Maitea several canoes arrived, selling produce such as plantains, breadfruit and coconuts. One of them told him that two ships had passed about three months before, but he knew nothing of what they were.

On 9 April 1792 the ships anchored in Matavai Bay. To his surprise Bligh was visited by a boat which had belonged to the whaler *Matilda*, which had been lost. Matthew Weatherhead had been Master of the ship and from him, Bligh learned many interesting things, not least the fact that Captain Edwards had been here with the *Pandora*. It seemed that the people of Matavai had stolen many items from the sailors of the *Matilda* and the natives of Oparre wanted them to share them. When they refused, there was war between the two districts which was still raging. [10] This was bad news for Bligh, whose project was to obtain more breadfruit plants and that might prove difficult in an atmosphere of civil war. Bligh could not hear more for at that times other canoes were boarding the ship.

There were joyful reunions. Tinah's wife, Iddeah, was one of the first to visit Bligh along with his brothers Oreepyah and Whydooah as well as the priest Tootaha. They were delighted to see Bligh again and a canoe had already been sent to Tinah to tell him the news and convey him back to Matavai with his parents. Some Oparre boats also arrived, bearing cargoes of hogs, breadfruit and other supplies; but the news from the *Matilda* worried him. On the next day he received the following:

Otaheite,

March 20th, 1792.

I beg you will rectify the wrongs I have received on this island by one Tabyroo ... after the misfortune of losing the *Matilda* we were six days in the boat. We landed at Matavai and put ourselves under the protection of this man. I had with me one box containing most of my papers, 407 dollars, 17 guineas, between 3 and 4 lbs. of English silver, and a bag containing a few necessary clothes. After being in the house six days I was turned out without anything, to shift for myself with only one shirt. Your obed. servant, Matthew Weatherhead. P.S. — Sir, the chief mate and carpenter will explain more clearly if required. — M.W. [11]

Two ships, the *Mary Ann* under Captain Munro and the *Matilda* under Captain Weatherhead had left England on 27 March 1791. They arrived in Port Jackson during August, then sailed off for the coast of Peru on 28 December. On 14 February 1792 both ships moored in Oaitepeha Bay, where they received supplies. After two days they sailed off, agreeing to part company and meet up later to hunt for whales. On the 25th they ran aground and escaped on the four boats; there were twenty-nine men, including a prisoner who had stowed away in New South Wales. Two arrived at Matavai Bay on 5 March, while the others landed at Oaitepeha and Attahooroo, but finding the natives unfriendly at the latter two places, they all ended up in Matavai.

Weatherhead decided that they should separate, so some of the men went to Oparre and others to Attahooroo. At each of the places the men were dispossessed of everything they had, but the greatest share went to Matavai. This was the reason for the present civil war. The men who commanded the theft was none other than Bligh's old friend, Poeeno and another chief named Tabyroo. The men from Oparre came to Matavai and destroyed many houses, pillaging as they went, but the Matavaians put up a stout resistance. The war paused on 25 March when a schooner, the *Jenny*, arrived from Bristol; they carried away Weatherhead, one man and two boys. At that moment all the twenty-one remaining men were treated with kindness and they were being looked after at Oparre.

While waiting for Tinah to return, Bligh discovered some information about Fletcher Christian. He had got rid of the breadfruit plants before returning to Tahiti and the natives were astonished to see the *Bounty* back so soon. They were suspicious when they found the Captain was not there and interrogated Christian as to what happened.

'Where is Bry?'

'He is gone to England.'

'In what ship?'

'In Toote's ship.'

'How came you to meet Toote, and where is he?'

'We met him at Wytootackee where he is going to live, and he, Toote, has sent me for all those who will come and live with him, and he wants the bull and cow and as many hogs as you will send him.'

'What has become of the breadfruit?'

'He has sent it home to England with Bligh.'   [12]

It infuriated Bligh to hear that through all of these lies Christian was given what he asked for and sailed off with provisions and several men and women.

In fact, Matavai had not been Christian's first destination. After the mutiny, the crew were in disorder and some of them had harsh words to say about the actions of Bligh's officers.

'The behaviour of the officers,' wrote Morrison, 'was dastardly beyond description. None of them ever making the least attempt to rescue the ship.'

One of the first things Christian did was to throw all of the breadfruit plants overboard. Then he set sail, not for Tahiti, but for Toobouai. It was not a good choice; the natives were hostile and there was a battle on shore during which twelve natives were killed and many more injured. It was then that Christian decided to make for Tahiti.

Here the natives, after being taken in by Christian's story, gave up 460 hogs, 50 goats, fowl and the cow and bull, although the bull did not survive. They returned to Toobouai and found the natives much more tractable, although Christian discovered what problems beset the master of a ship. Sumner and Quintal went ashore without leave and when they returned next morning Christian demanded to know why they had disobeyed orders. They replied:

'This ship is moored and we are now our own masters.'

'I'll let you know who is master,' Christian replied and pressed Bligh's pistol to the head of one of them.

The mutineers then began to build a stronghold, 'Fort George', while Morrison and two others plotted to escape in the cutter, but it was not seaworthy. The crew began to get more discontented, demanding women and more grog. The natives were also discontented, mainly on account of their women and they beat a party of men who had been sent to collect stock. This resulted in an all-out battle in which sixty natives and six women were killed. After a vote, it was decided that they should return to Matavai. Here, sixteen left the *Bounty* while eight decided to throw in their lot with Christian and sail off – they were Young, Mills, Brown, Martin, McKoy, Williams, Smith and Quintal. They were also joined by a young Toobouian chief Taroameiva and his two friends as well as a number of Tahitians.

Christian had read Carteret's account of a lonely uninhabited island – Pitcairn – and after some trouble the *Bounty* sailed into the bay – now known as Bounty Bay. It fulfilled all of their hopes – warm and fertile, inaccessible and free from hostile natives. Fearing discovery, someone – probably Quintal – set fire to the ship on 23 January 1790 and the mutineers were marooned there. It is said that Christian wanted to keep the ship, but Quintal argued, 'No, we shall be discovered'. [13]

The mutineers treated the Polynesians badly, dividing the land and allotting none for them. They were treated as slaves and were forced to share wives as the fugitives had selected their own. However, within a year the consorts of Williams and Adams had died and so they took the wives of Tararo and Oha from them – the women were called Toofaiti (Nancy) and Tinafanaea. Needless to say, the Polynesian men were furious and three of them – the two husbands and Titahiti – plotted to murder them. So in December 1790, Tararo and Oha were killed in retaliation.

For almost three years the remaining Polynesian men suffered being treated as slaves while sharing the one woman, Mareva. They hatched another plot and massacred a number of the mutineers – Williams,

Christian, Mills, Martin and Brown. Adams was shot but he survived.

By the time Bligh was passing the island on the *Providence,* the settlement was peaceful and continued to be so until around 1794 when McKoy worked out how to distil a powerful poteen from the *ti* plant. It destroyed him mentally and eventually after tying together his hands and feet, he threw himself into the sea. In 1799 Quintal got drunk and became threatening so he was killed by Young and Adams. When Young died from asthma in 1800, Adams was the sole survivor of the mutineers. He himself was addicted to the home-made *ti* spirit but one day after a religious conversion he became a changed man and was a respected leader of the community. The progeny of the Pitcairn mutineers live on to this day.

Going back to Matavai Bay, the mutineers who stayed there soon paired off with their old *tyos* and were scattered over the island. The islanders had been visited by a Captain Cox of the brig *Mercury*, who had told them of Toote's death, which put Bligh's original story in a bad light. Morrison decided that they should built a boat of their own and sail in her back to England and confided his plan to McIntosh and Millward, who agreed to help. They decided to tell everyone that it was to be a pleasure-boat for cruising around the islands and enlisted the help of the armourer, the cooper and the carpenter's mate.

Thompson was living at Point Venus with Coleman and one day he abused a local girl, so in revenge her brother knocked him down and ran away. Thompson was in a fury and swore that he would take his displeasure out on the first person who crossed him. Some natives mobbed around him out of innocent curiosity, but having told them to go away he fired his musket, killing a father and child while breaking a woman's jaw. Thompson, Brown and Churchill compensated the widow but the natives were aroused and one day the brother of the dead man grabbed Peter Heywood, mistaking his man, and would probably have killed him if one of the others had not pointed out his error.

On 15 March one of the chiefs, Vyeooreedee, had died and the natives elected Churchill as their new leader. But Churchill and Thompson had a violent argument which culminated in Thompson shooting Churchill. Soon after Patirre – the friend of the native Thompson had killed – went to his house and named him the new Chief and when he was unawares Patirre killed him by smashing his skull with a large stone.

After these killings, life resumed to normal; Heywood was compiling a dictionary of Tahitian while Stewart had a daughter by his consort Peggy. By 1 July the boat was ready and named *Resolution*; Morrison and his friend took her out for a trial around Oparre, along the coast and as far as Morea. On 21 March 1792 a party of seven sailed in the *Resolution* for Papaara, where they met Burkitt, Sumner, Musprat and Brown. They had just reached the *morai* when a messenger came to inform them that Captain Edwards and the *Pandora* had anchored off Matavai Bay.

Immediately Heywood and Stewart went on board and surrendered. Interested in finding his old *Bounty* messmate Thomas Hayward on board, he thought he might help. He didn't, as Heywood wrote later to his mother:

Having learned from one of the natives that our former messmate, Mr Hayward, now promoted to the rank of Lieutenant, was on board, we asked for him, supposing he might prove the assertions of our innocence. But he (like all worldlings when raised a little in life) received us very coolly, and pretended ignorance of our affairs. Appearances being so much against us, we were ordered to be put in irons, and looked upon – oh infernal words! – as *piratical villains*.

Later Skinner and Coleman also came on board ship and Edwards learned that the others had gone to Papaara, so he send his pinnace and launch – under Lieutenants Corner and Hayward – in pursuit. Morrison argued that they simply meant to avoid the boats then sail back to the *Pandora* and give themselves up. They did land Brown and Byrne on shore and they quickly surrendered. Meanwhile Morrison, Norman and Ellison stayed with the boat while the others fled to the mountains, hoping for the protection of the chief Tommaree. The three moored the launch and walked along the shore until they found the ship's launch with all men fast asleep. They woke Lieutenant Corner and surrendered. Later Corner took a party of armed men and captured the remaining mutineers. [14]

This was as much as Bligh would find out on his visit to Tahiti in 1792. But if the men had thought Bligh was a bad Captain, he was nothing compared to the sadistic and brutal Edwards. He confined all of the prisoners in a specially constructed cell – 'Pandora's box' – on the quarter-deck and treated them with contempt and savagery throughout the voyage home – even the ones that Bligh himself had written down as being innocent. [15]

His ship came to grief in the Endeavour Straits, as Bligh feared it would. On 28 August they hit the reef and water poured into the hold. Some of the prisoners – Coleman, McIntosh and Norman - were let out of their irons to help out at the pumps. The ship violently heeled and turned onto her side. At Pandora's box sentinels were placed and ordered to fire if there was any motion, while the prisoners, newly set in irons, begged for mercy. At one point they heard a voice shout:

'Fire upon the rascals!

'For God's sake don't fire!' one replied, 'What's the matter? There is none here moving…' [16]

At daybreak they saw that the boats were being launched and they cried that they should not be forgotten. Edwards ordered that Musprat, Skinner and Byrne be sent aloft but as they rose up, the scuttle slammed shut. Morrison begged the master-at-arms to leave the scuttle open and he replied:

'Never fear, my boys, we'll all go to hell together!' [17]

Soon after the boatswain's mate heard their cries and opened the bolt and threw the scuttle off to allow them to scramble out. Four of them subsequently drowned – Stewart, Sumner, Skinner and Hillbrandt, their hands still manacled.

The boats took them to Timor, but Edwards' cruelty never relented. He had Ellison and Morrison tied up and lashed to a boat's bottom and when asked why, he said:

'Silence, you murdering villain, are you not a prisoner? You piratical dog, what better treatment do you expect?' [18]

The treatment continued, then from Coupang, the survivors sailed to Batavia on the *Rembang*, to Cape Town on the *Vreedemberg* and finally to Spithead on the *Gorgon*. Here, after a voyage of the most inhuman punishment, they prepared to face a court martial for mutiny.

That is a short account of the *Bounty* mutineers. Back in Tahiti, Bligh's mind was full of thoughts of the breadfruit plant and how to get as many as possible on board the *Providence*. He was still aware that he had to behave with political correctness and he was in the middle of a civil conflict as well as a suit from the *Matilda* to have its property returned. Nothing could be done smoothly without the friendship of the chiefs and fortunately Bligh had fostered long-standing amities on his last visit. Now even Otoo accepted his visit to Oparre; back in 1780 he was a weak-looking little boy and while little yet than a youngster he had grown into a hardy child. Bligh gave him gifts of iron tools and shirts, for which the chieftain was grateful.

His old friend, the wife of the chief Teppahoo, Terrano, visited with tears in her eyes and clinging on to him in a fond embrace. With her sister, she thanked God for his deliverance after the *Bounty* mutiny, but she herself was full of tales of woe. Teppahoo was dead and that news was sad for Bligh, who had forged a strong friendship with the chief and he was a main figure in whom he could trust. He also learned that Tinah's eldest daughter had also died as had his uncle Moworoah. His other friend Odiddee had gone with Captain Edwards to the rest of the Society Islands. These were all a loss to Bligh.

As to the war, Bligh kept to a strict policy of non-interference. Skirmishes were still happening near the borders and Otoo wanted Bligh to join his army, but Bligh refused to assist unless the people of Matavai invaded his country. This was pleasing news to those of Oparre, but Bligh also needed to help the people of the *Matilda* so he sent their surgeon with a chieftain to parley with Poeeno and Tabyroo, with a message from Bligh to tell them that they were to return Captain Weatherhead's things if they wished to stay on good terms with him. [19] When they arrived they were nervous because the natives seemed very agitated and were armed, but the answer came that everything would be returned, except the muskets which were needed for the war, although they would happily comply if the opposing faction also laid their arms down to Bligh.

In Matavai Bay, Bligh grumbled about the absence of Tinah. The way things were, he did not dare send a party on shore for the plants, yet the only person of importance he had spoken with was Oreepyah. Oreepyah had advised him to wait and when Iddeah came to visit again she implored him to send a boat out for her husband. She said that if he refused to send one, he would not return and Bligh easily saw through her plot. He insisted that she sent for him herself – if she wished to retain his friendship. Iddeah saw she was in a dilemma and if she did not acquiesce then she would risk the friendship of the most powerful man in the region – and that was not a good idea when civil war was still raging. She set off in her own boat, promising to return within two days.

Bligh then advised Oreepyah that he did not intend to wait any longer for Tinah and was determined to set up a shore camp as soon as possible. He also told him it was in his people's interests to help him, as he wanted no more fighting. In the company of Oreepyah and Tootaha, he chose a piece of ground of advantage for the plants, about four hundred yards from Point Venus and began to erect a fence and a shade for the trees. They also prepared to make makeshift houses and ordered the marines to get ready for guard service. On the 15th, Tinah at last arrived. He was welcomed with a ten-gun salute.

Since they last met, Tinah had married again and now his two wives were Iddeah and Whyerreddee. Whyerreddee was Iddeah's younger sister and had been married to Whaeahtuah, a Chief of Tiarraboo, until his death. They remained the best of friends as well as sisters. Tinah had brought Cook's picture, which he kept safe with him everywhere. In another canoe came his aging father, Otow. There was a friendly greeting and Tinah had many questions to ask his old friend.

'We all thank the gods,' he said to me, ' that you are safe. We were told that you were put into a little boat and sent adrift without anything to eat or drink, and that you must perish. You have a fine ship now. Have you good men? Is there a bad man among them? Have you seen King George? What did he say to you?'

There was one burning question in Bligh's mind.

'How did you come to be so friendly with Christian?'

Tinah was disturbed by it, but replied:

'I really thought you were living, and had gone to England until Christian came back the second time. I was then away from home, but all my friends, who heard you were lost from the men who came on shore, from that time did not profess any friendship to him, and Christian knew it so well that he only remained a few hours and went away in such a hurry that he left a second anchor behind. One of the anchors we got I gave to the *Pandora*, to Captain Edwards.' [20]

This seemed a reasonable explanation so Bligh let it pass and they became fast friends again, Tinah constantly smiling and laughing. On political matters, Otow and Tinah had developed a strong dislike for the people of Matavai and asked Bligh to wage war on them, which Bligh obviously refused. It would interfere with the business he was sent on, he explained, but he still had a problem with the natives who withheld the *Matilda*'s arms and money.

Bligh had gifts for them all, which delighted them. He gave the men suits of crimson cloth with gold lace and a calico gown to each woman; he also gave them iron and trinkets.

Things had changed in the paradise of Tahiti and it was not all due to the fighting. Although Tinah brought him a gift of hogs and fruit, the old customs were beginning to wane and Bligh blamed the European visitors for it. Even the language was altering, made coarse with oaths learned from their guests and their speech was intermingled with fragments of English. Bligh regretted that in the future few people would experience their traditional way of receiving visitors. He also noticed how the people were addicted to spirits, which he had tried to dissuade as much as he could but with no effect. At one time the Tahitians dressed with clean cloth in their traditional way; now there was such an abundance of cast-off clothes that many had taken to wearing filthy shirts and waistcoats. It was all very depressing.

Bligh's men got on with the task of potting breadfruit plants and in the meantime continued to entertain guests; sometimes Otoo would come, carried on a man's shoulder (the custom would continue 'until he was a man'); sometimes Tinah and his wives. The Captain was glad that not many of the Matavai people were around as he was still suffering from his illness, his 'nerves and headache being at times scarce bearable.' One day he saw George Stewart's daughter, only a year old and 'a very pretty creature, but had been so exposed to the sun as to be little fairer than an Otaheitan.'

Once again Tinah changed his name, as did Iddeah – now they were both known as Pomarre. They told how they had lost their eldest daughter Terranaoroa from some disease which they called '*marre*' and described by coughing. It happened at night – '*po*', so the parents, as was the custom, named themselves after the disease, *po-marre*. [21] Such a change of names was difficult for Bligh to grasp, so he continued to call him 'Tinah'. The two were regular visitors to the *Providence*, Tinah having lost none of his appetite. Bligh noted that while Iddeah had given him another child – a boy named Oroho – Tinah was 'a perfect fool' to his newer wife and she ruled him in any way she pleased. Iddeah seemed perfectly happy with her lot and her share of influence.

There was a breakthrough in the war; Matavai made concessions and it was all over by 26 April. Poeena and Tinnah had a conference after which it was agreed that Poeeno would come again to live at Matavai; they also – again – promised to return Weatherhead's money. As part of the agreement, Otoo moved his residence from Oparre to Matavai too – which meant bringing the Temple of Oro. It was brought by double canoe on whose prow were a baked hog, a dog's head, a fowl and a piece of sugar cane. Hammene-manne the priest – who was called Tootaha when Bligh was last here – made a prayer which he did by chanting to the accompaniment of drums, to the effect that neither King George, Bligh or Portlock would be in need or defeated in battle.

On the 27th came the ceremony of the temple, which was orated by Hammene-manne. There was a sacred bundle – the *etuah* – and a dead body wrapped in a coconut branch and tied to a pole. The bundle was unwrapped and revealed yellow and red feathers along with four rolls plaited with coconut fibre, to which they gave the name of over ninety gods. When the priest made a prayer, which Bligh wrote down as:

We have sacrificed a man. We have presented one of his eyes to you as a token of your power and one to our King, because it is by your will he reigns over us. We display our feathers! We present our hogs to you! We do this O Oro, because we know you delight in it! Our wish is to do as you desire: prosper therefore our undertakings. Let us conquer our enemies and live in plenty. [22]

Later in the day Tinah asked Hammene-manne to perform a ceremony solely for their visitors; so he collected leaves and wrote their names upon them and gave them to Otoo. Then each man was called in turn and Bligh, Bond and Harwood helped with the ceremony, Tinah telling them what to say.

On 2 May Bligh met a woman with a young child, who claimed to have been the wife of McIntosh. She had gone with Christian and the *Bounty* to Toobouai and described their problems there; McIntosh had known her as 'Mary'. She had heard all about the mutiny and knew the facts as well as Bligh did – maybe more. She also said that while in her company McIntosh, Coleman, Hillbrandt, Newman, Byrne, and Ellison 'scarce ever spoke of Bligh without crying', whereas Stewart, Heywood and the rest were perfectly happy about the way things turned out.

'They deserved to be killed, but I hope those who cried for you will not be hurt.' [23]

Everywhere, Bligh saw the evidence of the mutineers. One day he saw the house in which 'the villain' Peter Heywood had lived, at the bottom of a hill commanding a splendid view of the bay. He had set out some fine gardens and there was an avenue of shaddock trees. It was evident that while Bligh had faced the terrible voyage on the launch, the mutineers had been living in some comfort. They had been, as Bligh put it, 'entrapped through their own seduction' and that at least gave him some sense of justice.

Two days later Bligh met another old friend, Tinah's mother, Oberreeroah, who arrived from Morea with her daughter Wow-wo, who was now completely cured of her skin complaint after her treatment by Dr Ledward, whom she remembered with great affection. Oberreeroah was now so fat she had to be hoisted on board the ship; Wow-wo's husband, erstwhile chief of Morea, had died and was succeeded by Oberreeroah's nephew, Mahow, who seemed to be well-liked by his people. This was only honorary as the chief's heir was Tettoanovee – but he was only four.

On the 7th word came from Tabyroo that Weatherhead's money had arrived from Tabyroo, so Bligh instructed a Mr Norris to go and collect it along with members of Matilda's crew. The next day brought disappointment – Norris returned with no muskets and with 182 dollars, three half-crowns and a watch. That amounted to less than half of what they had expected. Salt was added to the wound the next day when a native bought a knife for a guinea which turned out to be part of the missing money.

Most of the month was spent peacefully enough. More and more plants were potted; the marines continued to do their exercises (to the endless amusement of the islanders) and the crew did some fishing. There were some problems later; on the 18th a native - one of Oreepyah's people – threw stones and dirt at some of the crew who had gone for water – he was clapped in irons and the natives said he deserved to be killed. On the 19th a native pulled the sheet off Bond's bed while he was sleeping. A day later a native gave a seaman a black eye and Bligh allowed him to be revenged, something he would not normally do. Bligh took the prisoner out of irons and awarded him 36 lashes – 'he received the punishment without wincing' – and put him back in irons until he was forgiven after the entreaties of Tinah. [24] It did little good as a deterrent – three days later another native crept in and stole clothing.

On 28 May, Tinah's daughter Tahamydooah died after some friends had taken her to see a *haiva* at Papaara. She caught a cold and died on her return. Tinah seemed little concerned about the death but Iddeah shed some tears. Iddeah took her body, wrapped in scarlet cloth – to a raised stage called a *teappapow*, decorated with leaves, flowers and cloths. There she would stay until the flesh had rotted away after which her bones would be laid in the earth. Sadly, her youngest was also ill and when Bligh told her she should take better care of her infants, she replied, 'Let Whyerreddee do it!' Bligh asked his surgeon to look at the child.

On 4 June the natives were delighted by a firing exhibition to commemorate King George. The marines fired three volleys and later the ships fired twenty-one guns each. Bligh served liquor to everyone and twelve sky-rockets were set off. The natives were overjoyed and kept shouting:

'*Mahannah no Earee Prittannee ! King George!*' ('The King of Britain's birthday! King George!')

By June supplies were becoming more difficult to get and lurking islanders became a problem at night. One native was discovered stealing and ran off so that a sentinel fired at him. He winged him through the shoulder and he set off at once back to Tettaha. Entertainments continued at intervals, *haivas* and wrestling matches but Tinah, Oreepyah and Whydooah were drinking *ava* so avidly they were almost constantly drunk, so Bligh made them promise to cut down on their drinking. Bligh was also pained to see that human sacrifices were more common than he thought and was a customary way of pleasing a chieftain who had been wronged.

By the middle of June Bligh was thinking of leaving, so Otow and Otoo sailed off to find hogs and cloth to sail to the ships to promote friendship – and to barter with. On the 20th Bligh went off to sound the bay but was 'seized with burning heat', which brought on a fever. Some worried natives brought him coconuts and apples and he recovered a little, but left the rest of the work to Portlock. The next day the fever was gone but Bligh was left with a stinging headache and kept clear of the sun.[25]

Bligh was happy to see supplies now more plentiful, but less happy when a thief managed to sneak past the guards and steal a bundle of Guthrie's clothing. Tinah promised to retrieve them, but it took some time and even them only part of the stuff was brought back. At that moment Bligh was considering the *Matilda*'s whale-boat which was at that time at Attahooroo and, thinking in would be useful in case of accident, he sent Portlock after it. He did recover it, but it was not a universally agreed decision and there had been some deliberation. A factor which helped was the present Bligh had sent to the chief which was gratefully received and it seems that the people of Oparre and Matavai had purposely prevented them from having any meetings with the people of that island. They were happy in that Bligh had sent a message assuring them of his friendship.

Once again Tinah was disconsolate to learn of Bligh's preparations for departure and was annoyed at his refusal to take him along. As a gesture, Bligh did agree to take one of his men, a servant called Mydiddee. The news that the visitors were leaving soon spread and Otoo cut his visit short to return. Tomaree, chief of Papaara, refused to come because he knew that Bligh was annoyed with him. Not only had he possession of some of Bligh's books from the *Bounty* – some of which he offered to send if Bligh sent him cartridge paper – he also had powder and arms from the *Matilda*. A wrestling match was performed for the crew and this was returned with a firework display.

Tinah and his family were distressed at the leaving, but most of the natives felt that they were guests which had stayed too long and were indifferent. Bligh promised to seek permission for Tinah to be brought out on the next ship that sailed and gave him a musket and 500 rounds of powder and shot. As they prepared to go, Otoo burst into tears. By 17 July throngs of natives began to come to the ship, begging for some remembrance. The ship's crew was augmented by that of the *Matilda*:

- **Chief Mate:** *John Marshall*

- **Surgeon:** *Joseph Norris*

- **Boatswain:** *Robert Atkinson*

- **Boys:** *John Smith, Thomas Baillie*

- **Carpenter:** *John Potts*

- **ABs:** *John Smith, David Mouet, Joshua Harper, John Thompson, Samuel Dennis, John Hopkins, Stephen Regrove* [26]

Two others, John Witstaff and Joseph Gilbert, went on board the *Assistant*. There was to be one more addition to the Providence's complement. They found a man – Bobbo – hidden between the decks and Bligh did not have the heart to ask him to jump overboard – so he remained. The total sum of plants they had on board was 2126 breadfruit plants and 508 of other assorted plants.

Bligh sent his written order to Portlock:

Being now ready for sea and thus far the object of our voyage fully completed, you are to proceed with me as in all former cases in our intended route home. Having furnished you with a copy of my orders

and shewn you how uncertain my route will be between here and Timor, you will readily perceive what an attention is requisite to keep company and observe such signals as I may make to you.

Should accident separate us before I reach the Friendly Islands I shall cruise twenty-four hours for you in sight of the islands Caow and Tofoa. I shall then pass to the north of Bligh's Islands, of which you have a map, and proceed round those I discovered off the New Hebrides, where in Lat. 14° 30' I shall also cruise in sight of land for twenty- four hours. This is the last place of rendezvous I can fix with any certainty, and you must cruise twenty-four hours if you get there before me.

Coupang in Timor is the place I propose to complete my water, and it is situated 10° 12' S. 124° 41' E. of Greenwich. As the time of the westerly monsoon is advancing fast upon us, I with much concern give up the power of examining strange lands but what will not detain us. I shall therefore make the coast of the Louisiades, and take the most direct and effectual means to pass on to Timor with the utmost dispatch, where you may wait for me such a time as you think advisable and best for His Majesty's service. I shall wait for you eight days and leave such directions as I may think will satisfy you how to proceed.

Given under my hand on board His Majesty's ship *'Providence'* in Matavai Bay, July 15th, 1792. Wm. Bligh.

Once again Tinah and his wives spent a last night on board before their affectionate farewells. And again, the ship's crew gave three cheers to the Tahitians, which were returned.

Chapter Nine. The Rocky Road

The ships sailed past Morea and Huaheine then Ulitea, after which Bligh determined to take a closer look at Wytootackee to find out more about the *Bounty* and the *Pandora* and also to seek for a safe harbour on the west side. Here, he was successful; there was a three-mile strip of shore which was good for shelter. A number of canoes gave out to greet them, the natives particularly anxious to obtain hatchets and willing to trade spears, breastplates, fish-hooks and rudimentary necklaces. Bligh also learned that no white man had ever set foot on their island. [1]

They passed Savage Island on 26 July and made towards the Friendly Islands; but Bligh had some more discoveries to make. He had information that in 1781, Captain Francisco Antonio Maurelle, on board the *Princessa,* had passed this way and spotted many islands, the northern group of which he called Don Martyn Mayorga Islands and the southern Don Jon de Galvey's Islands. Bligh reckoned that Mayorga stood at the same meridian as the northern Friendly Islands and that the Southern Islands were also part of the same group. What's more, Bligh had discovered several other small islands on his launch, so he was determined to find out the truth of the matter.

On 3 August they spotted what they assumed to be Maurelle, the northernmost of the islands and soon saw that they were two. The northern shore comprised steep cliffs but the southern was much shallower. Soon after that they saw two other islands (Fanua Lei and Lette) which were both very tall. Bligh had no doubt that these were the islands first seen by Maurelle and did not change their names.

After this the ships ventured into largely unknown territory, although some of it had been traversed by Bligh in his launch voyage. From this point, as he discovered more and more islands he began an unfortunate manner of naming them by letters of the alphabet. These were Fiji, or as they were then known, Bligh's Islands. The first two – A and B – were Mothe Island and Oneata through which Bligh meant to pass but found the breakers too dangerous. Some of the natives came from Mothe and bartered coconuts for small iron pieces such as nails. They found the west of Mothe cut off by three reefs which joined it to three other islands, F, G and H (Komo, Olorua and Thakau Viute).

Another island, C (Lakemba) was the largest they saw and another small island, Aiwa, stood between it and Oneata. Bligh made constant observation, comparing his rough calculations on the launch with his new positions as accurately marked on board the *Providence.* On 7 – 8 August they made many new discoveries in the form of new islands, M – Z (M - Naiau, N - Thithia, or Favourite Island, O - 'Gibraltar Rock' or Vatu Vata, P - Moala, Q - Yathata, Taviuni (R and T), S – Koroso, U - Nairai Island, V - Ngau Island, W – Mbatiki, X – Wakaya, Y -part of Ovalau. W, Mbatiki. X, Wakaya, Y – Ovalau, Z -Viti Levu). By the time they reached Ngau, the scenery was truly beautiful; surrounded by a reef it had placid waters and a fine sandy beach. They could also see plantations of plantains and coconut trees, dwelling-huts scattered among them. Flinders called it 'Paradise Island'. [2]

By this time Bligh had run out of letters and began to use numbers – 1 being Mbengha Island. By 11 August, after passing through dangerous waters, they found a number of rocky keys – 2 (Kandavu Island and the Astrolabe Reefs). These were the discoveries made by Captain Bligh on his voyage through the Tonga Islands. Little credit was later given to him.

It must have been satisfying for Bligh to make all of these discoveries from the relative comfort of the ship. The last time he had sighted the islands he was starving and cramped in the *Bounty*'s launch; now he could appreciate and survey them at his leisure. He meticulously charted everything he saw and made careful notes for the benefit of those explorers who would come after him. He fully realised the importance of the new finds and recorded all that he saw for posterity.

Bligh now navigated to the forty islands which make up the New Hebrides and first sighted Banks' Islands, which the launch had passed by and which Bligh thought – wrongly – was another new discovery. However, Quiros and Torres had not only seen them but named them. Bligh also passed by the Torres Group on their southern side. Of the Banks Group, Bligh wrote:

In pursuance of my plan to verify my observations made during my distressing voyage in the '*Bounty*'s Launch', I directed my course to make the islands I had then discovered to the northward of the New Hebrides. [3]

He surveyed a number of these islands, starting his alphabet again and paid attention to islands A-D (Mota Island, Valua Island, Vanua Lava and Ureparapara or Bligh Island). The largest was Vanua Lava, whose peak soared into the clouds. On 20 August he surveyed three more, E – G (Tog or South Island, Lo or Saddle Island, Tegua and the North Island). They were now nearing some of the most perilous waters in the world – Torres Strait and its hazardous coral reefs. As Bligh began his perilous venture he wrote:

This track should be taken with great caution, and I recommend whoever may follow me, not to run in the night but to keep the ship on a wind under such sail as will render her manageable. [4]

First of all they spotted a water-spout, which joined with a column of water 'the size of a church tower'. The first sign of danger was a ship's boom floating in the water and by the 29th Bligh was preparing for emergencies. Both ships sailed with caution, although Bligh realised it was now getting late in the season and he had the delivery of his plants to worry about. At last they reached the entrance to the Strait which is called Bligh's Entrance. Steering carefully to avoid rocks and hidden reefs, on 3 September they saw a sandy key about six miles ahead so they proceeded with utter caution. They saw another island (Errub) and a sandy key at which they decided to anchor (Anchor Key). From then on they carefully sounded, to make sure they were not caught unawares. They passed some of the Murray Islands and Bligh sent out boats to examine their passage.

One of the boats, under Tobin, almost came to grief. Four native canoes began to give chase and eventually blocked their progress; one offering a coconut. When Tobin explained they should take it to the ship, they began to become hostile and pulled out bows and arrows. At first they shot at the sails, but Tobin, realising his situation was critical, fired a musket among them. This astonished them but three other canoes joined them and they raced to cut off the boat from the *Providence*. Matthew Flinders watched the race from the deck of the ship, but the boat was rescued by the pinnace which had sailed to its aid. Bligh wrote: 'This was the most melancholy account I have received,' and fretted over the loss of good feeling between his men and the islanders. According to Flinders, they were lucky to escape with their lives:

No boats could have been manoeuvred better in working to windward, than were these canoes of the naked savages. Had the four been able to reach the cutter, it is difficult to say whether the superiority of our arms would have been equal to the great difference of numbers, considering the ferocity of these people and the skill with which they seemed to manage their weapons. [5]

Little by little the ships went on. They sailed between a key called Canoe Key and Errub but Bligh was unsure how far the reef stretched, so he head north between Nepean island (Attagoy) and Hogar. Portlock was sent to sound the passage between Errub and Attagoy while canoes headed for the Providence and traded. Their friendliness suggested that Tobin's incident had not soured possible relations with the natives. The *Assistant* found a passage, so the *Providence* followed on and then anchored by Attagoy, being sheltered by Stephen's and Campbell's Islands.

On 8 September they sailed further, as the north and west seemed clear, but after an hour there were shoals, so Bligh steered for Rennel Island (Mauar) and sighted Marsden Island, Keats Island and the Yorke Islands. They headed for another island, Dalrymple's, where they did a little trading and the natives, like all others, were mostly interested in *toorick*, or iron. Sea-food seemed to constitute their staple diet. Although they were armed with bows and arrows they were a peaceful people.

Bligh then sailed to the most dangerous part of his voyage. Shoals seemed to be threatening in every direction and a continuation of the reef seemed to join Warrior Island (Tutte) and not far away lay Dungeness Island (Jeaka); there was also a third: Arden's Island (Garboy). As they slowly sailed for Dungeness, they met an extensive reef; as they approached they found the tide ran at three knots and the sea bottom was very risky. It seemed that the best approach was between Dungeness and Warrior Island, but the passage was fraught with peril. To make matters worse, natives sailed towards them in nine canoes and their intentions were far from friendly.

The natives began to fire arrows at the crew of the *Assistant,* so they raised the flag for help and began to fire. Three men were wounded. 'It was not a time to trifle', wrote Bligh and he needed to get the situation under control as soon as he could. He fired two of the quarter-deck guns loaded with shot and grape then the canoes, astonished, quickly disappeared. Fires were soon lit on Warrior Island and Bligh decided to anchor under Dungeness, as the natives did not live there. [6]

On the 12th Bligh found new hazards. He intended to go around a high rock of an island known as The Brothers Hills Island (Gabba) but found shoal water just to the north. In a quandary he decided to send the Second Lieutenant and the Master to sound the area between the Brothers and a sandy key (Bligh called this Nichols Key) and luckily there was a good passage. They spotted some more high islands – Mount Cornwallis, Long Island and Cap Islet – before hitting more shoaling. Once again he sent out boats to see if there was a passage between this shoal and an island Bligh would call Turn Again Island. Finding poor reports, he then sent another party to explore a passage round some islands to the south-west. Guthrie returned with the news that there were five to six fathoms and a good bottom. Bligh decided to try that way.

To make life even more difficult, they were now beset with bad weather. By the evening of the 15th a gale was blowing and the sky was dark and stormy. Next day it got worse and the ships were pitching and tossing in the fierce winds. On the 16th, when the weather had moderated, Portlock could find no way through the reef and Bligh doubted whether the channel would be enough to sail the *Providence* through it. They were stuck.

The situation was desperate. Bligh had already noted that 'The month of October advances on us and every thing urges me to get on.' Now there seemed to be nowhere for them to go. The Torres Strait had defeated them and what was worse, they were running very short of water. What there was needed to be given to the plants, as should they die, the project was doomed. The crew began to grumble – unlike Bligh they had not suffered the heroic voyage in the *Bounty*'s launch and were not used to such privations. Flinders recalled that he and his comrades would lick the drips from the watering-cans and to be given a sip was a great favour. Someone maliciously watered the plants with sea-water and when Bligh found out he was livid and threatened to 'flog the whole company.' [7]

Bligh considered his next step. He saw wide spaces around Banks' Island and sailed there, noting two other islands on the way – Jervis Island and Mulgrave Island. To the south-west Bligh saw a familiar sight – an island he had seen on the launch and had named the Peaked Hill. It was one of many small islands which Bligh called Clarence's Archipelago. Guthrie landed on the northernmost and called it Possession Island. Bligh now took thought and decided that if there was a possibility of escaping from the Strait - the most likely passage lay between Mulgrave and Jervis Islands. Gingerly they passed the Black Rock and Passage Island and saw several other islands near the opening between the islands, but here the reefs overcrossed and both ships needed to anchor as the flow tide was very strong.

The situation was difficult as the tide drew everything in its path. Boats were flying distress signals in every direction and Bligh found his anchorage was poor enough to threaten the ship being drawn towards the reefs and rocks. Portlock did not dare signal for the *Providence* to follow him, but she did have a more solid bottom and a more sheltered position so Bligh bore towards him. The tide was worse, running at 'a fearful rate' so the *Providence* bore to and tried to anchor, the cable flying from them. When they pulled up the half cable they were horrified to see it had the dogstopper on and the ship was heading towards the rocks. Bligh just had time to throw down a second anchor which stilled the ship. Interestingly, he wrote:

The men who had done this were no more faulty than the officer who was in command so I did not punish them. [8]

The passage was extremely hazardous, with shoals appearing everywhere as well as perilous rocks; even so, they needed to anchor for the night and none of the crew knew whether the ships were able to stay clear of the rocks around them. The next day the ships needed to find safer seas so they slowly crept away from the islands. Fearing a disaster in these untamable waters he sent the boats forward to check the waters and report back on the condition of any channels through the labyrinth of rocks and reefs. On the 18th they gave the signal for good anchorage so, following the *Assistant*, Bligh reached the narrows – to find the information he had been given was false:

Lieutenant Guthrie met me as I was passing the first narrows, and I now found we had neither good anchorage nor a convenient passage for the ships.

Our situation was worse than before. Rocks all around us and a dreadful tide running. Night obliged me to anchor with little certainty of keeping off the rocks. [9]

They survived the night and the next day they made a further attempt to defeat the Strait. Portlock carefully led the way until they sailed through a channel between keys off Mulgrave Island – known as Bligh's Channel –

and at last they found themselves in open sea. It was a tremendous achievement and even Flinders was full of praise:

No space of 3½ degrees in length presents more dangers than Torres Strait, but with caution and perseverance the Captains, Bligh and Portlock, proved them to be surmountable, and within a reasonable time. [10]

Before Bligh, only Tasman and Cook had made any discoveries among the Fiji Islands. Tasman had seen Nuku Mbasanga, Taveuni and about a dozen other islands while Cook had seen Vatoa, which he named Turtle Island. It was Bligh who discovered around forty islands including the largest of them all, Vanua Levu (of which Tasman only saw at a distance)

There was to be one tragedy - on 24 September William Terry died from the arrow wound he had sustained on the *Assistant* – but by 2 October the crews arrived at Timor, where Bligh's old friend Wanjon was still in charge and gave them a warm welcome. Here, Bligh was to discover the fate of the *Pandora* and other news. Bligh was pleased to meet his old friends at Coupang, but his stay was marred by a recurrence of his fever. On his former visit, he had already written:

During my stay here I had not a moment's intermission from a violent headache and touches of fever at times ; from 8 in the morning till 5 in the afternoon I dare not expose myself to the heat of the sun. The houses, too, from the red tiling were heated like ovens, so that morning and evening were the only parts of the day at all bearable.

The illness made the voyage insufferable for Bligh, who wrote to his wife, saying that he meant to make no more. He added:

I love you dearer than ever a Woman was loved... every joy and blessing attend you, My Life & bless my Dear Harriet, my Dear Mary, my Dear Betsy, my Dear Fanny, my Dear Jenny & my Dear little Ann. I send you all many Kisses on this paper & ever pray God to bless you – I will not say farewell to you now, my Dear Betsy, because I am homeward bound – I shall lose no time. Every happyness attend you my Dearest Life and ever remember me your best of Friends & most affectionate Husband. [11]

He also counted up his losses with respect to breadfruit and found that 224 had perished. He made up for some of these at Timor and also planted 'Mangoes, *Jambelang Jambos, Balumbeng, Chermailah, Karambola, Lemon Moresang, Cosambee, Cattahpas*, Bread-fruit, *Seereeboah, Penang* or Beetle Nut, *Dangreedah* trees with which they perfume, *Bughnah,* and *Kanangah.*'

After watering, the ships got under way on 11 October. As to the plan, they headed for Madagascar but the unhealthy climate of Timor took its toll on at least one of the crew – Thomas Lickman, mate, died on 6 October and was committed to sea the day after. [12] Four days later, Bligh had the chance to pull in at Madagascar, but Wiles and Smith felt it would be too risky for the plants. They rounded the Cape of Good Hope and seas became heavy on 19 November. By 17 December they sighted St Helena and the Second Lieutenant was sent to inform the Governor, who gave a fifteen-gun salute which was returned.

Bligh now went to visit Lieutenant-Colonel Brooke, the Governor and presented him with ten breadfruit plants with the King's compliments – they were taken to the nearby valley known as Plantation House. On the 23rd they were offloaded and planted; Bligh gave one each to the Lieutenant-Governor, Major Robson and another to the First in Council, Mr Ringham. He also brought them mountain rice and the sago plant. They did not recognise the latter, so the native Tahitians came and prepared a pudding from its root.   After supplies were taken on board, the ships sailed on past Ascension Island and on 23 January they landed at Kingston Bay, St Vincent. The Superintendent, Dr Anderson, came on board and when General Seton arrived it was agreed that the negro slaves should carry the plants up to the Botanic Garden, about two miles from the beach. In all, Bligh left 544 plants and received 465 pots and two tubs of plants for Kew gardens. The next day the Honorary Council and Assembly waited on Bligh and presented him with a resolution and a piece of plate valued at one hundred guineas. They also laid on a dinner for all the officers of the ships.

While in port, Bligh lost two men. One was John Thompson of the *Matilda*, who deserted and the other Henry Smith who fell in the sea and drowned.

On 30 January the ships sailed off to their last port of call, Jamaica. On 5 February they landed at Port Royal Harbour and the next day Bligh put himself under the command of Commodore Ford while Guthrie waited on Governor-General Adam Williamson. At a meeting of the 9th it was decided that the plants should be divided between the counties but that two nurseries should be set up for them, one at East Garden and the other at Bath. Wiles was selected to act as Gardener at Bath and to be assisted by Bobbo. The plants were taken to Port Morant via the *Providence* and to Savannah la Mar via the *Assistant.*

The Committee wrote the following to Bligh:

Sir, I am authorised in the name of the Committee appointed to act in the reception of the Bread Fruit and other valuable plants lately received, to assure you in their name of the high sense they entertain of

your exertions and great merit in bringing to so happy a conclusion the beneficent object of our most gracious Sovereign in this most arduous task committed to your charge. I am, etc., Henry Shirley. [13]

It was over. At last, after so many years, Bligh had completed his mission. It had been a difficult process and he had endured mutiny, starvation, sickness, humiliation, a court martial and two long sea voyages. It must have been a triumphant Bligh who watched the last of the plants being delivered to their final destination. Had the Admiralty listened to him before his first voyage and given him marines, he could have been spared much hardship. That was all over and he could look forward to a well-earned rest before the long voyage home. At least, that is what he thought.

Bligh sailed back to Port Royal, where he heard startling news, which had arrived by means of the *Duke of Cumberland* packet. The National Convention of France had declared war on Britain. As the country was now at war, Ford commandeered the ships to do duty there. The *Assistant* was often used to convey vessels into port and many of His Majesty's ships were to arrive: the *Persephone, Penelope, Spitfire, Hyaena, Europa, Serpent* and *Fly*. They would give chase to any French vessels and thus Borrell, Commandant of the *Port au Prince*, was captured.

On 10 June Bligh was finally given orders to sail for England, but not straight away. First he had to participate in the war effort and he was told to sail to San Antonio, Cuba with the *Assistant* and take any ships of the Honduras fleet. The *Providence* set out for Bluefields, where the *Assistant* was, but received a letter from Portlock telling him he was assisting a ship called the *Roehampton* and would meet him at Grand Cayman Island. Here they met on 17 July and reached San Antonio on the 20th.

Bligh was to see no action. Finding no Honduras sails, Bligh headed home in the company of the *Antelope*, the *Roehampton*, the *Clemenson* and the *Thomas*. On the 26th he saw the coast of Florida, passed through the Florida Channel and sailed north-east towards Cape Clear on the Irish coast. They reached the Downs on 2 August 1793 and on 7 August. Bligh's last log entries were somewhat depressing:

Friday, August 9th, our Otaheitan friend Mydiddee became so ill that I was obliged to send him to lodgings and sick quarters at Deptford.

Wednesday, September 4th, our Otaheitan friend died.

Friday, September 6th, our Otaheitan friend was buried at Deptford New Church Yard in the parish of St. Paul's. I shall ever remember him with esteem. [14]

The quest was over. For those wishing to find evidence of Bligh the tyrant, the voyage had been singularly disappointing. Throughout the whole of the two years, he gave only a dozen men the lash and only twice did he award more than twelve lashes. He held his crew in high regard and promised to do whatever lay in his power to advance their careers. The project had been a success and Bligh had achieved what he had set out to do. After he had published his narrative of the *Bounty* mutiny, his name was a household word. Now he had returned again, with more adventures to tell and success in his wake. He must have expected that the world was his. His log ended:

This voyage has terminated with success, without accident or a moment's separation of the two ships. It gives the first and only satisfactory accounts of the pass between New Guinea and New Holland, if I except some vague accounts of Torres in 1606 ; other interesting discoveries will be found in it. (Signed) WILLIAM BLIGH, Captain. September 9th 1793.

As he left the ship, his crew cheered him on his way to his interview with the Commissioner. But Admiral Lord Chatham refused to even see him. His narrative would not be published. Things had changed since he boarded the *Providence*.

Chapter Ten. That *Bounty* Bastard

What can have happened for Bligh to have lost so many folds of favour? It all began over a year before his return when the Admiralty held the court-martial to try the *Bounty* mutineers. Of all the men on trial, Heywood probably had the strongest allies – his uncle was Captain Pasley, who had many contacts – and the undying support of his beloved sister Nessy, who first wrote in June 1792:

Oh! my ever dearest Boy, when I look back to that dreadful Moment which brought us the fatal Intelligence that you had remained in the *Bounty* after Mr. Bligh had quitted her & were looked upon by him as a Mutineer! when I contrast that Day of Horror with my present Hopes of again beholding you such as my most sanguine Wishes cou'd expect. I know not which is the most predominant sensation — pity Compassion & Sorrow for your sufferings, or Joy & Satisfaction at the prospect of their being near a Termination; & of once more embracing the dearest Object of our Affections! [1]

Naturally, Nessy turned to her Uncle, who was best situated to promote the cause of her accused brother. Pasley promised to do what he could, but he had already cast an eye over the accusations and he was very pessimistic of the outcome:

I cannot conceal it from you my dearest Nessy, neither is it proper I shou'd, your Brother appears by all Accounts to be the greatest Culprit of all, Christian alone excepted. — every Exertion you may rest assured I shall use to save his Life — but on Trial I have no Hope of his not being condemned. — three of the ten who are expected are mentioned in Bligh's Narrative as Men detained against their Inclination — wou'd to God! your Brother had been one of that Number... [2]

Despite the dreadful warnings, Nessy was determined to persuade Pasley to exert himself to the utmost for his nephew. Heywood's pathetic letters were loaded with cries of anguish and suffering, which had convinced her more than anything else of his innocence. Thinking his words would have the same effect on her uncle, she sent her last letter from him to Pasley, with a short note:

Let it speak for him — the perusal of his artless & pathetic story will I am persuaded be a stronger recommendation in his Favor than any thing I can urge.

Pasley knew that the outpourings from his nephew's heart would hardly sway the tribunal and that he needed more concrete evidence if he were to save him. He needed witnesses to testify in Haywood's favour and he needed to prime the judges as best he could. Straight away used all the influence he had and made it his business to visit other members of the *Bounty*'s crew to discover if any proof could be gained from them. He then wrote two letters to his nephew:

I have seen Mr. Fryer & Cole — rest assured of every Exertion in my Power to serve you — let me hear from you, & be particular in any thing in which you think I can serve you – bear your present situation with Patience & Firmness...

I have seen Mr. Fryer the Master, & Cole the Boatswain, both favorable Evidences. to Day I set off for Woolwich & Deptford to endeavour to see the Gunner & Carpenter, & shall try e'er I return to see Hayward & Hallet.... [3]

Pasley's efforts encouraged Nessy to be optimistic and she wrote a letter full of hope to her brother. Heywood, however, knew he was in a spot and that several of the witnesses could make things hot for him; those who had seen him standing with his hand on the cutlass, for instance. He wrote back to Nessy:

Cease to anticipate the Happiness of personal Communication with your poor but resigned Brother untill wished-for Freedom takes the indignant shackles I now bear.

On 15th July, Pasley was confident was his nephew would be acquitted, writing: 'Have Courage my dear young Friend & hope the best.' His activities seem to have gone well and he added: 'I have no Doubt we shall see you acquitted whenever your Court-Martial takes Place.' A week later, he finally received Bligh's letter which Nessy had sent him, telling her mother that Heywood was guilty of ingratitude and the blackest treachery.

On Bligh's return, she had written to him asking about the fate of his son; Bligh replied 'His baseness is beyond all description, but I hope you will endeavour to prevent the loss of him, heavy as the misfortune is, from afflicting you too severely.' As to his whereabouts, Bligh imagined that 'he is, with the rest of the mutineers, returned to Otaheite.' Heywood must have expected something of the like from Bligh, but in his return letter to Nessy he pretended that he was utterly horrified.

... Did he then write to you to that Effect! — Alas! — & had he so mean an Opinion of my Disposition & Morals? — But — I forgive his Cruelty, & may God do the same! — Yet I think he might have known me better. — Ah! Nessy — wou'd to God this Letter had not come to my Hand! — till now I had almost said my Fears for my reputation & good Name were groundless; but Alas! by it they are verified — that he, the first Commander I ever was with, deemed me a *Mutineer* — Oh! Heavens! — The Thought is almost insupportable! [4]

At least his apparent despair brought forth a poem which, while not of any literary consequence, at least reflects his feelings at the time:

Oh! Hope — thou firm support against Despair
Assist me now stern adverse Fate to bear;
And Teach me, when by Troubles sore opprest,
To think they happen to me for the best;
To waft from off my Soul the Clouds of Woe
And make the big swol'n Tear forget to flow:
And Oh! remind me that the Time draws near
When from these Chains! once more I shall be clear:
My long-felt Troubles then perhaps will cease
And past Distress be crown'd by future Peace. [5]

Peter and Nessy continued to correspond and the letters contained a few more poetic offerings – such as *The Dream* – as well as tokens of love and esteem.

By 28 August Pasley had hired Graham – a very good friend - as his nephew's lawyer; he had some experience in court-martial defence and 'he has a thorough Knowledge of the Service, uncommon Abilities & is a very good Lawyer.' On 6 September he wrote to Heywood asking him to follow Graham's advice, 'of whose Abilities I have the highest Opinion; – & trust your Cause to him, with a Confidence I shou'd hardly have done to any man in England — the whole Bar of Council not excepted.' The court martial was to take place six days later.

The trial was presided over by Lord Hood, Vice Admiral of the Blue and Commander in Chief of His Majesty's Ships and Vessels at Portsmouth and Spithead. The Court consisted of Captain Sir Andrew Snape, George Montagu, John Bazely, John Thomas Duckworth, John Knight, Richard Goodwin Keats, Captain John Colpoys, Sir Roger Curtis, Sir Andrew Snape Douglas, John Nicholson Inglefield and Albemarle Bertie. Nessy had already contacted Emma Bertie, Albemarle's wife and Pasley was friends with Montagu.

Those called as prosecution witnesses gave the account of the mutiny, how they came to know of it and named those defendants who were seen as bearing arms. Fryer gave a complete account, including many of the conversations which passed between himself and various crew members, but he contradicted himself so much that some of the presiding officers felt that he should have faced trial himself. The prisoners knew that their best defence was to insist that they had intended to retake the ship after the launch was cast off and Morrison took the opportunity to ask Fryer:

'Do you recollect that I said, "I will do my endeavour to raise a party and rescue the Ship?"'

Fryer answered: 'No.' [6]   :

The next witness was the boatswain William Cole, who had nothing bad to say about Bligh, directly or indirectly. He recalled Fryer's words with Christian:

' Then Mr. Fryer came upon Deck and asked Mr. Christian what he was about (the particular Words I do not recollect) - he then told him that if he did not approve of the Captain's behaviour to put him under an Arrest and proceed on the Voyage. He told him that if that was all he had to say to go down to his Cabin again, for he had been in hell for weeks and weeks past.' [7]

The court questioned Cole about Heywood.

'You say you saw Peter Heywood overhaul the Forestay Tackle fall. Do you think he did it voluntarily or not?'

'Yes, I do.'

'Do you think he was influenced by threats of People under Arms?'
'No.' [8]

It might have been expected that Purcell nursed a grudge against Bligh following his own court-martial, but he did not speak against Bligh. He declared that he saw the defendants with weapons, but the Court wanted to gain definitive proof that Heywood was part or the conspiracy or not.

'Do you upon the solemn oath you have taken, believe that Mr. Heywood by being armed with a cutlass at the time you have mentioned, by any thing that you could collect from his gestures or speeches, had any intention of opposing or joining others that might oppose to stop the Progress of the Mutiny?'
'No.' [9]

On the other hand, Purcell 'looked upon him as a person confused and that he did not know that he had the weapon in his hand, or his hand being on it, for it was not in his hand.'

When Hallet took the stand, he was able to recount all the men he saw in arms - Ellison, Morrison, Burkitt, Hillbrandt, Sumner, Skinner, Christian, Young, Churchill, Thompson, Smith, Mills, McKoy, Williams, Brown, Martin and Quintal. Although he did not see Heywood with arms, he did comment:

'Captain Bligh said something to him, but what I did not hear, upon which he laughed, turned round, and walked away.'

This was noted by the Court.

Hallet also made accusations against Morrison, who took advantage of the cross-examination to question him.

'You say you saw me under arms on the taffrail and that I did sneeringly say, 'Tell my friends if they enquire that I am somewhere in the South Seas' — can you positively declare before God and this Court that it was me and no other Person whom you saw under arms and to whom I declared the said sneering message?'

Hallet replied: 'I have declared it, but did not remark that the message was said to any particular Individual.' [10]

Captain Edwards also gave some evidence at the trial, telling the Court how Coleman had given himself up and a brief interview with and Heywood, who had asked to talk with Hayward. Hayward 'treated him with a sort of contemptuous look.' First Lieutenant Larkin briefly stated in which order the prisoners were taken and Second Lieutenant Corner explained that there was no resistance.

Peter Heywood opted to have a long harangue read out which had been written – or at least, signed by him, then he was given the opportunity to cross-examine a number of witnesses.

The Court's verdict was:

That the Charges had been proved against the said Peter Heywood, James Morrison, Thomas Ellison, Thomas Burkitt, John Millward and William Muspratt, and did adjudge them and each of them to suffer Death by being hanged by the Neck, on board such of His Majesty's Ship or Ships of War, at such Time or Times and at such Place or Places, as the Commissioners for executing the Office of Lord High Admiral of Great Britain and Ireland etc. or any three of them, for the Time being, should in Writing, under their Hands direct; but the Court, in Consideration of various Circumstances, did humbly and most earnestly recommend the said Peter Heywood and James Morrison to His Majesty's Royal Mercy — and the Court further agreed That the Charges had not been proved against the said Charles Norman, Joseph Coleman, Thomas McIntosh and Michael Byrn, and did adjudge them and each of them to be acquitted. [11]

Although found guilty, Emma Bertie lost no time in writing to Nessy Heywood.

I have the happiness of telling you that the court-martial is this Moment over, & that I think your Son's Life is more safe now, than it was before his Trial: — as there was not sufficient Proof of his Innocence, the Court cou'd not avoid condemning him: — but he is *so strongly recommended to Mercy*, that I am desired to assure you (by those who are Judges) that his Life is safe; — all the principal Officers of the *Bounty*, who were called as Evidence; gave him the highest Character imaginable; — therefore for God's Sake, whatever you may hear, believe Nothing but what you hear from hence. [12]

Heywood refuted the four points of evidence for which he was convicted. Firstly, he helped to hoist out the launch; here he insisted that he was acting as the Captain's friend, because if they had launched the cutter they would have been in a much worse condition. Second, Purcell saw him with his hand on a cutlass; Heywood argued that he placed his hand on it in a kind of 'stupor' and removed it when he realised it might be thought he was a mutineer. Third, he 'laughed' at Bligh; he argued that he was too far away to hear him clearly and in any case it was dangerous to assume a man's mind from his looks:

Tears have often been, nay generally are, the relief of excessive joy, while misery and dejection have, many a time, disguised themselves in a smile; and convulsive laughs have betrayed the anguish of an almost broken heart. [13]

Fourth, he remained on the ship; but he said that he wished to go into the boat but was prevented by Thompson.

It is strange that all commentators view Heywood as an innocent who had suffered by the Mutiny. In fact, his confused evidence strongly suggests the opposite. He did not refute the fact that his hand was on a cutlass. The question remains – where did he get it from? He did not even go down the well-trod road of blaming the mutineers or claiming that they – at least the ones not in court – had forced it into his hand. He claims that when Purcell saw him with the weapon, he took his hand away in case he might be thought of as a mutineer, which is more credible and suggests that he did not realise the carpenter was close by. It also suggests that he did not want anyone in the launch to see him acting in Christian's rebellion and it has to be remembered that Heywood and Christian had become 'bosom friends.' If Christian was to rely on anyone for friendship alone, that would have been Heywood.

How far Heywood was involved in the plotting of the mutiny is conjecture.

His excuse for helping the mutineers to launch the boat was ludicrous – that he was actually helping Bligh because the launch would have been much more comfortable than the jolly boat. Whether it would or not, the fact remains that Heywood did indeed help at the launch – he never denied it – and so the charge was proven from his own mouth. It is clearly ridiculous to claim that he put out the boat in which Bligh was to be cast adrift from a sense of duty or from any care of his Captain. He did not even maintain that the mutineers forced him to perform this 'friendly action' and the evidence shows that he did it voluntarily. He swore that he had been forcibly kept from the boat, yet in court he said that it would have been an 'act of suicide' to have gone.

On the point which seems to have swayed the court – that he laughed and turned away after Bligh had called to him – once again he did not even deny it. Instead he put forward two lame excuses – first, that he was too far away to hear Bligh's words and second, one cannot judge a man by his countenance. But Bligh was addressing him – no-one argued about that, not even Heywood – and it is hard to imagine that the blustering Lieutenant would not have made himself heard or his intentions clear. Bligh had been accustomed to address the crew at all parts of the ship and knew how to bellow if need be. Heywood does not even deny that he laughed but construes this as a contradictory sign of grief, a bizarre explanation which cut little ice at the Court Martial.

It is also important to note that Bligh, whose tempests normally faded in minutes, nursed a grudge against Heywood whom he painted as the blackest of the villains. While this is usually put down as vindictiveness, it is also out of character and can only be satisfactorily explained if he seen him with cutlass in hand; if he had begged him to save his own reputation and was laughed at and ignored; or if he had seen any other signs which were incontestable proof of his complicity in the mutiny. What's more, he had seen or heard enough to convince him beyond any doubt that Heywood was voluntarily in league with the rebels. This alone could explain the curt note he sent to Heywood's mother when he arrived back in England. Besides, Heywood had admitted that he had 'lost his head'. On the *Pandora*, Hayward had refused to befriend him and treated him as a mutineer; not, one may suspect, without good reason.

McIntosh's 'wife', Mary, told Bligh that Heywood had shown no remorse on his return to Tahiti. Mcintosh, Coleman, Hillbrandt, Newman, Byrne, and Ellison scarce ever spoke of him 'without crying', whereas Stewart and Heywood were perfectly satisfied with their situation and so were the rest of them.

'They deserved to be killed,' she had said, but she 'hoped those who cried for Bligh would not be hurt.'

Heywood and Morrison were both pardoned. Morrison was threatening to write his own 'memorandum' of the voyage but this was unlikely to sway the Court. More serious was Heywood's threat to bring a counter court-martial against Bligh, one which Morrison also put forward. At this point no-one had pointed a finger of blame at Bligh and this was the first hint of a smear campaign against the commander of the *Bounty*. If Heywood was going down, he would drag Bligh with him – and Heywood knew that such a legal action would be of great embarrassment to the Navy. He had already begun to gather evidence, but after his reprieve a court martial would seem like malice.

Four sailors were facing the sentence of execution, although Musprat was reprieved on a technicality. Burkitt, Ellison and Millward were hanged on the *Brunswick* on 29 October.

Heywood had escaped punishment, but that was not enough for him. He was thirsting for revenge and now took it upon himself to write to Christian's brother, Edward, a barrister at law:

I am sorry to say I have been informed you were inclined to judge too harshly of your truly unfortunate brother; and to think of him in such a manner as I am conscious, from the knowledge I had of his most worthy disposition, and character, (both public and private,) he merits not in the slightest degree: therefore I think it my duty to undeceive you, and to re-kindle the flame of brotherly love (or pity now) towards him, which, I fear, the false reports of slander and vile suspicion may have nearly extinguished.

Excuse my freedom, Sir: — If it would not be disagreeable to you, I will do myself the pleasure of waiting upon you; and endeavour to prove that your brother was not that vile wretch, void of all gratitude, which the

world had the unkindness to think him; but, on the contrary, a most worthy character; ruined only by having the misfortune, (if it can be so called) of being a young man of strict honour, and adorned with every virtue; and beloved by all (except one, whose ill report is his greatest praise) who had the pleasure of his acquaintance. [14]

Edward Christian had shown no signs of even contemplating a rebuttal of Bligh's claims as published in his book. It was Heywood who decided to contact him and his anger against the 'one, whose ill report is his greatest praise' is obvious. Heywood knew the men who had grudges against their old Captain and he was also aware that Morrison was about to publish a 'memorandum' to defame Bligh. He himself – along with Morrison – had threatened an action of court-martial against Bligh; however, Heywood still had friends in the Navy, including Pasley, who would ensure that his dear nephew would find a billet in his ship the *Bellepheron*. Heywood was too crafty to appear in the limelight of a lurid court case – so he turned to Christian.

After the interview Christian determined to rescue the family name. On 15 May 1794 he began to collect evidence from – he claimed - Fryer, Hayward, Peckover, Purcell, Smith, Lebogue, Coleman, Thomas McIntosh, Michael Byrne, Heywood Musprat and Morrison. He then wrote an account which was later to act as an *Appendix* to the published court-martial minutes and which was to be a template in the art of character-assassination.

The *Appendix* begins by the assertion that Bligh used to call his officers 'scoundrels, damned rascals, hounds, hell-hounds, beasts, and infamous wretches'; which may or may not be the truth, knowing his bursts of sudden anger; but the suggestion that when the ship arrived at Endeavour Straits, 'he would kill one half of the people, make the officers jump overboard, and would make them eat grass like cows' is in the realms of fantasy. Christian advances the preposterous story by claiming that Fletcher was as afraid of the Straits as 'any child of a rod.' It is doubtful whether Christian 'bore the brunt' of Bligh's rage all of the time, although the idea that he 'shook his fist in his face' may conceivably be accurate as Bligh had a way of gesticulating when in anger. Edward Christian, however, decided to excuse his brother's position as head of the mutiny by arguing that Bligh made his life utterly unbearable, which was wholly false. It was highlighted, however, in an imaginary conversation between Purcell and Christian, when the latter saw him weeping like a baby:

'What is the matter Mr. Christian?'

'Can you ask me, and hear the treatment I receive?'

'Do not I receive as bad as your do?'

'You have something to protect you, and can speak again; but if I should speak to him as you do, he would probably break me, turn me before the mast, and perhaps flog me; and if he did, it would be the death of us both, for I am sure I should take him in my arms, and jump overboard with him.'

'Never mind it, it is but for a short time longer.' [15]

'In going through Endeavor Straits, I am sure the ship will be a hell. I would rather die ten thousand deaths, than bear this treatment; I always do my duty as an officer and as a man ought to do, yet I receive this scandalous usage. Flesh and blood cannot bear this treatment.'

Christian stresses the incident of the coconuts and Bligh's command to lessen the yam ration, although he makes the incidents overflow with ripe language and pompous cruelty. Bligh's major fault – his temper –would always come back to haunt him yet Christian never once remarks on any acts of kindness done by the Captain for his crew. Christian's account of the coconuts is as follows:

'Damn your blood, you have stolen my cocoa nuts'; Christian answered, 'I was dry, I thought it of no consequence, I took one only, and I am sure no one touched another.' Captain Bligh then replied, 'You lie, you scoundrel, you have stolen one half.' Christian appeared much hurt and agitated, and said, 'Why do you treat me thus, Captain Bligh?' Captain Bligh then shook his hand in his face and said, 'No reply'; and called him 'a thief,' and other abusive names. He then ordered the quarter masters to go down and bring all the cocoa nuts both from man and officer, and put them upon the quarter deck. They were brought. The Captain then called all hands upon deck, and desired 'the people to look after the officers, and the officers to look after the people, for there never were such a set of damned thieving rascals under any man's command in the world before.' [16]

While representing Bligh as a martinet and a sadistic monster, Edward Christian paints a portrait of his brother as the flower of manhood and a man whom all the mutineers followed out of reverence and admiration. He even argues that while at Tahiti he had no women at all, which was plainly fictional. If such a suggestion was meant to show him in the light of a moral and upright character, then Heywood also fell foul, as he was one of the first to contract venereal disease.

Christian rounds off the article with:

The sufferings of Captain Bligh and his companions in the boat, however severe they may have been, are perhaps but a small portion of the torments occasioned by this dreadful event: and whilst these prove the melancholy and extensive consequences of the crime of Mutiny, the crime itself in this instance may afford an awful lesson to the Navy, and

to mankind, that there is a degree of pressure, beyond which the best formed and principled mind must either break or recoil. And though public justice and the public safety can allow no vindication of any species of Mutiny, yet reason and humanity will distinguish the sudden unpremeditated act of desperation and phrenzy, from the foul deliberate contempt of every religious duty and honourable sentiment; and will deplore the uncertainty of human prospects, when they reflect that a young man is condemned to perpetual infamy, who, if he had served on board any other ship, or had perhaps been absent from the *Bounty* a single day, or one ill-fated hour, might still have been an honour to his country, and a glory and comfort to his friends.

Often ridiculous in its excess, Christian's *Appendix* nonetheless had a huge impact on the way the country now viewed Bligh. There is little doubt that it was published as a direct conspiracy to blacken his name, with Christian, Heywood and Morrison as ring-leaders. Morrison had little to lose and before long his own 'journal' was ready for publication with hammered more nails into the coffin of Bligh's reputation.

Morrison describes the incident of the cheese and bluntly states that the two missing cheeses had been sent to Mrs Bligh's residence while she was waiting for the *Bounty* to set sail from Portsmouth.

Mr. Bligh without making any further inquiry into the Matter, ordered the Allowance of Cheese to be stopp'd from Officers and Men till the deficiency should be made good, and told the Cooper He would give him a dam'd good flogging If He said any More about it. [17]

The story is ridiculous as supplies were always short and it was impossible that Bligh could charge thefts with the deficiency. Besides, if he had proportioned the cheeses to his own use, it would have been foolish for him to blame anyone else. Bligh himself explained that the cheeses were counted, then at a second examination were found to be short.

Morrison next writes that Bligh told the crew they were to have one pound of pumpkin in lieu of two pounds of bread and they refused it. Bligh then stormed:

'You dam'd Infernal scoundrels, I'll make you eat Grass or any thing you can catch before I have done with you.' [18]

Bligh again explained the situation; he offered two pounds of pumpkin for a pound of bread – only for those of the men who liked it. The rest was therefore a fiction.

Next, the men's provisions were kept light and the casks of meat had never been weighed when opened. Furthermore, the choice pieces of meat were taken for the Captain, while the seamen had to make do with what they had. They had 'to stand the Wrangle in the Gally for their Pease, &

Oatmeal, which was served in very sparing quantities—So sparing that there never was any of either left for the Hogs who must have Starved but for bread & the Indian Corn purchased for the Poultry.' [19] Monstrous Bligh stated that he was the best judge of what was right or wrong, and threatened to flog the next man to make a complaint.

In his defence, Bligh argued that every cask was counted after broaching and he never ate anything more than the common man. Everyone had more than enough to eat and he even provided hot breakfasts, which was never heard of before. His ship's log is eloquent in its defence.

In Tahiti, Morrison complains of Bligh's avarice when taking hogs on board:

The Market for Hogs beginning now to slacken Mr. Bligh seized on all that came to the ship big & small Dead or alive, taking them as his property, and serving them as the ship's allowance at one pound pr. Man pr. Day. He also seized on those belonging to the Master, & killed them for the ships use, tho He had more than 40 of different sizes on board of his own, and there was then plenty to be purchaced: nor was the price much risen from the first, and when the Master spoke to him, telling him the Hogs were his property, he told him that 'He Mr. Bligh would convince him that every thing was his, as soon as it was on board, and that He would take nine tenths of any mans property and let him see who dared say any thing to the contrary', those of the seamen were seized without ceremony, and it became a favour for a man to get a Pound extra of His own hog. [20]

He also stated that the natives would hide their hogs as Bligh was in the habit of simply taking whatever he pleased. Once again, this is a nonsense; the hogs were bought or traded for by Bligh and his men and were part of the communal foodstock. The hogs were more often given as gifts than anything else. [21]

The conspiracy among Heywood, Christian and Morrison succeeded beyond their wildest expectations. Never had a character been muddied so much by so few. The figure of the heroic Bligh was unceremoniously hauled down and a mythical beast supplanted it, one which years hence would become a caricature of cruel barbarity. The native idolatry blurred into indignity and repulsion as these new revelations sped through grapevines, none so easily as in the Admiralty. Bligh soon had inklings of his fall from grace when Lord Chatham blanked him and it was not long before he read the libels of Fletcher Christian's brother.

Bligh did reply to Christian's *Appendix*, but as befitting his station he did so with dignity, refusing to be drawn into a public newspaper brawl – or to be taken unawares by the legal traps it had set for him. However, his honour was at stake and so, as he wrote:

The respect I owe to that Public in whose service I have spent my life, as well as regard to my character, compel me to reply to such parts of Mr. Christian's Appendix, as might, if unnoticed, obtain credit to my prejudice. [22]

Bligh did not get involved in a literary debate: he simply appended several documents to prove his innocence from all charges, including a letter from Hallet and affidavits from Coleman, Smith and Lebogue, contradicting Christian's 'evidence'. These documents were:

- Orders issued upon the Arrival at Tahiti, to regulate Intercourse with the Natives. — October 25th, 1788.

- Orders respecting the confinement of the men who had deserted from the ship. — Date, January 24th, 1789.

- Letter from the deserters thanking Bligh for his clemency — January 26th, 1789.

- Examination respecting the Loss of his Majesty's Ship the *Bounty*, by the High Court of Judicature at Batavia. — October 13th, 1789.

- Descriptive List of the Mutineers. — Dated 28th April, 1789.

- Orders given to Mr. John Fryer, the Master, on leaving him at Batavia. — October 14th, 1789.

- Letter from Mr. Peter Heywood, Midshipman, to Mrs. Bligh. — July 14th, 1792.

- Extract from Mr. Peter Heywood's Defence, on his Trial by a Court-Martial; held August 12th, 1792, at Portsmouth.

- Letter from Mr. Peter Heywood to Mr. Edward Christian, published in the Cumberland Packet, and Whitehaven Advertiser, November 20th, 1792.

- Letter published in the *Times*, July 16th, 1794, from Mr. Edward Harwood, late Surgeon of his Majesty's ship Providence.

- Affidavit of Joseph Coleman. — July 31, 1794.

- Affidavit of John Smith. — August 1, 1794.

- Affidavit of Lawrence Lebogue. — August 2, 1794.

- Letter from Lieutenant John Hallet. — August 1,1794.

- Letter from Mr. Edward Lamb, Commander of the *Adventure*, in the Jamaica trade. — October 28th, 1794. [23]

These documents were examined by Edward Christian, who decided to write *A Short Reply to Captain Bligh's Answer* which was not as persuasive as his *Appendix*. He found he had no answer to the first two affidavits, but he declared Lebogue's as 'the most wicked and perjured affidavit that ever was sworn before a magistrate, or published to the world.' [24] He then had his friends, John Atkinson and James Losh, write a certificate claiming they were present at the interviews with Byrne, Coleman, Lebogue and Peckover, which included the assertion that 'Mr. Christian had no favourite or particular connection among the women.' As to Bligh's complaint that the *Appendix* failed to ascribe the testimonies to individuals, Christian claimed that at least one of the men had received threats, but failed to indicate from which source. [25] Bligh mentioned that some evidence spoken at court was not referred to by Christian, who made the rather lame excuse that the 'minutes did not extend beyond the evidence for the prosecution.' He also took exception at Hallet's opinion that 'Christian did not appear to have received any portion of classical learning, and was ignorant of all but his mother tongue' and attested that he 'was an excellent scholar, and possessed extraordinary abilities.'

Possibly Bligh felt the riposte was too poor to merit a reply; in any case he wrote none. The mud was destined to stick and the poison did its work. Later, naval ratings, as was their wont, would give their Captains nicknames – and Bligh was '*Bounty* B'. It was a while before he realised that they referred to him as 'that *Bounty* bastard.'

Chapter Eleven. A Very Delicate Business

On 13 April 1795 Bligh received his next commission from the Royal Navy as Captain of the *Warley*, which was later changed to the *Calcutta*, a 24-gun ship under the command of Admiral Adam Duncan. The main purpose of the ship was to join Duncan's fleet in the North Sea on watching for Dutch ships trying to break through to the Baltic. 1

During that year Bligh had a brief joy followed, within a day, by tragedy. Betsy gave birth to his first sons, twins named William and Henry. Within twenty-four hours they had died.

Very little else of note happened during his time on board the *Calcutta*. By 1 August, one of his Lieutenants, Thomas Russell, had absconded from the ship taking with him £21 2s 6d. Later another Lieutenant, David McDonald, failed to join ship and yet another had written to say that he would join up when money problems had been settled. This letter was written from the Gun Tavern at Deptford, leading Bligh to 'suspect he is under some arrest for debt.' 2

Although Bligh was on duty with Duncan's fleet watching the Dutch ships in the Texel – along with nineteen ragged Russian ships, twelve of the line and seven frigates – he saw no action for the whole of 1795. During that October, there was a mutiny on board the *Defiance* and Bligh helped to restore order.

The *Defiance* problem was the harbinger of worse to come. The men's grievances were, according to Bligh, the presence of a new Captain (George Home) and Lieutenant, few opportunities for shore leave and the grog 'mixed with less than five waters'. Lord Gordon deployed 200 troops from Scotland but they did not make a direct assault. Bligh took charge and led them in boats to the *Defiance*, where they took control with little resistance. The mutiny was not yet over as the Scottish troops were not allowed to serve outside their country and troops from the 134th regiment were drafted in. Four were hung and nine flogged. But the brewing resentment among the sailors was growing. 3

On 4 January 1796 Bligh was transferred to the *Director*, a fourth class ship of the line with sixty-four guns and 491 men. For the rest of the year the fleet played a waiting and strategic game but Bligh had little to do. Between January and February 1797 the *Director* was in port either in the Humber or in Yarmouth Roads.

At this time the Navy made use of Bligh's talents in the field of surveying and ordered him to the Humber, where he prepared a chart of the stretch of water from Spurn to Sunk Island, containing a 'correct plan of the entrance' and the cut at Grimsby. At Helford Harbour, his actions with sextant and compass brought him to the attention of the local bargemen, who assumed he was spying for the French. One day they ambushed him and led him in triumph to the vicarage as their prisoner. Bligh's outburst of fury and the bargemen's red faces may only be imagined. 4

A slack time is always a good one for sailors to mull over their grievances and at that time they had many. A major complaint was one of pay and here they had good cause to gripe. Ordinary seamen earned 19s a month and ABs £1 2s 6d, which was a pittance and had not risen since the days of

Charles II. To make matters worse, army wages had been increased, as had the pay of the officers. On top of this there were many other things to moan about – their provisions were of poor quality and often deficient, as seen on the *Bounty* when Bligh counted out the contents of each barrel. Vegetables were not issued to sailors when in port. The care of the sick was usually inadequate and the men often grumbled that the surgeons stole their necessities while the purser would take the opportunity to cheat the crew and accrue a small fortune. Discipline was harsh on board ship, floggings were often extreme and they were treated with brutality by the officers. Confinement and imprisonment caused much hardship. After months at sea, the sailors were often refused leave to go into harbours. After a conflict at sea, prize money was awarded to the officers but no bonuses were given to the ordinary seamen. If wounded, the men were given no wages until they were either cured or discharged.

There had been rumblings of discontent until, in 1794, occasional mutinies began to crop up among the fleet. One was stamped out by Captain Thomas Troubridge, on board the *Culloden*, which was followed by others on the *Caesar* and on the *Windsor Castle*. Then, in 1797, trouble began to spread.

In March, the *Director* joined the main fleet on the outer Road of the Texel. Bligh recorded that the crew behaved excellently until April. On the 10th six men either neglected their duty or refused to perform it altogether, so the Captain resorted to punishment – a dozen lashes each, apart from one sailor who received eighteen and another six. This did not suppress the mutinous atmosphere and between the 12th and the 17th another five men 'neglected their duty' and were rewarded with between a dozen and two dozen lashes. The next day, a mutiny involving all ships at Spithead began.

A week later, the *Director* pulled into port. Much had happened in that week. The sailors had forwarded their list of grievances to the Admiralty who were in the cleft stick of appearing weak and submitting to the demands or risking a spread of mutiny. They were not prepared to alter anything in the running of the ships or discipline, but conceded that the complaint of wages was a fair one. They therefore agreed to raise wages by 5s 6d a month, which was quite substantial. When Bligh arrived in port on 25 April, he read the proclamation to his men.

Perhaps realising that the Admiralty would now be more amenable to the rest of their demands, discontent rose. On 2 May Thomas Norton was given 24 lashes for drunkenness, William Roland 12 for insolence to a sentinel and William McDougall 12 for insolence to a superior officer on board the *Venerable*. On the 9th Lord Howe arrived at Spithead armed with the Proclamation and a new Act; an old hand at the diplomacy game, he offered free pardons for all who returned to duty and his silver tongue won the day.

Whereas his Majesty has been most graciously pleased to issue his royal proclamation, dated the 11th instant, and thereby to declare that all such seamen and marines on board any ships of the fleet who may have been guilty of any act of mutiny, or disobedience of orders, or neglect of duty, and who have returned, or who shall, upon notification of such his Majesty's proclamation, return to the regular and ordinary discharge of their duty, shall be discharged and released from all persecutions, imprisonments, and penalties incurred by reason of any act of mutiny or disobedience of orders, or any breach or neglect of duty previously committed by them, or any of them. [5]

Meanwhile, the *Director* had sailed to Nore for a refit.

On 12 May, the Mutiny at the Nore began in earnest. The sailors had organised themselves in committees of twelve men, one for each ship and each committee appointed two delegates to represent the men. All of the committees were responsible to the President, a malcontent called Richard Parker. Parker's recommendations were sent to each committee and from the beginning they played tough and demanded that all officers they hated should be sent ashore; from the *Director* they demanded the dismissal of two Lieutenants, Church and Ireland, as well as the Master, Birch. The next day Bligh wrote in his log that the *Sandwich* had hoisted a red flag and immediately his crew rushed to the poop to take up arms. It is interesting that Bligh was not sent off the ship until a week later. Lieutenant McTaggart was put in command and as he left the ship, Bligh's thoughts must have flown back to the last time he was ordered off a ship by mutineers. At least this time he had no hands tied behind his back. Nor a terrible open boat voyage ahead of him.

As was protocol, Bligh sent a letter informing the Admiralty of all that had occurred.

Being without any resource I was obliged to quit the ship. I have stated the whole transaction to Admiral Bruckner, and now wait their Lordships'; directions, being ready to meet any charge that can be brought against me or such investigation as they may think proper to direct. I have reason to believe the whole has originated with the *Sandwich*'s crew – hitherto never did a ship's company behave better or did ever a ship Mr Purdue, Mr Blaguire, and Mr Eldridge, Midm, are also turned on shore for being too much noticed by their Captain & Mr Purdue particularly because he did his duty like a spirited young officer – I know of nothing dishonourable they can be accused of.[6]

Bligh was contacted by the Admiralty as their man on the spot and he became a useful go-between. On 26 Lord Spencer sent him to consult with Admiral Duncan at the Nore, with this letter:

Private. We send you Captain Bligh on a very delicate business on which the Government is extremely anxious to have your opinion. The welfare and almost the existence of the country may depend upon what is the event of this very important crisis, but till we know what we can look to from your squadron it will be very difficult for us to know how to act. [7]

The members of the Admiralty found themselves in a difficult situation. Bligh returned the next day with news that the mutineers had spread their discontent as far as the ships in Longreach and were persuading them to join the rebellion. If diplomacy would not work, they would need to resort to violence and their Lordships were pondering over the strength of Duncan's squadron. The order for military intervention would be given if necessary. Meanwhile, they sent Bligh on a spying expedition around the shipyard. His report arrived after four days:

The *Standard* and *Lion* refused to obey the Admiral's orders, but afterwards complied and sailed. *Nassau* refused to obey the sailing order on account of the pay due to the people. The ship's company observed, on being questioned whether they would resist mutiny in other ships, that every Captain should keep his own ship quiet.

***Montagu* claims pay although but a month due. The ship's company went to their quarters and shotted their guns when the *Venerable* got under weigh.**

The ships in the road will only permit their own boats to come alongside, and no strangers. The Captain of Marines of the *Standard* turned on shore and a Lieutenant of the *Repulse* got into the Admiral's ship by command of the people.

The *Glatton*'s Company have a remarkably loyal and good character.

The delegates arrived from the Nore, but Admiral Duncan was informed of eighteen coming round in the *Cygnet* Cutter, and he had given orders to prevent their communicating with any of the ships (dated 26th May).

It appeared to me very doubtful and hazardous what would be the conduct of the favourable party of seamen, if employed against the other.

> The *Standard* and *Lion* wanted to send delegates to the other ships, but they were refused admittance.

> When I received Admiral Duncan's letters for their Lordships, I thought it advisable to return without a moment's loss of time *Montagu* and *Nassau* only in the Road. [8]

Duncan was furious. He had his duty to attend to, the blockading of the North Sea, and no-one to help him. Cursing the mutiny, he set off with only two sail, the *Venerable* and the *Adamant,* to reconnoitre the Texel Road. When he got there he was horrified to find fifteen ships waiting under the command of Admiral de Winter. In an impossible position, with only two ships to contain a whole fleet, he turned to subterfuge. He ordered the two ships to raise flags in the pretence that they were signalling the main fleet. Luckily the Dutch were fooled and did not sail; but it was only a matter of time before they realised they had been tricked.

Back at the shipyards, the Captains realised how dangerous the situation was, although they could not know the dreadful predicament Duncan was in. Bligh, the same Captain who had been denounced as a tyrant, walked around the ships and talked to everyone he saw, mostly the ordinary seamen and chatted to them man to man, discussing their grievances and trying to persuade them, in their own best interests, to return to duty. Ironically, on 30 May, the *Director* gave a nineteen-gun salute to commemorate the restoration of Charles II and a twenty-one gun salute for the King's birthday on 5 June. Later, the Admiralty officially thanked Bligh for his efforts.

While Bligh tried to talk the men into returning to work, delegates from the Admiralty met with delegates but made no progress. The feelings of the mutineers were summarised by Henry Long of the *Champion*, who wrote to the Lords Commissioners:

> Damn my eyes if I understand your lingo or long proclamations but in short give us our due at once and no more of it, till we go in search of the rascals the enemies of our country.

Parker decided that it was time to turn the screw so the mutineers began to blockade the Thames and, as supplies were running out, turned pirate to attack merchant ships. This was too much for the Admiralty, who rushed through two new Acts of Parliament to crush the rebellion, set up barriers at the Thames estuary and order ships to fire on the mutineers. This began a widespread panic. Parker tried to open negotiations through the Captain of the *Monmouth,* the Earl of Northesk, to no effect. Fighting broke out on most ships and many of these conflicts were bloody affairs. By 13 June, most of the ships had surrendered, the *Director* being the last to do so; they hauled down the red flag and replaced it with the Union Jack as the crew gave three cheers. [9]

Other ships tried to flee. The *Leopard* reached as far as the Thames. The *Repulse* crew surrendered to their First Lieutenant and were told to sail up the Medway but were stopped by the *Monmouth* and the *Director* who, knowing only that this was a mutineers' ship, opened fire.

With peace now restored, Keith was able to write to the Admiralty with the good news.

The Mutiny which prevailed among the ships at the Nore seems to be quite extinguished. [10]

There were inevitable repercussions. Parker and some of the ringleaders were executed. Some were jailed in the Marshalsea, while some were transported to Botany Bay, where a penal colony had been instituted – one of these was a doctor called William Redfern who later acted an Assistant Surgeon in New South Wales. [11] A number of mutineers were flogged on board the several ships and others were imprisoned on the *Eagle* until the King pardoned them four months later.

Bligh was not yet back in command of his ship so on 15 June Keith went on board the *Director*, arrested ten men and sent them on shore to be guarded by Admiral Bruckner. That same day Bruckner had sent a message asking all the commanding officers to submit a list of their men, as well as an opinion on their levels of guilt. Despite his reputation, Bligh was not vindictive and felt that there had been punishment enough. He replied:

I beg leave to state to you that Lord Keith having been on board and particularized with the opinion of the officers 10 men who went on shore and are now in prison, I conceive the intent of your order is fully answered, except that part respecting good men, which I shall with much zeal particularize as soon as I can with consistency discover them and consider myself free of error in my representation. [12]

Unfortunately, Lieutenant McTaggart was temporarily in command and he obeyed Bruckner's instructions to the letter, with a complete list of the men and notes referring to their individual participation in the mutiny. As a result, when Bligh regained command, Keith wrote to him asking about the '29 men represented to have been the most violent' so that proceedings may be started against the worst of them. Bligh defended his men:

I considered from the moment you went on board in my absence, and pointed out from the opinion of the officers ten men who had been most active in the Mutiny, that the remaining persons were to expect a pardon

and when I was afterwards sent out to take command again of the Director, Adml Buckner told me of what your Lordships had done and that a pardon would be sent, but it could not be said positively what day. – In consequence, I conceived any report from me would be like a desire to counteract your Lordship's humanity in considering ten great offenders to be a sufficient example when brought to punishment. [13]

The matter did not rest. When the pardons were issued, Vice Admiral Skeffington Lutwidge wrote to Bligh telling him that he had pardons for all his ship's crew with the exception of thirty-one. These represented the twenty-nine already indicated plus two more who had been detained by the civil powers. Bligh protested so much that the matter was referred back to the Admiralty, who asked Bligh for his account of the matter. Bligh replied that the ship's company had been assured that they would receive the King's pardon and that only the ten chosen by Keith would be brought to trial. At last Lutwidge directed Bligh to muster his crew and...

...obtain from them individually a solemn promise to persevere in future in a regular and orderly discharge of their duty and obedience to their officers, and that they will not engage in future in any mutinous assemblies, nor take an oath of any kind whatever excepting such as may be administered to them by persons legally authorized to do so, acquainting them at the same time that their Lordships, having been furnished with such information as will enable them to distinguish the men most active in the mutiny and those who have been instrumental in exciting those to mutiny who might otherwise have conducted themselves in a different manner. [14]

In some ways, the men got some of their demands - but at a heavy price. Lord Howe recommended the removal of over a hundred officers most hated by the seamen and the mutiny died. It did flare up again on board the *Director* in October, when a John McHeugh was court-martialled for 'endeavouring to excite mutiny and for disobeying the lawful commands of his officers when at sea.'

Chapter Twelve. A Heart Of Oak

In 1797 the French and Dutch were formulating plans to attack the English and had already been in touch with Wolfe Tone, the Irish republican. The Dutch fleet was to rendezvous with the French at Brest then sail on to Ireland; but by the middle of August, after he had been fooled by Duncan and the winds had changed, de Winter found the plan was impractical. Wolfe Tone moaned:

The destiny of Europe might have been changed for ever . . . the great occasion is lost, and we must do as well as we can. 'Le vin est tiré, il faut le boire.' [1]

Duncan returned to Yarmouth on 1 October to refit, but he sent some of the ships back to the Texel two days later to watch the Dutch. The small fleet – the *Adamant, Beaulieu, Circe, Martin* and the cutter *Black Joke* – were commanded by Captain Henry Trollope in *HMS Russell*. When they arrived, they saw that de Winter's ships were ready to sail – sixteen ships of the line with other smaller vessels. The British shadowed the Dutch ships at a wary distance, having sent a message back to Duncan. [2]

Despite several attempts, de Winter could not shake off the enemy ships and having failed a rendezvous at the Maas, they sailed for home. By this time, Duncan was waiting. After receiving reports of the Dutch fleet, a game of cat and mouse ensued, de Winter having heard of Duncan's arrival and changing course towards the village of Scheveningen. Duncan sailed on in pursuit. He spied the Dutch ships near Camperduin.

Although the weather was poor, with wind, squalls and heavy seas, at 9 am on the morning of 11 October Duncan hoisted the signal to prepare for battle, while de Winter formed his solid defensive line. As they did so, Duncan changed his plans; he had intended for each ship to manoeuvre between two opponents but now the defensive formation and the closeness to the shore changed his mind. He ordered his ships to form a line and sail with the wind behind him, to the south-east; but then he became concerned that the Dutch would make the shore, so signalled the fleet to bear southwards and advance on the enemy. Allowing slower ships time to close up any gaps, he noticed the Dutch formation heading slowly towards the shore, so he abandoned all former signals and ordered the fleet to steer for the fleet and engage.

The poor visibility and mixed signals led to much confusion and the British fleet ended up in two groups; the Scottish Captain John Inglis gave up trying to understand the signals threw his code book on the deck and cried out:

'Up wi' the hel'lem and gang into the middle o't!' [3]

The northerly group, comprising eight ships of the line (including the flagship *Venerable*, the *Triumph,* the *Ardent* and the frigate *Circe*, aimed for the Dutch flagship *Vrijheid*, fifth in line of the defence fleet. The southern group was led by Admiral Richard Onslow on *HMS Monarch* and they concentrated on the rear of the enemy line. A few small vessels followed behind to repeat Duncan's signals. But the conditions were so poor that most could not be seen.

The sudden advance shook de Winter, and in the confusion gaps appeared in his line. The Dutch commander ordered some of the van to fall back and aid the rear, but there was no time. However, he did have a second line of well-armed frigates which were poised to fire on any ship attempting to break through the gaps. Then at 12.05, Admiral Duncan called for close engagement.

The *Monarch*, Onslow's flagship, sought to break through the Dutch line between the *Jupiter* (commanded by Rear-Admiral Hermanus Reijntjes) and the *Haarlem* but soon the ship was under fire from the entire rearguard. The *Monarch*'s Captain, Edward O'Bryen could not see how they could smash through but Onslow replied:

'The *Monarch* will make a passage.' [4]

Although injured, the *Monarch* turned back to the attack and forced its way, raking both ships before turning to lay alongside the *Jupiter*. As it did so, the Dutch frigate *Monnikkendam* and the brig *Daphné* moved from the second line to fill the gap, but the *Monarch* fired on them, damaging both vessels so that they had to fall back. In the meantime HMS *Powerful* under Captain William O'Bryen Drury, passed through the same gap, then fired on the *Haarlem* again and finished off the ailing *Monnikkendam*. Attention now turned to the next two ships, the *Alkmaar* and the *Delft*; the *Montagu* fired on the first, the *Russell* on the second while the *Monmouth* passed between the two, sending raking fire into both ships. Bligh was not idle; he steered after the *Haarlem* and engaged it at close range. Because of the confusion over signals, the *Adamant* and the *Veteran* joined the fray late.

Only one ship remained aloof and took no part in the battle – the *HMS Agincourt*. She was Captained by John Williamson, the same man who had remained in his boat and given no assistance on the day Captain Cook was killed. He had escaped court-martial and here he was at the Battle of Camperdown, as indecisive – or cowardly – as ever.

As dark rainstorm clouds loured overhead, the battle became more and more ferocious, many Captains afraid that, in the terrible visibility, they might fire on their own ships. The British fleet now had the advantage and the Dutch were overwhelmed, *Jupiter, Haarlem, Alkmaar* and *Delft* all surrendering to Onslow while what was left of the *Monnikkendam* was taken by the frigate *Beaulieu*.

In the van, the southerly group was having a tough time of it. Duncan had decided to ram a gap between the *Vrijheid* (de Winter's flagship) and *Staaten Generaal* (under Rear Admiral Samuel Story). Seeing the manoeuvre, Story closed up the gap and both ships fired hard so that Duncan was obliged to find a way behind the *Staaten Generaal*. Meanwhile the *Ardent* under Richard Rundle Burges was attacked by both the *Vrijheid* and the *Admiraal Tjerk Hiddes De Vries*. The crew 'fought like maniacs' but suffered over a hundred casualties, among them Burges himself. By this time the *Venerable* had turned and raked the *Staaten Generaal* twice and caused it major damage; as it drifted away, Duncan turned on the *Vrijheid*.

The arrival of the *Venerable* have the *Ardent* a much-needed respite, but before long both ships were isolated and at the mercy of continuous fire. The *Bedford* and the *Triumph* sailed in, attacking *Admiraal Tjerk Hiddes De Vries* and the *Hercules* respectively while Inglis sailed his *Belliqueux* in the gap between the *Beschermer* and the *Hercules*, raking both ships. By now the Dutch central division joined the fray and the British were soon outnumbered. Now the *Venerable* found herself against *Vrijheid, Staaten General, Admiral Tjerk Hiddes De Vries* and *Wassenaar* all at once, Duncan rallying his men and fighting like a demon. Things eased a little when two enemy ships, the *Beschermer* and *Hercules* were knocked out of action, the *Hercules* catching fire which brought some enemy ships out of the contest as they raced to relieve her.

Hearing that the van was in danger, Admiral Onslow ordered the fittest ships to sail to the rescue and the first to arrive were the *Powerful* and the *Director*. The tide began to turn; several Dutch ships surrendered and parts of the enemy fleet retreated. However, de Winter carried on fighting and then came face to face with Captain Bligh. Bligh lost no time – he raked the ship and fired broadsides, slicing away every mast she owned, as he wrote in his log:

At 3.5, we began the action with him, lying on his larboard quarter within 20 yds, by degrees we advanced alongside, firing tremendously at him, & then across his bows almost touching, when we carried away his foremast topmast t.g. mast & soon after his mainmast, topmast & t.g. mast, together with his mizzen mast, & left him nothing standing. The wreck lying all over his starboard side, most of his guns were of no use, I therefore hauled up along his starboard side & there we finished him, for at 3h 55 he struck and the action ended. – We believe 9 line of battle ships to have struck, the rest ran off. [5]

De Winter was not a man to give up easily. After dismasting the *Vrijheid*, Bligh sailed to within twenty yards of the flagship and asked if de Winter was ready to surrender. He replied: 'What do you think?' and tried to send signals for reinforcements. He also ordered his carpenter to fix the barge so he could sail off and rejoin the battle. Bligh now turned to Duncan and asked for his orders – which were to take the ship:

Adm[l] Duncan, who we knew had been severely engaged with the van of the enemy, had wore, and was now on the starboard tack standing from the shore abt half a mile to leeward of the Dutch Admiral. I

therefore bore up to speak to him, when he hailed me to take possession of the *Vrijheid*, the ship we had just beaten, & I sent my first Lieutenant on board in consequence. The Dutch Admiral, Mr de Winter, was taken on board of Adm^l Duncan, & as the Cap^tn could not be removed owing to a death wound, my first lieu^t sent to me the cap^tn lieu^t, who was next in command. As soon as the action ceased, my officers came to congratulate me, & to say there was not a man killed who they knew of, & of such good fortune I had no idea, for it passed belief – we had only 7 men wounded. Before we got up with the Dutch Adm^l, we had a share with the *Veteran* in making a Dutch ship strike, & we passed close to leeward of a Dutch ship of the line on fire. [6]

When Bligh's men boarded the *Vrijheid*, they conducted what was left of her crew on boats bound for the *Venerable*. It was a fearful sight – the decks were covered with bodies, mostly dead but many wounded. They found de Winter trying to help his carpenter with the barge; when they told him he was a prisoner, he replied:
'This is my destiny not foreseen.' [7]
Among the prisoners was one Captain Siccame, who told Bligh of the tide of events prior to their capture.

Captn Siccame informed us that before the *Director* came up, they had about 10 killed, 20 wounded, he could not say with certainty the number, but the slaughter was very great from us, and when he left the ship, the decks were full of wounded men, and he feared there had been 200 men killed and wounded... Lieut. McTaggart, who I sent to command the *Vryheid*, sent me word there were 58 killed and 98 wounded. [8]

De Winter was taken to see Duncan and when he met him he held out his sword as a token of surrender. Duncan shook his hand instead, saying:
'I would much rather take a brave man's hand than his sword.' [9]
Because of the poor weather, Duncan decided not to hunt down the rest of the Dutch fleet but ordered his men to secure the ships they had taken and head back to England. The British had their own casualties to look after and many men were in urgent need of medical assistance. Dr Robert Young of the *Ardent* wrote:

Melancholy cries for assistance were addressed to me from every side by wounded and dying, and piteous moans and bewailing from pain and despair. In the midst of these agonising scenes I was able to preserve myself firm and collected... Many of the worst wounded were stoical beyond belief; they were determined not to flinch and, when news of the shattering victory was brought down to them, they raised a cheer and declared they regretted not the loss of their limbs.

It was time to head for home. The Battle of Camperdown had been a savage conflict, British casualties amounting to 228 killed and 812 wounded while the Dutch suffered 540 men killed and 620 wounded. On board the *Venerable*, Duncan gathered all men for a divine service then – even at the age of sixty-six – he stayed on duty for twenty-four hours, finding time to play de Winter at an after-dinner game of whist. Duncan won, leaving de Winter to moan:

'It's hard to be beaten twice in one day by the same man.'

The return home brought its own tragedies. The gale of 12 October inflicted a lot of damage on the already injured Dutch ships and on board the *Delft* were a small crew of 69 men along with 76 wounded Dutch sailors. In command were the British Lieutenant Charles Bullen and the Dutch Lieutenant Heilberg. Despite being towed by the *Veteran* it was soon obvious that the ship would never make England, so a large board was produced and held up, on which was chalked:

THE SHIP IS SINKING

Bullen offered Heilberg a place in the first rescue boat from the *Veteran*, but he replied:

'But how can I leave these men?'

Bullen answered: 'God bless you, my brave fellow! Here is my hand; I give you my word I will stay her with you!' [10]

Twice the rescue boat transferred men, but Bullen waited with Heilberg and thirty injured men for the next. Sadly the ship foundered and Heilberg perished, although Bullen managed to swim to safety on board the *Monmouth*.

They lost two other prizes: *Monnikkendam* was ready to sink and she made her way to the Dutch coast - the British were taken to a prison boat at Flushing. Another frigate, the *Ambuscade*, also ended up on Dutch land.

News of the victory had reached Britain and Duncan was the darling of the nation. As one sailor said:

'They say they are going to make a Lord of our Admiral. They can't make too much of him. He is a heart of oak; he is a seaman every inch of him, and as to a bit of a broadside, it only makes the old cock young again.' [11]

The King wished to meet Duncan personally and tried to reach him by royal yacht on 30 October, but strong winds forced him back. Duncan was made Viscount Duncan of Camperdown and Baron Duncan of Lundie. He was also given a pension of £2000 a year as well as being made freeman of many towns. Admiral Onslow was made a baronet and Captains Henry Trollope and William George Fairfax were knighted. As part of the celebrations, the King pardoned the mutineers still imprisoned on board the *Eagle* and gold medals were minted for all Captains. All Lieutenants were promoted to Commanders. There was a public subscription was taken up for the widows and wounded and raised £52,609 10s and 10d. On 23 December the King led a thanksgiving procession as well as a ceremony in St Paul's.

It was not all congratulations. John Williamson was court-martialled for his inactivity at the battle, accused of failing to do his duty by Captain Hopper of *Agincourt*'s Royal Marines. The trial took place on 4 December 1797, at Sheerness aboard the *Circe,* on the charges of 'disobedience to signals and not going into action' and 'cowardice and disaffection'. Bligh was asked to give evidence.

'Did you make any observation on that day, on the *Agincourt*'s conduct, in making sail during the action, so far as you were in a situation to observe her?

'No; I made no observations on the *Agincourt* making sail. I don't recollect making observation of the *Agincourt* but once and that merely momentarily during the action, when the ships were engaged, and I fancied at that time the whole rear division was engaging. They seemed much crowded.'

'If the *Agincourt* had lain to a mile and a half to windward of the Fleet for half-an-hour, under her topsails, and her main topsail aback, after the Vice-Admiral had commenced the action, would you not have seen her?'

'I did not see her in that situation.' [12]

Williamson was found guilty of the first charge, resulting in his demotion and a prohibition from naval service.

The battle did encourage a new wave of patriotism and praise for the battle was found on every lip – even in song:

St Vincent drubbed the Dons, Earl Howe he drubbed Monsieur,
And gallant Duncan now has soundly drubbed Mynheer;
The Spanish, French and Dutch, tho' all united by,
'Fear not,' Britannia cries, 'My Tars can beat all three.'
Monsieurs, Mynheers and Dons, your country's empty boast,
Our tars can beat all three, each on his native coast. [13]

Bligh himself was criticised in some of the press for delays in action and some asked what he was doing during most of the battle. His log book is evidence enough and most people would agree that he served his country well and deserved his share of praise. But this is William Bligh and general praise would come seldom to a man whom the public loved to despise.

For a while Bligh rested on his laurels and turned inventor. In August 1798 he presented the Admiralty with a model 'and description & use of an instrument invented by Capn Wm Bligh to regulate naval evolutions &

for the readily taking bearings of land or ships when sudden emergency will not allow of time to use a compass for that purpose'.

It is a hollow wood tube two feet long and an inch core fixed on a semicircle moving at its centre at a pedestal scored to receive it, & has a circular plate at the base with two diameters to mark the position it is required to have the instrument in. The whole stands on a stool of convenient height, the top of which is divided on the periphery of a great circle into 32 divisions, called points, which are equal to those of the compass and for convenience are counted up to eight each way, being the quarter of the circle. [14]

During 1799, Bligh continued to serve in the North Sea under Duncan and his second-in-command, Vice Admiral Dickson. At times he saw action – once he chased American and Danish vessels from the Texel and had them detained at Yarmouth for searching. These flashes of excitement were relatively few as the latest action had somewhat chastened their Dutch foes. On another occasion Bligh was involved in a mission of mercy; as the Anglo-Russian invasion of Holland had got under way, Lady Rodney and her two daughters were detained at the Helder. Admiral Storey had arranged for them to be transported out of the country on a galliot, which was flying a flag of truce when confronted by Bligh and three other ships under his command. Bligh took the ladies on board and then sent a message to the Admiral, who arranged a passage to England for them on board the sloop *Ranger*.

Sometimes there were problems of insubordination. Bligh had some trouble with one member of his crew, the Master Joseph Ramsay, who argued with Bligh then remarked:

'If I am not able to work the ship, it is better to have some person else here.'

After the court-martial of 25 June, Ramsay was found guilty and dismissed.

Bligh also logged the punishment of a marine, John Keller, who was 'flogged round the squadron' for sleeping on duty and for striking a corporal. He managed to endure 150 lashes.

In September 1799, Bligh was sent to sea with sealed orders which he opened two days later. He was instructed to proceed to the remote island of Saint Helena and to escort a convoy of East India Company vessels home to England. Saint Helena was a common stop for traders on their way back from voyages to India or China; most of the population were slaves but the acquisition of slaves had been made illegal seven years previously. It would be more than a decade before coolie labourers began to arrive from China to boost the workforce.

The passage to Saint Helena was not an easy one; the ship met with storms and gales which delayed them considerably. On 1 November they crossed the Line, Bligh giving permission 'for Neptune to frolick'. He even allowed the ducking part and every person was 'in high glee'. The *Director* anchored in St James' Road on 28 November, thirteen days later than the date stipulated by the Admiralty. Bligh was expecting to meet the Captains of the *Belvedere*, the *Great Wycombe*, the *Thetis*, the *Worcester*, the *Walpole*, the *Seringapatam Extra Ship*, the *Marquis Cornwallis* and a couple of whalers, but this was not to be. On 15 November the Governor, Brooke, had decided he could detain them no longer and they had sailed off. This was the very day that Bligh was expected and he was both mortified at his failure and surprised at the speed with which the fleet was dispatched. [15]

Bligh was not well and his stormy passage had not helped. To make things worse, there were no lodgings for anyone in the town, but Brooke offered Bligh a room in his own house. Here he slowly gathered his health; every night the company sat by a large open fire and retired at 9.30 pm, to rise for breakfast at eight. Here they swapped stories and news, the most exciting being the death of Sultan Tippoo, the most implacable enemy of the East India Company. The 'Tiger of Mysore' had been besieged in his capital Srirangapatna and refused to fly, stating:

'One day of life as a Tiger is far better than thousand years of living as a Sheep.'

Feeling a little better, Bligh's mind turned to his beloved wife and he made shopping expeditions, buying a shawl and various silks and cloths. He was also on the lookout for tropical plants – the Admiralty had decided to make use of his expertise and ordered him to bring home plants for the King's Gardens at Kew. He found little of value, but did take some bulbs and seeds, fearing that 'Sir Joseph' would be very disappointed otherwise. Apart from his personal feelings at visiting this lonely place, the trip could be considered as an unmitigated disaster.

The voyage home, after this fruitless expedition, was a stormy one and at one point a leak caused water to pouring at the rate of eight inches per hour. Nevertheless he made it home and moored at the Downs on 23 January 1800. Soon after wrote to Betsy telling her that he would 'be in constant flutter & expectation' till he heard from her. Towards end of year, he worked on *A Map for the Purpose of Exhibiting the Track of* HMS Director *in a Voyage to St Helena and Return to England, by Capt. Wm Bligh.*

By September, Bligh's surveying talents were in demand again. Lord Castlereagh had wanted a survey of Dublin Harbour and Bligh was the best man to send. This took him the rest of the year, but while he was busy it was thought a good idea if Bligh could also survey Holyhead Harbour on his return. The idea was to build a deep water harbour where boats could be ready to leave at any time. Meanwhile the Board of Navigation at

Dublin had made it clear that Bligh's map should be published, so he wrote to Nepean from Durham Place:

The Board of Navigation on Dublin, having particularly requested by letter that I would publish my survey of Dublin Bay, stating it as their opinion 'it would be of infinite importance to their navigation, it being a work so correct and of such authority' – I have to request you will do me the honour to represent the same to my Lords Commissioners of the Admiralty and that I hope their Lordships will permit me to do so, as thereby I will come more correctly before the publick, than by being published in Dublin, and be of some advantage to myself.

It was eventually published in 1803.

By 13 March Bligh had been transferred from the *Director* to the *Glatton*, after which he performed his survey at Holyhead. His main problem was getting any payment for his work, so in the end - on 12 May 1800 - he wrote to the Admiralty:

I beg leave to request of you to represent to the Lords Commissioners of the Admiralty that having, in compliance of their letter of 14th January last, surveyed the Harbour of Holyhead and presented a plan and memoir of its present state, and improvements it is capable of receiving, I hope their Lordships will be pleased to allow me such compensation as they may deem proper, having been employed four days in completing the work, and not having received any payment from the Irish Government. [16]

Chapter Thirteen. Blind Eye

Bligh had already seen action under the national hero, Admiral Duncan and acquitted himself with honour; now he was about to fight under one of the greatest of all English naval heroes – Admiral Horatio Nelson. In 1801, Nelson was not in favour due to his scandalous relationship with Emma Hamilton while Admiral Hyde Parker had just married a girl of eighteen, he being sixty-one at the time. Parker was in no great hurry to leave port at that moment. [1]

While the French Revolutionary Wars were in full swing, Britain retained superiority over the waves and would prevent other nations from trading with France. This was not to the liking of the Russian Tsar Paul, who formed a League of Armed Neutrality with Denmark, Sweden, Prussia, and Russia - their function was to revive trading with France by means of force. Not only did this threaten the British blockade, it also put their Scandinavian timber supply at risk. The Admiralty ordered Hyde Parker to take on the Danish and smash the League through diplomacy or by battle. Nelson was in favour of sailing for Russia and dealing with the problem at the source whereas Parker was content to take on the extra ships and continue the blockade. Now their minds were made up for them.

The fleet set sail, Nelson on board his 98-gun *St George*, Bligh on the *Glatton*. On 19 March 1781 they heard that the Danes had rejected their ultimatum, so the only prospect was war. On 30th, the ships passed the narrow between Sweden and Denmark, the Swedish batteries not firing. Parker's delay, due to indecision and possibly his young wife, meant that the Danes had had plenty of time to arrange their defences. Off the coast of Amager Island, the fleet was intermingled with old ship hulks and the line stretched between the island of Amager to the Tre Kroner – a fort with 68 guns. To make things harder for the British, a large shoal, the middle ground, hampered ships trying to enter the harbour. On the night of 31st, Thomas Hardy, Captain, was busy sounding the channel.

The shallow sea was a problem and Parker gave Nelson the twelve ships of the line with the shallowest draughts, which is why Nelson transferred from the *St George* to the *Elephant*. Finding the defences strong – land batteries were more reliable than floating cannon – they formed their plan. The ships would form a line parallel to the enemy's; the foremost would anchor alongside the first ship and engage. The next would pass them and anchor at the next; and so on. The frigate *Desirée*, along with smaller gun-ships, would rake the southern end of the Danish line while the *Amazon* would do the same at the northern end. Should the southern enemy line be breached, their bomb vessels could approach within range of the city. Bligh tells of the beginning of the battle:

At 7 am, signal for all Captains. At 7.45, signal prepare for battle and anchor by the stern, with springs on the cables. At 9.45 prepare to weigh. At same time *Edgar*, *Ardent* and *Glatton* to weigh, and the other ships in succession. After engaging from the south end of the enemy's line, we anchored precisely in our station abreast of the Danish Commodore. At 10.26 the action began. At noon, the action continuing very hot, ourselves much cut up. Our opponent, the Danish Commodore, struck to us, but his seconds ahead and astern still keep up a strong fire. At 11.24, our fore top-mast was shot away, seven of our upper deck guns disabled by the enemy. The *Bellona* and *Russell* got aground and could not take their stations. The *Agamemnon* could not weather the middle, so our line did not extend so far to the north as it was intended by three ships. Lord Nelson our second ahead. [2]

While the ships consecutively weighed alongside their opposite numbers, there was no manoeuvring and the two simply slogged it out with broadsides until one of them was defeated. The British had not counted on the low-lying floating batteries and the Danes fought with determination. Their ships might have been old, but they more than made up for that with their gun strength. *Prøvesteenen* would have destroyed the *Isis*, but the *Desirée* raked it with the aid of the *HMS Polyphemus*. *Holsteen* and *Sjælland* both opened fire on the *Monarch,* which was badly damaged.

Both fleets were enveloped in a huge cloud of gunsmoke so that Parker could not see what was going on. He did see that three ships had run aground and were flying signals of distress but did not have any way of judging how the battle was proceeding. He told his flag Captain:

'I will make the signal of recall for Nelson's sake. If he is in condition to continue the action, he will disregard it; if he is not, it will be an excuse for his retreat and no blame can be imputed to him.' [3]

While Parker could see little of the action, Nelson saw Parker's signal and it irritated him. Then he turned to his own flag Captain, Thomas Foley and made his famous speech:

'You know, Foley, I only have one eye — I have the right to be blind sometimes,' and then, holding his telescope to his blind eye, said 'I really do not see the signal!' Or perhaps he said: 'Damn the signal! Keep mine for closer battle flying! That's the way I answer such signals. Nail mine to the mast!' [4]

Whatever he said, his flag remained unchanged.

Bligh also saw Parker's signal and looked to the *Elephant*. Seeing that Nelson was still flying his 'close action' flags, he also ignored Parker's order and continued with the battle. The rest of the fleet followed Bligh's signal, except for Riou, who saw Parker's and withdrew from his bombardment on the Tre Kroner fortress. Unluckily for him; as he retreated heavy fire killed him.

The guns kept firing and smoke still rose to the skies but by early afternoon the British guns had won the day. The bomb ships moved through the southern line and now threatened the city. The Danish were in disarray; *Nyborg* tried to leave the line with *Aggershuus* in tow, but both sank. Commodore Olfert Fischer moved from *Dannebrog* at 11:30 am, when it caught fire, to *Holsteen*. When *Indfødsretten,* the ship to the north of the Commodore, struck her colours, the *Holsteen* moved on to the Ter Kroner to fight the ships there. By now Fischer was fighting a lost cause. Some ships began firing after they had surrendered, which forced Nelson to write a note to Crown Prince Frederick:

To the Brothers of Englishmen, the Danes. Lord Nelson has directions to spare Denmark when she is no longer resisting, but if firing is

continued on the part of Denmark, Lord Nelson will be obliged to set on fire the floating batteries he has taken, without having the power of saving the brave Danes who have defended them. Nelson. [5]

Prince Frederick sent his Adjutant General, Hans Lindholm (a Danish member of parliament), asking for the reason for Nelson's letter:

If your guns are not better pointed than your pens, then you will make little impression on Copenhagen. [6]

In reply, Nelson wrote a note:

Lord Nelson's object in sending the Flag of Truce was humanity; he therefore consents that hostilities shall cease, and that the wounded Danes may be taken on shore. And Lord Nelson will take his prisoners out of the Vessels, and burn and carry off his prizes as he shall see fit.

Lord Nelson, with humble duty to His Royal Highness the Prince of Denmark, will consider this the greatest victory he has ever gained, if it may be the cause of a happy reconciliation and union between his own most gracious Sovereign, and His Majesty the King of Denmark. [7]

A twenty-four hour cease-fire was agreed. Soon after, the Danish flagship *Dannebrog* exploded, killing 250 men. Lord Nelson requested that Bligh visit him on board the *Elephant* and personally thanked him for his support. The last word on the battle may be left with him:

PM The action continuing very hot. At 2.45, it may be said to have ended. Lord Nelson in the *Elephant,* our second ahead, did me the honour to hail me to come aboard, and thank ,me for the conduct of the *Glatton.* All the ships to the southward of the Crown Battery struck their colours; some of the floating batteries were sunk and some burnt. We destroyed the Danish commander's ship, the *Danebrog,* by setting fire to him with our carcasses... About three, we slipped our sheet cable and sailed out ... into the Road, where the Commander-in-Chief, Sir Hyde Parker, was with his squadron. Anchored at 4 ... Saw the Danish Commodore blown up. Our loss 17 killed, 34 wounded. Mast very dangerously wounded. Rigging and sails shot to pieces. Seven upper deck guns and two lower disabled by the enemy's shot. Received 52 Danish prisoners from the *Daneborg.* [8]

Both fleets had almost been reduced to floating wrecks. Danish casualties were in the region of 1800, while British figures were 953, of whom 264 were killed. Only the *Holstein* was considered seaworthy enough to be taken back to England. Bligh described the *Glatton* as the 'most cut up of any ship'.

'Our lower masts must be double fished and mast heads secured by reefing the top masts. If there had been a fresh breeze we must have been a mere wreck.'

The next day, Nelson secured an agreement with the Prince and by the 8th Nelson returned with his Agreement. Bligh asked him for a recommendation to Admiral the Earl of St Vincent; Nelson wrote:

Captain Bligh (of the *Glatton*, who had directed the *Director* at Camperdown) has desired my testimony to his good conduct, which, although perfectly unnecessary, I cannot refuse; his behaviour on this occasion can reap no additional credit from my testimony. He was my second, and the moment the action ceased, I sent for him on board the *Elephant*, to thank him for his support. [9]

On 12 April 1801, before returning to England, Bligh was made Captain of *HMS Monarch*, whose Captain had been killed. On 8 May he was promoted to the *HMS Irresistible*, a 74-gun ship which had been Nelson's flagship at the Battle of St Vincent. On 21 May he was given another honour – he was elected to a Fellowship by the Royal Society 'in consideration of his distinguished services in navigation, botany, etc.' This was due partly to his own merit but he also had a friend in high places – Joseph Banks was the Society's President.

Little happened during his tenure with the *Irresistible*, although he once sentenced a man to 'Running the Gauntlet twice round for Stealing £25.'

On 25 March 1802 the Peace of Amiens was signed and this brought a temporary end to the war between France and Britain. On 22 April, by order of Lord Cornwallis, Bligh mustered his men and gave them thanks for their meritorious conduct during the war. On 28 May he was retired on half pay. There was something to celebrate - his daughter Harriet Maria married Henry Aston Barker of Bitton, Gloucester during that year. She had been introduced to him through the Taubmans, family friends in the Isle of Man, and one of their children had also married a Barker. Barker was an artist of some merit and also a shrewd man of business, designing the celebrated Panormama in Leicester Square. In 1799 he had met Lord Nelson and Lady Hamilton, which must have given Barker and his future father-in-law something to chat about.

1803 came and went and by 9 March Bligh was writing to the Admiralty offering his services 'to command any of His Majesty's ships'. There was some work for him to do – between September and October he was given the cutter *Swallow* to survey the harbour of Dungeness; in November he examined and reported on the coast of Flushing; and for the rest of the year he surveyed the port of Fowey. This was because France had fallen out with England again and the Admiralty wished to know if their ships should be used there in a defensive role. The survey was to be top secret.

The next year brought another Captaincy, this time of the *Warrior*, a 74-gunner and one of the finest ships in the Royal Navy. It was also during his time with the ship that he was brought to be tried at another court-martial. It was brought about by the Warrior's Lieutenant John Frazier.

On 18 October 1804, Frazier had fallen between some casks in the Warrior's launch and subsequently hurt his leg. Frazier, known as a malcontent who harboured a grudge, asked Admiral Collingwood to 'survey' his lameness with the hopes of leave from duty. This was to be performed on reaching port and as the surgeon could now give him no attention, he was taken off the sick list. Frazier sulked and was put on watch duty, but Bligh allowed him a chair so that he could sit and rest his leg. One day Frazier was telling off a steward for playing cards on deck in such a loud tone that Bligh came to investigate. This turned into an argument and Bligh fell into one of his rages, using strong language and accusing Frazier of neglect of duty. The row became so heated that Bligh eventually placed him under arrest and had him court-martialled for 'contumacy and disobedience of his Captain.'

The case was admittedly a weak one and Frazier was acquitted, but that was not enough for him. Instead, he called for a court-martial for Bligh, accusing him of 'insulting, bullying and tyrannising his crew.' Lord Cornwallis did not relish trying a man of Bligh's calibre and seemed to consider it a piece of nonsense. However, proceedings began on 25 February 1805 on board the *San Josef*, off Torbay.

Of course, 'that *Bounty* bastard' had a reputation and it was all too easy for the accuser to drag up the same old accusations, some of which did carry weight and which could be put down to Bligh's bane, his hot temper. Frazier accused Bligh of insulting terms, but this was the early nineteenth century when a ship's Captain was almost expected to use ripe language at times. If not, the entire Navy fleet commanders would be on trial. He was accused of calling midshipman Knowles and Frazier 'a parcel of villains and scoundrels'; he once shook his fist in Frazier's face, he called him a 'rascal', a 'damnation or a damn'd impertinent fellow' and that he once called the gunner 'a damn'd long pelt of a bitch'. Frazier put much stress on the way the boatswain had been treated, but when Samuel Jewell gave evidence, he said he 'put no interpretation' on such abuse:

'Captain Bligh was hot and hasty, but I believe the words were no sooner escaped him than his passion ended.'

He also said he would rather serve under Bligh than any other Captain, which dulled the edge of Frazier's attacks.

There were two counts of cruelty – one on Frazier, when Bligh forced him to keep watch with a sore leg, but he was allowed to sit and rest

during this duty. Second, he forced his carpenter to work while ill, but
Bligh had consulted with his surgeon over whether work would prejudice
his health and he only gave him a supervisory task to do.

Bligh summed up his defence with some candour:

I candidly and without reserve avow that I am not a tame &indifferent
observer of the manner in which Officers placed under my orders
conducted themselves in the performance of their several duties; a signal
or any communication from a commanding officer have ever been to me
an indication for exertion & alacrity to carry into effect the purport
thereof, & peradventure I may occasionally have appeared to some of
those officers as unnecessarily anxious for its execution by exhibiting
any action or gesture peculiar to myself to such: Gentlemen, I do not
now appeal to you, Mr president & the members of this honourable
Court, who know & have experienced the arduous task of responsibility
and that of the magnitude of one of His Majesty's seventy-four gun-
ships, which will, I am persuaded, acquit me of any apparent
impetuosity & would plead in extenuation for my imputed charges:
attributing the warmth of temper, which I may at intervals have
discovered, to my zeal for that service in which I have been employed
without an imaginary blemish on my character for upwards of 35 years
and not with a premeditated view of any personal insult to my
Prosecutor or reducing the rank which he holds in it concerning an
incumbent duty in out relative situations to render that rank mutual
support which its dignity indispensably requires, as without such
impressions, discipline could not ensure obedience in ships of war.[10]

It was a good defence, although his abusive language could not be
doubted and so the case was in part proven and Bligh was admonished to
be in future 'more correct in his language.' To show that the Admiralty
dismissed the matter without a thought, he was returned in command of
the *Warrior*. [11]

Within a fortnight Bligh received a letter from his old friend which was
like a bolt of lightning. He had been talking to his influential friends about
the colony of New South Wales; it was in everyone's minds in government
circles as the Governor King has resigned and wanted to return home.
They were looking for a man 'who has integrity unimpeached, a mind
capable of providing its own resources in difficulties without leaning on
others for advice, firm in discipline, civil in deportment and not subject to
whimper and whine when severity of discipline is wanted to meet
emergencies.' Luckily, Banks knew just the man.

I can, therefore, if you chuse it, place you in the government of the new
colony, with an income of £2,000 a year, and with the whole of the

Government power and stores at your disposal, so that I do not see how it is possible for you to spend £1,000; in truth King, who is now there, receives only £1,000 with some deductions, and yet lives like a prince, and, I believe, saves some money; but I could not undertake to recommend any one unless £2,000 clear was given, as I think that a man who undertakes so great a trust as the management of an important colony should be certain of living well and laying up a provision for his family. [12]

Bligh must have thought he was dreaming. A major problem was the fact that Betsy was no traveller and could not undertake such a long journey on board ship. However, his daughter and son-in-law would be prepared to ravel with him if he could manage to wangle him a plum job in the colony. He also feared that he would be throwing away all of his service in the Navy and prevent further promotion – as well as his half pay. It was therefore decided that he would take command of the ships of New South Wales on full pay and that his son-in-law would accompany him as his Lieutenant. This was better than he expected and so he decided he would accept the offer. As he was preparing to leave, he heard news of the victory at Trafalgar and the death of Nelson. 'Alas, poor Lord Nelson is gone!' he wrote to Banks.

Soon Bligh was ready to leave and he must have congratulated himself on negotiating such a good deal for himself. He does not seem to have considered why he was given double the usual pay with so many benefits. In fact, as he would soon find out, he was entering the snake pit.

The voyage to New South Wales was not without incident. Bligh was on the *Lady Madeleine Sinclair* with his daughter and they were accompanied by three convict ships. Mary's husband was ordered to serve on board the *Porpoise*, the convoy ship, and as they were newly married she was bitter about it. John Short, the Captain of the *Porpoise*, was of the opinion that he was in charge of the expedition, but Bligh was the senior officer and flew his broad Commodore's pennant. Trouble began when Bligh asked for Putnam to be transferred to his ship and Short stated that if the request were put in writing, he might consider it. This resulted in Bligh boarding the *Porpoise* and a bitter argument with Short, whose temper matched his name. Later, Bligh ordered the *Lady Madeleine Sinclair* to alter course and Short ordered Putnam to fire across her bows and, if she did not obey, fire upon the ship itself. Mary was indignant, stating that:

'Such an inhuman thing as making a man fire at his father and his wife was never done before.' [13]

Later, Short was court-martialled but acquitted. [14]

It had been an undignified and unduly ugly squabble – but at least it gave Bligh a taste of things to come.

Chapter Fourteen. A Question Of Rum

To understand the problems Bligh was about to face, we must look at the whole problem of New South Wales at that time and some of its history.

The penal colony at Botany Bay was planned by Lord Sandwich and Sir Joseph Banks, to facilitate attacks on Spanish interests in Chile and Peru. In 1786 Arthur Philip was appointed Captain General and Governor-in-chief of the colony and a subsidiary colony to be founded on Norfolk Island. Philip was given the *Sirius* and set sail 13 May 1787 with eleven ships, some marines and other officers as well as 772 convicts (mostly from London slums) of whom 40 died. Among the officers was Captain John Hunter - who had cut his naval teeth under Admiral Durell and had been involved strongly in the battles for American Independence – and he was to succeed Philip if he were absent or died. The second Lieutenant on the *Sirius* was Philip Gidley King.

Philip had not been allowed persons with experience in building, framing or agriculture. Lord Sydney planned for a civil administration, complete with its own courts of law. Hunter led an expedition to explore the Parramatta River while in February 1788 King and some officer took convicts to set up the colony on Norfolk Island. They cleared land, planted crops, built huts and prevented a prisoner mutiny. King had a relationship with a convict, Ann Inett, with whom he had two boys, Norfolk and Sydney. Life was hard for convicts and the womwn were treated no better than prostitutes.

Philip had plans for the new colony; he was determined that it would be a free territory, with no slavery. He ingratiated himself with Eora aborigines, and ordered that anyone killing one of them would be hanged – he even struck up a friendship with the chieftain Woollarawarre Bennelong. A misunderstanding on Manly beach resulted in a native spearing Philip in the shoulder but he ordered no retaliation. The natives soon learned that as well as colonists, European diseases such as smallpox had also arrived. There was discontent too - officers wanted grants of land which Philip was not empowered to grant. There was food scarcity and an outbreak of scurvy, so Philip sent Hunter to Cape Town for supplies and instituted strict rationing. Flogging and hanging were common at that time and Philip bemoaned conditions there.

The living conditions need to improve or my men won't work as hard, so I have come to a conclusion that I must hire surgeons to fix the convicts.

Hunter, commanding the *Sirius,* was sent to Norfolk Island with a number of convicts, but the ship foundered in a storm (May 1790). Some returned on the brig *Supply*, but Hunter and others waited almost a year before returning to England on the *Waakzaamheid*. He was court-martialled on Apr 1792 for the ship's loss but was honourably acquitted. King also returned to England with his two boys, who were educated there and joined the Navy. He married Anna Josepha Coombe (his first cousin) on 1 Mar 1791 and had one boy and four girls.

By 1790 stabilisation at last arrived; there was a population of about 2000, all adequately housed. Food was being grown and Philip assigned land to a convict, James Ruse, at Rose Hill (now Parramatta); he succeeded and was given the first land grant. June 1790, more sick prisoners arrived, but when 2000 more arrived in July 1791, food ran short again and a ship needed to go to Calcutta for supplies.

Someone else also arrived that year. Born in Plymouth, John Macarthur joined Fish's Corps as an ensign bound for the American War, but war ended and it was disbanded in 1783. Living at a Devon farm on half pay, he read about rural occupations and had dreams of becoming an agricultural tycoon. He later secured an ensign commission in the 68th Foot, but negotiated with the War Office for a post in the New South Wales Corps. Sailing on the *Neptune*, he fell out with officers especially the Master, Captain Gilbert, with whom he fought a duel. He was transferred in the high sea to the *Scarborough* and finally ended up at his destination; he would be appointed commandant at Parramatta. [1]

Relations with the natives soured when Philip's gamekeeper, John McIntyre, was fatally injured by an Aborigine. William Dawes and Watkin Tench were disgusted by Philip's plans for a punitive raid, to kill and behead six. It was ordered for 14 Dec 1790.

King returned to Norfolk Island but was horrified by the actions of Major Robert Ross' strict regime; he listened to the men and improved conditions on prices and wages and encouraged settlers. By 1792 John Macarthur and others began sheep-rearing for wool. A sly, aggressive and selfish man, Macarthur was always on the lookout to advance himself – and his fortunes. His plan was to expand his territory and to ingratiate himself with the most important of the settlers. He had little to do with Philip – the Governor's health failed and late in the year he set sail for England with his friend Bennelong and another Aborigine, Yemmerrawanyea.

It was almost two years until another Governor stepped into Philip's shoes; Hunter had been accepted for the post but he was still serving at sea and was involved in the Glorious First of June, 1794. Meanwhile the military had taken control of Australia and set an example which caused the original rot of the colony. The Lieutenant-Governor was Francis Grose and he cared little about what his men got up to, so before long the prisoners were exploited, the officers controlled the lands and a great trade in alcohol had sprung up. There was no recourse to the courts, which were controlled by the army and were thus biased. Through these, Macarthur ruthlessly protected his commercial interests.

Macarthur certainly had the will and drive to get on. In February 1793, Grose granted him 100 acres of land at Rose Hill near Parramatta and in April 1794 he was awarded another 100 'for being the first man to clear and cultivate 50 acres of land.' He named the property Elizabeth Farm in honour of his wife, Elizabeth Macarthur. Eventually Grose appointed him as Paymaster for the regiment and as Superintendent of public works. Macarthur's star was beginning to rise. At Elizabeth farm he experimented by cross-breeding Bengal and Irish sheep.

By crossing the two breeds, I had the satisfaction to see the lambs of the Indian ewes bear a mingled fleece of hair and wool-this circumstance originated the idea of producing fine wool in New South Wales.' [2]

The military did not appreciate King's return to Norfolk Island and they conspired to be rid of him by accusing him of severity to officers and leniency to prisoners. King sent twenty to Sydney for court-martial, but was reprimanded by Grose instead, who put the military in command of all civilians. King returned to England, complaining of gout.

When Hunter arrived in 1795 the military – and Macarthur – already had a stranglehold on the colony. He tried to overturn the damage done by the military but they were too strong for him. When he sent two ships for supplies to the Cape, Macarthur asked the commanders Captain Waterhouse and Lieutenant Kent to look out for good sheep breeds and they managed to buy some fine merinos for him. [3] His sheep-breeding experiments went on and on. So did his campaign to oust Hunter and then officers wrote anonymous letters as part of a smear campaign, accusing Hunter of ineffective rule and that he trafficked in rum. Hunter was recalled and left in September, handing Governorship to Lieutenant-Governor Philip Gidley King. Unable to vindicate his character, he published *Remarks on the Causes of the Colonial Expense of the Establishment of New South Wales. Hints for the Reduction of Such Expense and for Reforming the Prevailing Abuses.*

On 28 September 1800 King became Governor and he did much for the colony. He formulated building plans, regulated prices and wages and increased the Government stock of livestock. During his tenure, whaling and sealing became important industries for oil production and education became a prime target for improvement, establishing workshops for convict children to learn trades. The first book, *New South Wales Standing Orders*, was printed as well as the first magazine, *The Sydney Gazette*. He did much to foster a good relationship with the natives, encouraged smallpox vaccinations and promoted explorations. As for the prisons, he began a programme of rehabilitation and gave appointments to deserving ex-convicts. He was careful in his business transactions, although he did benefit from cattle sales and land grants. He began to overhaul administration and appointed Major Joseph Foveaux as Lieutenant-Governor of Norfolk Island.

Inevitably he came to grief after a clash with the New South Wales Corps – and Macarthur and his cronies. When Macarthur and Captain Abbott had 'investigated a theft', they were assaulted by Lieutenant James Marshall of the Earl Cornwallis and given twelve months' imprisonment. Marshall had refused to consent to an officer of the New South Wales Corps from presiding, so King overturned the sentence and referred the case for trial in England. Macarthur began a boycott on King and when Colonel Patterson refused to be a party to his demands, Macarthur tried to blackmail him, leading to a duel at which Patterson was wounded. King arrested Macarthur then appointed him as Norfolk Island commandant, but Macarthur refused and demanded to be tried by his peers. King reacted by ordering his trial to take place in England, sending a weighty bundle of documents as evidence. This conveniently disappeared on the voyage on board the *Hunter*.

Macarthur made the most of his trip. In Indonesia, he befriended Robert Farquhar, son of the Physician in Ordinary to the Prince of Wales, who became his patron. He also brought some merino wool and the Committee of Manufacturers rated them as finer than any Spanish wool. He even purchased rams and ewes from the royal flock at Kew. Pushing his New South Wales interests, he found support in Lord Camden, the Colonial Secretary and persuaded him to allow him a grant of 10000 acres from anywhere in New South Wales. Joseph Banks saw through him immediately and managed to have the grant halved. [4]

As to the trial, King was given a ticking-off and told to manage the affair at home, so Macarthur was ordered to accept the commandant job. He refused, resigned his commission and afraid of repercussions in New South Wales, he waited until 1805 before returning home. By this time King had had enough of the disobedience and failed attempts to control the military stranglehold on illicit liquor trading. In 1806 he resigned. Knowing they needed a firm disciplinarian to tackle the situation, Banks looked to Bligh and hence his offer.

This was how things stood when Bligh decided to take the position and sailed off to New South Wales. While he was a conscientious man who took his duties seriously, it is doubtful whether he can have been fully cognoscent of the whole situation before him. Doubtless, Banks filled him in on many things; but the New South Wales Corps were still the military presence and Macarthur was now back to pull strings from backstage. However much he knew, Bligh was committed to his task and with him came his beloved daughter Mary and her husband, John Putnam, now Bligh's aide-de-camp. He also had his first written orders:

And whereas it hath been represented to us, that great evils have arisen from the unrestrained importation of spirits into our said settlement, from vessels touching there, whereby both the settlers and convicts have been induced to barter and exchange their live stock and other necessary articles for the said spirits, to their particular loss and detriment, as well as to that of our said settlement at large; we do therefore strictly enjoin you, on pain of our utmost displeasure, to order and direct, that no spirits shall be landed from any vessels coming to our said settlement, without your consent, or that of our Governor-in-chief for the time being, previously obtained for that purpose; which orders and directions you are to signify to all Captains or masters of ships immediately on their arrival at our said settlement; and you are at the same time to take the most effectual measures, that the said orders and directions shall be strictly obeyed and complied with. [5]

Almost immediately Bligh crossed swords with Macarthur, who was eager to promote his agricultural interests. Bligh had heard of this man and of his methods of manipulation as well as his involvement in the trading cartel. Banks had also told him about Lord Camden's grant. According to Macarthur, the conversation went:
'What have I to do with your sheep, sir? What have I to do with your cattle? Are you to have such flocks of sheep and such herds of cattle as no man ever heard of before? No, sir, I have heard of your concerns, sir, you have got 5,000 acres of land, sir, in the finest situation in the country, but by God you shan't keep it.'
When Macarthur reminded him that the grant hand been recommended by the Privy Council and ordered by the Secretary of State, Bligh boomed:
'Damn the Privy Council, and damn the Secretary of State, too! He commands at home, *I* command here!' [6]
While Bligh denied the words, they have a ring of truth about them. He had been given his position based on his performance as a ship commander. He had been told that his forthrightness and forcefulness were the qualities needed as Governor. Very well – that is exactly what Bligh gave them. He was under orders from the Government and under their jurisdiction – but Australia was his ship and he was Captain of it. As such, his word was law. He had been given *carte blanche* to rectify matters in New South Wales and whereas the Secretary of State ruled in England, Bligh ruled in the colony. His transition was seamless and he carried with him the same strengths and failings he had when he was a Captain. Those

who opposed him felt his wrath and heard his streams of abuse; those in need would be succoured. In the *Bounty*, he felt secure as the commander only to find that he would be prey to a mutiny. His lesson should have been learned; mutinies can occur anywhere and not only on board a ship.

Despite his troublesome temper and bombastic ways, Bligh took his new job seriously and in no time proved that he had many other things on his agenda than the agricultural and military heavyweights who wanted to feather their nests. His daily timetable shows this much. He would rise early each morning and ride out to survey the public works; then, after breakfast he put time aside for interviews and to his credit he would give little preference for status but would listen to anyone, rich or needy. The rest of the day would be spent dealing with official business. He also had a good information network, thanks to which he discovered a plot by Irish convicts to ambush the military, seize the town and kill the Governor as well as the leading inhabitants. He crushed the rebellion ruthlessly.

Bligh's main concern as Governor of New South Wales was the welfare of the settlers. They had a hard life and it was a difficult chore, pulling down stretches of forest to clear land for cultivation and those who managed to claim a stake on some land faced many hardships, not least those brought by the weather. Most of the alluvial lands on the banks of the Nepean and the Grose rivers were now farming land, but heavy rains caused water to gather on the Blue Mountains, which rushed down through the gorges to flood the river – sometimes by as much as seventy feet. Two floods, in March and August 1806, caused a disaster as most grain was cultivated here; meal and flour were sold in Sydney for more than 2s 6d a pound.

Bligh did what he could. He made a tour of inspection of the agricultural districts, meeting the people. This was not just a diplomatic gesture; he took stock of the situation to see where the Government could help. He decided that the crops should be purchased at a fixed price at the next harvest and settled on a very generous 15s per bushel. He slaughtered some of the King's herd and distributed the meat among the settlers. What's more, he agreed to sell whatever they wanted from the King's stores at prices dramatically lower than those of the dealers. This was not popular among the racketeers – nor the John Macarthur Gang. It was popular among the poor folk and one old-timer commented:

'Them were the days for the poor settler: he only had to tell the Governor what he wanted, and he was sure to get it from the stores; whatever it was, sir, from a needle to an anchor, from a penn'orth of packthread to a ship's cable'. [7]

Bligh was so popular that many of the settlers named their boys after him. Lord Castlereagh acknowledged his work, but also rather unfairly blamed the settlers themselves for not taking any necessary measures to guard against flooding. The Under Secretary of State wrote:

I am to express Lord Castlereagh's approbation of the measures taken by you to relieve the colony from the late calamities, occasioned by the imprudence of the colonists in not taking precautions against possible inundation. [8]

Some of the more unscrupulous still tried to make mileage out of the disasters. It was common practice for a buyer to send a promissory note to order corn at the harvest; before the flooding grain cost 7s 6d per bushel. Afterwards, because of scarcity, the price rose to up to £1 10s. Macarthur had a promissory note to buy corn from Andrew Thompson and insisted on paying the original value of the corn. Arguing that Thompson had not been affected by the flood, Macarthur took it to the Court of Appeal, where Bligh decided against him. From that moment, Macarthur became a mortal enemy of Bligh's – and he was an enemy who bore a grudge. If he was ever called to Government House, Macarthur would plead 'indisposition'.

Things worsened when Macarthur applied for something from the stores, which Bligh refused. Macarthur stormed out his threat:

'Governor Bligh is giving the Government property to the settlers, a set of rascals who would deceive him; it would be better if he gave it to me and some of the other respectable gentlemen of the colony; if he does not, he will perhaps get another voyage in his launch again.'

This comment was noted by Charles Walker, a sailor who had commanded one of Macarthur's ships. He would later repeat it in a court.

Despite Bligh's activities, rum was still the major currency of the time. The Sydney traders had a monopoly on spirits and would use it (as well as tea and sugar) to make a bargain – but it was sold at usurious profits. The new Governor had not forgotten his orders from home and made his first bid to stop the racketeering by banning the distillation of spirits:

The Governor, having received information from various quarters, that in direct disobedience of pubic orders, and in defiance of the consequence of detection, several persons in different parts of this colony have taken the liberty of erecting stills, and providing materials for the purpose of distilling spirituous liquors; and as it is well known to the whole colony that this destructive practice has long been forbidden in this settlement, and under the immediate authority of every officer who has commanded in it; it is scarcely necessary to say more on the subject than to call on the aid and exertion of the whole body of officers, whether civil, military, or naval, in suppressing it; and to desire, that wherever they may understand it to be continues to be

carried on or attempted, they may use every means in their power to detect the guilty person, and to seize or destroy the utensils they may have provided for a purpose so certainly calculated to ruin the present healthy state of the inhabitants of this territory. All constables, watchmen, and other persons, are hereby strictly enjoined, wherever they may have cause to suspect this forbidden trade is carried on, to make the same known to any magistrate or officer, in order that steps be regularly pursued for bringing any opposition to these orders to proof. If those persons who shall presume to carry on this noxious work after this information, do happen to be free people, every indulgence they may have hitherto received from Government shall be immediately withdrawn, and they shall be ordered to quit the colony by the earliest opportunity: - if a convict, they will receive such treatment for their disobedience, as their conduct, in the opinion of a Court, may appear to merit. [9]

The order was the cause of the next conflict between Macarthur and Bligh. In March1807, the ship *Dart* - owned by Macarthur and Blaxcell - arrived in Sydney from London. On seeing the manifest, Bligh saw two stills listed, one for a Captain Abbott of the New South Wales Corps and the other for Macarthur. Macarthur realised that these might be stopped at port, so he had the coppers filled with medicines and as such they were delivered to his home. When Bligh ordered the stills to be seized and kept in His Majesty's store for return to England, they had the worms and heads but not the coppers. For the time being, nothing was done.

When the *Duke of Portland* was ready to sail for England in October, the coppers were sought, then it was remembered that Macarthur still had them. Bligh ordered naval officer Robert Campbell to have them shipped, so he wrote to Macarthur's partner, Blaxcell. The reply came from Macarthur; they could do whatever they liked with the heads and worms, but he intended to keep the coppers for domestic use. As the coppers were parts of the original stills, Campbell sent his nephew, Campbell Jr, to take them away. Macarthur demanded a receipt. Campbell elder sent one for 'coppers with heads and worms complete'. Macarthur refused, as he'd never had anything but the coppers. Campbell sent his nephew back again with the same receipt. Macarthur told the young man:

'Take them at your own risk.'

Campbell did and was promptly prosecuted for 'illegal seizure of his property'. At the trial Macarthur took the advantage to make some political speech-making:

'It would therefore appear that a British subject, in a British settlement, in which the British laws are established by royal patent, has had his property wrested from him by a non-accredited individual, without any authority being produced, or any other reason being assigned, than that it was the Governor's order. It is therefore for you, gentlemen, to determine whether this be the tenure on which Englishmen hold their property in New South Wales.' [10]

November brought another dispute between Macarthur and the Governor. Another ship co-owned by Macarthur came to dock – the schooner *Parramatta*, under the command of Scotsman Glen. It had sailed to Tahiti; but a convict had managed to get aboard and stayed at the island. Missionaries complained to Bligh who took legal action and the bond which ship-owners had given the Government was deemed to be forfeit. When Macarthur refuted the decision the naval officers refused to board the ship and police prevented the cargo from being delivered. Macarthur responded by telling Glen that he had wiped his hands of the ship, so without provisions the crew were obliged to come on shore – which was against colonial law. When questioned, they explained the situation and Macarthur's old enemy, the Judge Advocate, wrote to him demanding his presence at ten o'clock the next morning to give an account of his actions. Macarthur replied:

Sir, I acknowledge receipt of your letter of this date, acquainting me that the master, mates and crew of the schooner *Parramatta* have violated the colonial regulations, by coming unauthorized on shore; and that they in their justification, say, I have deprived them of their usual allowance of provisions &c; for which conduct you require me to come to Sydney tomorrow, and show cause. I have only in reply to say, that you were many days ago informed I have declined any farther interference with the schooner, in consequence of the illegal conduct of the naval officer in refusing to enter the vessel, and retaining her papers, notwithstanding I had made repeated applications that they might be restored. So circumstanced, I could no longer think of submitting to the expense of paying and victualling the officers and crew of a vessel over which I had no control; but previously to my declining to do so, my intentions were officially made known to the naval officer. What steps he has since taken respecting the schooner and her people, I am yet to learn; but as he has had two police officers on board in charge of her, it is reasonable to suppose they are directed to prevent irregularities; and thereof I beg leave to refer you to the naval officer for what farther information you may require on the subject. [11]

Macarthur did not show up in Sydney which was tantamount to contempt so Atkins sent the Chief Constable of the Parramatta district (where Macarthur lived) – Francis Oakes – with a warrant to bring him to Sydney. Macarthur almost blew a fuse:

'Had the person who issued the warrant served it instead of you, I would have spurned him from my presence! If he comes a second time to enforce the warrant, he should come well-armed, as I shall never submit till blood is shed!'

Macarthur now saw a chance to attack both of his enemies at once and went off to write a reply, muttering:

'I have been robbed of ten thousand pounds; but let them alone, they will soon make a rope to hang themselves.' [12]

Macarthur's reply was hardly conciliatory – nor was it meant to be:

Dec 15: Mr Oakes, You will inform the persons who sent you here with the warrant you have now shown me, and given me a copy of, that I never will submit to the horrid tyranny that is attempted, until I am forced; that I consider it with scorn and contempt, as I do the persons who have directed it to be executed. [13]

Atkins' reaction on reading this openly insulting note can easily be imagined. He heard Oakes' report in front of a bench of magistrates and immediately a warrant was issued for his arrest, to be executed by the chief constables of Sydney and Parramatta. They were accompanied by three other men armed with sticks and cutlasses and they found him at the house of Mr Grimes, Surveyor-General of the colony.

The next day, 17 December, he faced the bench and was charged with 'high misdemeanours'. He was allowed bail; the Provost-General Gore was in charge of that. The indictment was prepared by the attorney Crosley, the lawyer who had been transported for perjury and later received a pardon from Governor King. There were four counts:

- That against the express order of the Governor he had detained the boilers of the two stills on his premises

- That he had intended to stir up the people of the colony to hatred and contempt of the Governor and government in the inflammatory and seditious words he had uttered before a bench of magistrates at Sydney, convened at his instance against Mr Campbell, Jr, for the seizure of the stills

- That he intended to raise dissatisfaction and discontentment in the colony, and a spirit of hatred and contempt towards the Governor and government, in inducing the master and crew of the *Parramatta* schooner to come on shore in direct violation of colonial regulations

- With seditious contempt of the authority of the Judge Advocate and with uttering false, scandalous, malicious defamatory and

seditious words, of His Excellency the Governor, in the paper he had given to chief constable Oakes, and in the expressions he had used in conversation with that functionary respecting the Governor and government.

There was over a month between the charging and the trial and Macarthur made good use of that. His first move was a formal request to Bligh, that Atkins be removed and replaced by a disinterested party. This was a ludicrous request. The Judge Advocate was appointed by His Majesty's Government and could only be dismissed by it. Moreover, the trial could not go ahead without his presence, which Bligh and Macarthur both knew.

Macarthur now rallied his troops – or rather the bootleggers and racketeers who were his closest friends – most of them belonging to the New South Wales Corps. The jury was to be composed of officers from the military and before the trial was convened – on 25 January – they were all primed and knew what to do. He also needed some assistance from the head of the Corps, Lieutenant Johnston, but he had little time for Bligh anyway and while he might have had some reservations he was won over. By the time Atkins swore in the jury, he was blissfully unaware that both he and Bligh were walking into a trap.

As per protocol, Atkins took the oaths from the jury and was about to take his own. At that point Macarthur loudly protested against his presence and Atkins told him that the case could not be heard without him.

Captain Kemp shouted on cue:

'You are a juryman as well as the rest and can be objected to!'

He then asked Macarthur to state his objections and he produced a written list of them which he had carefully prepared. It was useless Atkins trying to protest; Lieutenant Lawson cried out:

'We *will* hear him!'

As Macarthur read his rant, Atkins tried to regain control of the court by threatening to commit him for contemptuous language. Kemp called out:

'*You* commit? No, sir, *I* will commit *you* - to jail!'

Atkins had had enough and declared that the court was adjourned. As he walked off, other went to follow him until the officers yelled:

'Stay, stay! Tell the people not to go out! We are a court!'

Macarthur finished his protest. Basically he made four objections against Atkins: that because there was a suit pending between them, 'for the recovery of a sum of money that he unjustly withholds'; second, that Atkins held 'a rancorous inveteracy' against him; third, that he had 'long been the object of his vindictive malice'; and last, that he planned to destroy him by associating 'with that well-known dismembered limb of the law, George Crosley, and others of as wicked minds.' He also gave eight 'authorities' for objecting to a judge, using a small number of legal tomes as his sources.

After this, the men got ready to leave the court. The police would be waiting for him, Macarthur knew, so he said:

'Am I to be cast out at the mercy of a set of armed ruffians – the police?'

The men gave him an armed guard [14]. Gore saw this as a rescue of his prisoner, so he went to Atkins and three other justices and received a warrant to arrest Macarthur.

It may be wondered why Macarthur went to all of this trouble. He knew the entire jury was on his side and the court case was a travesty anyhow – he would certainly have been declared innocent. By now, the trial was unimportant. It was merely bait with which to catch two big fish - the Judge Advocate and the Governor of the Province. Once Macarthur was safely stowed, the officers began to write to Bligh.

> **We, the officers composing the Criminal Court of Jurisdiction appointed by Your Excellency, beg leave to state to you, that a right of challenge to the Judge Advocate, Richard Atkins, Esq., has been demanded by the prisoner John Macarthur, Esq, which we, as a Court, after mature and deliberate consideration, have agreed to allow as a good and lawful objection. We therefore submit to Your Excellency, to determine on the propriety of appointing another Judge Advocate to preside in the present trial. We farther pray Your Excellency's protection in the execution of our duty, having been grossly insulted and threatened by Richard Atkins Esq, with a seeming view to deter us in our proceedings. We have the honour to be Your Excellency's faithful and humble servants, AF Kemp, Capt, NSW Corps, J Brabyn, Lieut, NSW Corps, Wm Moore, Lieut, NSW Corps, Thos Laycock, Lieut, Wm Minchin, Lieut, Wm Lawson, Lieut. [15]**

Bligh replied, explaining the legal implications of dismissing a Judge Advocate. He sent his note at half past noon:

> **In answer to your letter just received, I conceive that there could have been no cause for challenge to the Judge Advocate, who is the officer appointed by His Majesty's patent, and without whose presence there can be no court.**

> **And I consider that the Judge Advocate had a right to commit any person who might commit any gross insult to him, while he was in his official capacity as Judge of the Court. I do not consider the Court to be formed without the Judge Advocate; and when legally convened, I have no right to interpose any authority concerning its legal acts.**

I therefore can do no otherwise than direct that the Judge Advocate take his seat, and act as directed by His Majesty's Letters Patent, for the constituting of the Court of Criminal Jurisdiction; which, being authorised by an Act of Parliament, is as follows:

'And we farther will, ordain, and appoint, that the said Court of Criminal Jurisdiction shall consist of our Judge Advocate for the time being, together with such six officers of our sea and land service, as our Governor, (or, in the case of his death or absence, our Lieut. Governor), shall, by precept issued under his hand and seal, convene from time to time for that purpose.' [16]

The officers ignored the legal ramifications and continued to ask Bligh to dismiss Atkins from the trial of Macarthur, 'well knowing the hostile enmity which has existed between them for the last thirteen or fourteen years'. The Judge Advocate now told Bligh that the men had seized the papers associated with the trial which Atkins had left behind when he left. At 2.15 pm Bligh wrote:

In reply to your second letter of this date, I require that you deliver to Mr William Gore, Provost General, and Mr Edmund Griffin, my Secretary, who accompanies him on the occasion, all the papers that the Judge Advocate left on the table, and which were refused to be sent to him by the constable; and also those which the prisoner John Macarthur has read before you, that they may be delivered to the Judge Advocate, His Majesty's legal officer.' [17]

Letters now crossed; the officers had written to state that the laws 'had been grossly violated by Mr Richard Atkins' in threatening 'to commit John Macarthur, Esq, the prisoner at the bar, who was pleading his own cause by the Court's order, to jail, as a common felon.' By now they had received the note demanding the papers.

With all due submission to Your Excellency's commands, we beg leave to state, that we are not defensible in giving up the papers alluded to, to any person, unless Your Excellency thinks proper to appoint another Judge Advocate to proceed on the trial of John Macarthur, Esq. [18]

Bligh could smell as mutiny; he had had plenty of practice. He therefore wanted the men to give him a yes or no – in writing – to his demand.

I have required the Judge Advocate's papers, with those that were read by Mr John Macarthur, and I now demand finally your answer, in writing, whether you will deliver these papers or not; and I again repeat, that you are no Court without the Judge Advocate. [19]

The men wavered – they did not want to defy the Governor in writing as this would put them in a bad light at a future date. They did offer copies, but insisted on the replacement of Atkins, which was out of Bligh's power. It was time for Bligh to act – the mutineers on the *Bounty* had succeeded because he had no militia; he did not want to repeat the same mistake. He asked his secretary, Edmund Griffin, to write to Lieutenant Johnston at 5.30pm and deliver the letter to his home, some four miles out of town:

His Excellency, under particular public circumstances which have occurred, desires me to request you will see him without delay. I have the honour to be, Sir, Your most obedient humble servant, Edmund Griffin, Secretary. [20]

It was a message which Johnston had expected. He gave a verbal reply, that he 'was too ill to come to Sydney, and that he was unable to write, having fallen from his chaise'. While drunk, Bligh supposed, as that would not have been unusual. It was a big disappointment; but if Johnston could not come and sort out his officers, then the next-in-command would have to do it.

Early in the morning of 6 January, Gore committed Macarthur to jail. This, as would be expected, stirred the officers to write again, enclosing a copy – not of the letters, but of Macarthur's protest speech.

It is with much concern we have learned by the inclosed deposition made before us by G Blaxcell, Esq and N Bayly, Esq that the body of John Macarthur, Esq, the prisoner arraigned before us yesterday, has been forcibly arrested from the bail which the Court remanded him in; which illegal act of the Magistrates, (grounded on the false deposition of Mr William Gore, Provost Marshal), we beg leave to represent to Your Excellency, is in our opinion calculated to subvert the legal authority and independence of the Court of Criminal Jurisdiction, constituted in this colony by His Majesty's letters patent; and we therefore pray that Your Excellency will discountenance such magisterial proceedings, pregnant with the most serious consequences to the community at large; and that Your Excellency will be pleased to take measures to restore John Macarthur, Esq, to his former bail, that the Court may proceed on his trial. [21]

The officers were taking over the role of judge and jury and Atkins warned Bligh that the six men were guilty of 'crimes amounting to a usurpation of His Majesty's government, and tending to incite or create rebellion, or other outrageous treason, in the people of the territory'. Bligh needed to be decisive – he had to constrain these men to appear at a magistrates' bench to see if there were grounds to proceed with criminal proceedings. It was the proper and lawful thing to do. Bligh therefore sent the following:

The Judge Advocate having presented a memorial to me, in which you are charged with certain crimes, you are therefore hereby required to appear before me at Government House, at nine o'clock to-morrow morning, to answer in the premises. [22]

It was a wild card to play and Bligh knew it. He had to enlist the help of the New South Wales Corps and to do that he needed someone to command it. Hurriedly he sent another letter to Johnston:

In answer to my letter of yesterday I received a verbal message by my orderly from you, that you were rendered by illness totally incapable of being at Sydney; I apprehend the same illness will deprive me of your assistance at this time; and the Judge Advocate having laid a memorial before me against six of your Officers, for practices which he conceives treasonable, I am under the necessity of summoning them before me, and all The Magistrates have directions to attend at none o'clock to-morrow morning.

I leave it for you to judge whether Capt. Abbott should be directed to attend at Sydney, to command the troops in your absence. [23]

Johnston replied that he would try to get a person to write an answer in the evening. It was an answer designed to lull Bligh into an ill-advised sense of security; meanwhile, thanks to a miraculous cure, Johnston drove straight off to the barracks. The whole Corps wanted him to take over the Governorship and his first act was to free Macarthur, who quickly rode up to see Johnston. The Colonel was worried about the act of committing the Governor and he said to Macarthur:

'God's curse! What am I to do, Macarthur? Here are these fellows advising me to arrest the Governor!'

Macarthur replied, '*Advising* you? Then, Sir, the only thing left for you to do is to do it. To advise on such matters is legally as criminal as to do them.' [24]

Johnston still demurred. To remove a Governor as an act of righteousness was one thing, but for an arrest, this would need to be explained to the British Government and Johnston insisted on some kind of request in writing. No sooner said than Macarthur did:

Sir, The present alarming state of this colony, in which every man's property, liberty and life are endangered, induces us most earnestly to implore you instantly to place Gov. Bligh under arrest, and to assume the command of the colony. We pledge ourselves, at a moment of less

agitation, to come forward to support the measure with our fortunes and our lives. [25]

Macarthur's name appeared at the top of a list of no more than nine people which much later swelled to 151. But at the time the rebellion was being planned, the only ones who signed were those who had issues with Bligh: Blaxcell, Macarthur's co-owner of the schooner; John and Gregory Blaxland, who did not get the land or labour they felt they deserved; Simeon Lord, who right to land nearly government property had been questioned; D'Arcy Wentworth, publicly reprimanded by Johnston at a court martial and who therefore suspended by Bligh from his job as assistant surgeon; Nicholas Bayly, who by a mistake had been given no office under the Governor. The resurrection had begun and the trap finally snapped shut on Governor Bligh.

From Government House, Bligh's people could see the regiment moving towards him. They were led by Johnston, the drummer was drumming and music was playing. As they approached the house, Lieutenant Bell's leader of the Governor's Guard, knew that the end was in sight so he joined up by the Corps. There was one brave figure who tried to keep out Bell and his men single-handedly – Mary Putnam. Bligh's newly-widowed daughter, arms outstretched, tried to block the advancing men. They marched on and entered the house with one thing on their mind – to find Bligh.

Bligh also knew that there was nothing he could do, so he kept a cool head. He went to his room and gathered together some important papers and documents which he did not want the rebels to get their hands upon then returned to the stairs with his Commissary, Palmer. As soon as they got there they heard the sound of soldiers invading the house and then, as Palmer went downstairs, he saw them coming.

'These men' he later swore, 'were in an infuriated state, with their muskets, and bayonets fixed.'

Bligh now went to a small apartment of two rooms at the end of the house and made his way to the inner one. Here he thought about his escape and he decided that he must make his way to Hawkesbury, forty miles distant, where he would find soldiers and hundreds of settlers who would doubtlessly support him.

While he planned his escape he also gave thought to hiding the papers he had brought with him. There were too many to hide under his waistcoat, so he had to make a choice as to which needed to be preserved and which to destroy. While stuffing documents under his clothing and ripping up many others, he suddenly heard the door of the outer room open and the voice of Lieutenant Moore.

'Pooh! pooh! You need not come in here, the Governor is not here. The

Governor is not in here! The Governor is not to be found here!' [26]

As Bligh continued to destroy some papers, he heard the Regiment bustling about the house while others went outside to search the grounds and the out-houses. Then he heard a 'halloo-balloo' and the voice of Sergeant Whittle:

'Damn my eyes, I will find him — soldiers! come up stairs again, I will have another search!'

Once again he heard the door of the outer room open but this time they came into the room where Bligh was standing behind a cot. There was a mighty cry and cheering from outside. Bligh stated that he was 'a little confused' by arranging the hidden papers, so he put his right arm to his chest to stop them falling through; at once a solider pointed his bayonet at him:

'Damn your eyes, if you don't take your hand out of there, I will whip this into you immediately!'

Bligh called to the sergeant: 'Keep the man off, I have no arms. Stand off!'

Minchin then came through the crowd 'on his hands and knees', according to Bligh, and taking him by the arm, led him downstairs. He was taken to the drawing room and then the adjoining dining parlour; here he found troops lined up against the wall, 'just like a Robespierrean party, or a revolutionary tribunal'. Then Moore brought him a letter, signed by Johnston. It was the order for his arrest.

Sir, I am called upon to execute a most painful duty. You are charged by the respectable inhabitants of crimes that render you unfit to exercise the supreme authority another moment in this colony; and in that charge all the officers under my command have joined.

I therefore require you, in His Majesty's sacred name, to resign your authority, and to submit to the arrest which I hereby place you under, by the advice of all my officers, and by the advice of every respectable inhabitant in the town of Sydney. [27]

The men decided to make profit from Bligh's actions and announced that they had found him hiding under a bed, from which they dragged him. It was a tale one of them would later repeat in London. An anonymous artist drew a cartoon showing the scene, a soldier pulling Bligh from under the bed while two soldiers watched. The soldiers were, of course, gentlemen and Bligh the coward was not fit to govern. Despite Bligh's version, it was widely believed and once again Bligh's name became the source of derision. It is strange to consider that a man who had faced cannon-fire at Camperdown and Copenhagen would show fear when confronted by a troop of arresting soldiers.

On Saturday 26 January, Johnston styled himself Lieutenant-Governor. That night, his friends celebrated. Bonfires were lit and effigies of Bligh and Gore were burned while the military band played *The Silly Old Man*. The ladies joined in the festivities, which ended in a drunken riot.

On the 27th Johnston issued a statement to the military:

> **Soldiers! Your conduct has endeared you to every well-disposed inhabitant in this settlement! Persevere in the same honourable path, and you will establish the credit of the New South Wales Corps on a basis not to be shaken. God save the King! [28]**

That certainly smacked of the French Revolution. It was a time for conspirators to be given rewards. Liquor was freely distributed to Macarthur's supporters and the racketeering recommenced in earnest. All the main conspirators were given plum jobs which were announced in a General Order to the Public:

> **Richard Atkins, Esq, Judge Advocate, is superceded from that office, and Edward Abbott, Esq, is appointed Judge Advocate during his suspension. Anthony Fenn Kemp, Esq, John Harris, Esq, Thomas Jamieson, Esq, Charles Grimes, Esq, William Minchin, Esq, Garnham Blaxcell, Esq, John Blaxland, Esq, and Archibald Bell, Esq, are appointed Magistrates; and those persons who heretofore performed the duties of that office are to consider themselves dismissed. Lieut. Lawson is appointed Aide-de-camp to his Honour the Lieutenant-Governor. Nicholas Bayly, Esq, is appointed Secretary to His Honour the Lieutenant-Governor, and to be Provost Marshal during the suspension of William Gore, Esq, who is hereby suspended from that office. John Palmer, Esq, Commissary, is suspended from that office; and James Williamson, Esq, is directed to take upon himself the charge of His Majesty's stores, and act as Commissary during his suspension.**

> **Robert Campbell, Esq, is dismissed from the office of Treasurer to the public funds, naval officer, and collector of taxes, and is hereby directed to balance his accounts, and to deliver them to His Honour the Lieutenant-Governor. Thomas Jamieson, Esq, is appointed naval officer.**

Macarthur wrote to his wife in glee:

> **I have been deeply engaged all this day in contending for the liberties of this unhappy Colony, and I am happy to say I have succeeded beyond what I. expected. I am too much exhausted to attempt giving you the particulars, therefore I must refer you to Edward, who knows enough to give you a general idea of what has been done. The Tyrant is now no**

doubt gnashing his Teeth with vexation at his overthrow. May he often have cause to do the like! [29]

It was also a time for reprisals and everyone who had supported Bligh or Atkins was punished with severity. Gore was imprisoned for 11 weeks and 4 days, on a charge of 'having made affidavit that Mr Macarthur was out of his custody on the 25th'. Crosley the attorney was sentenced to seven years' transportation. As for the Rev Fulton:

The Rev Henry Fulton is suspended from discharging in future the office of Chaplain in the colony.

The Officers, civil and military, are ordered to attend divine worship on Sunday next, at the New Church, and every well-disposed inhabitant is requested to be present to join in thanks to Almighty God, for his merciful interposition in their favour, by relieving them without bloodshed from the awful situation in which they stood before the memorable 26th instant.' [30]

On 2 February a travesty of a court case was held – Macarthur's trial, at which he was acquitted by his friends. The Surveyor general, Charles Grimes, played the part of Judge Advocate and even Captain Abbott – who had come to refer to Macarthur as 'The Leader' – complained at the shambles which passed as a Court of Law.

Within a week a meeting was convened in St Philip's Church to discuss the idea of sending a delegate to England so that the colonists' (in reality, the rebels') case might be put to the Government. Much drink was taken and a sword was presented to Johnston as well as a vote of thanks to him, Macarthur and the NWS Corps. Of course Macarthur was voted as delegate and his crony Blaxcell suggested a subscription list be put up to defray expenses - £1095 5s was promised. In the cold light of sobriety none of this was forthcoming so the plan was temporarily shelved.

It was resuscitated soon after. On 10 February Macarthur was appointed – or appointed himself - a Magistrate and Colonial Secretary, virtually taking over the running of the Colony with Johnston as a mere puppet. Immediately he chose his son as his delegate and sent him to London to give his version of events – and to take a bale of wool. The British woollen mills were desperate for wool at the time because of the Napoleonic blockade, and the Australian bale sold for a record price.

Edward also curried favour with some influential people such as the Duke of Northumberland and stated that Bligh's friends all wore 'gloomy countenances'.

For Macarthur's opponents, a Reign of Terror continued and the general feeling was one of fear, especially among the settlers. A magistrate called

Arndell wrote a letter praising Johnston, but wrote to Bligh that he had done it because he was afraid. There was general consternation over what was about to happen in the colony.

Chapter Fifteen. In Limbo

When the settlers discovered what had happened to Bligh they were incensed and wrote to Johnston's superior, Colonel Paterson in Dalrymple, complaining that the whole of the Government seemed to be under the control of Macarthur. Describing Macarthur as a 'turbulent and troublesome character' who had argued with every Governor since his arrival, they requested Paterson to go to Sydney and take command. They were not the only ones to feel this way. Some years later, the *Gazette* described Macarthur's Gang as 'the rebel, the stay-making asses; the craven-hearted rebels; the public thieves; wretches of no mind, who ruled with a fear that generates cruelty, with an ignorance that produces the most grotesque parody on law and justice.' It further stated that they should have been hanged:

The aristocracy, as they were then called, would have dangled nobly as skeletons on the fort; their bleached and rattling bones would have taught the virtue of constitutional obedience to some of those petty mushrooms, who have since drunk a sort of libellous infection from the impunity which their ancestors and others were allowed to escape the halter. [1]

Strong stuff indeed and only one side of the coin; but the settlers would have applauded the sentiment. They also wrote to Johnston, expressing their alarm at finding Macarthur had been given the post of Colonial Secretary. Having already felt the weight of the tyranny of the racketeers, they dreaded the all-too-familiar oppression of the new regime. Bligh had protected them against their excesses, but now they had free reign to exercise complete control.

The bad name Bligh had acquired in the colony had been almost exclusively due to his quarrel with Macarthur and his cronies. The attitude of the common man – the settler who had come to the new land in search of a new life – had never changed since his arrival. Bligh was no less than a saviour – he had succoured them in time of disaster and need as well as protecting them from the excesses of the racketeers. Under his government, they had begun to prosper in their affairs and a poll of the population would have been overwhelming in favour of their Governor.

In fact, just before his arrest, 833 settlers and land-holders wrote the following to him days before his arrest:

May it please your Excellency,

We the undersigned free and principal proprietors of landed property, and inhabitants of the rising and extensive colony of New South Wales, beg leave, on the beginning of another year, to approach your Excellency, and express the fullest unfeigned sense of gratitude for the manifold great and essential blessings and benefits we freely continue to enjoy from your Excellency's arduous, just, determined and salutary government over us, happy evinced by the present plenteous and flourishing state of this country, rapidly growing in population, opulence, and all improvements calculated by a wise and patriotic Government to make a large colony of people happy and rich in all their internal resources; and while enjoying, from year to year, such inexpressible benefits under your Excellency's auspicious and benign government, we feel and hold ourselves gratefully bound, at the risk of our lives and properties, at all times (as liege subjects) to support the same. And ever prove ourselves worthy of a continuation of your protection, attention and encouragement during your Excellency's gracious government over us, which may God long continue! [2]

Finding himself at the head of the colony, Macarthur might have felt a temporary satisfaction, but his triumph was not destined to last. 'The Leader', who had been the darling of the rebels, was shocked to see his popularity quickly wane. In fact, taking the reins of Government had been his biggest mistake because now his unbounded ambition was plain for all to see. The main actors in the deposition drama wanted their share of the wedge and more – it was becoming increasingly difficult to satisfy them. Abbott, Grimes and Bayly were turning against Macarthur, because he had refused some of the men's requests. The leadership was in turmoil: Johnston was every day expecting a visit from one of his superiors; Paterson from Port Dalrymple or Foveaux, Lieutenant General of Norfolk Island, who had been on leave but was now on his way back from England. This wasn't turning out to be the paradise that Macarthur had dreamed it to be and Johnston had had to write to the officers, asking for the reason for their apparent dislike of the Leader.

Johnston was liked by his men but was a weak and ineffectual Governor. He did try, but soon discovered the woes which had beset the former governors as he made some effort to reduce public expenditure and conserve stock while the officers pressed for more and more. It would not be long before Johnston realised that to run a colony he needed discipline and his supporters would not respond to it, now that the good old days had returned. He wrote ruefully to Castlereagh:

I am now, my Lord, arrived at the most painful part of my task – an explanation of the causes that have prevented me from preparing a better and arranged statement of the transaction in which I have been engaged: it is with deep concern I find myself obliged to report to your Lordship that the opposition of those persons from whom I had most reason to expect support, has been one of the principal obstacles I have had to encounter. [3]

As for Bligh, his tenure of Governorship was finished. He was under house arrest and could only wait and see what would develop. He pinned most of his hopes on the coming of Foveaux from England, when there was every chance he would be reinstated. Under house arrest, he had been treated with little courtesy and with more disdain and he described his guard, Daniel McKay, as a 'merciless and ferocious gaoler'. McKay himself owned a public house and he put up a new sign, depicting a female handing a cap of liberty to Johnston, whose foot trampled a snake.

On 28 July 1808, Lieutenant Colonel Foveaux at last arrived but Macarthur was too quick for Bligh. Johnston and Macarthur were allowed on board his ship while Bligh's welcoming party – Griffin, Palmer and Fulton, were left kicking their heels. There was time for the two cronies to convince Foveaux of Bligh's incompetence and tyranny, so that when they left his mind was already made up. When he visited Government House Bligh – assuming his original dignity- gave orders for Foveaux to suppress the mutiny using his utmost power. Foveaux simply ignored him. He did not even make full investigation into the rebellion, but continued the house arrest and fell in with the New South Wales Corps. He then took over the role of Lieutenant-Governor while Bligh fumed to Admiral Pellow:

This is not only rebellion but mutiny, and it is of so black a hue as all England must indignantly bring the principal actors to condign punishment. [4]

It can easily be imagined that there was a battle of words between the new self-appointed head of the colony and the Governor. Officially, as far as Britain was concerned, Bligh was still the colonial Governor and so he gave appropriate orders to Foveaux's men. As the rightful ruler, Bligh would spare no effort to regain that which had been taken from him by force of arms. When Foveaux discovered what Bligh was up to, he sent him a severe reprimand:

Some of the overseers having reported to me that you have thought proper to give them orders respecting the execution of their duty, I must acquaint you that should you do so again, I shall be under the necessity of taking some very effectual method of preventing any interference on your part in anything whatever relative to the affairs of this colony.

Foveaux wanted Bligh to go back to England but Bligh would not entertain the idea. Leaving him still under arrest, the Lieutenant Governor went ahead with his administration. Finding that the officers had turned against Macarthur, he also became his enemy. Now that any hopes he had were now at an end, Macarthur considered Foveaux as being 'unprincipled' and the chief cause of the mischief at that time. Meanwhile Bligh responded to Foveaux's veiled threat by appealing to Paterson, Lieutenant Colonel of the New South Wales Corps, to bring the mutiny to heel. Paterson, however, was a cautious man and awaited instructions from Britain. He advised Bligh to leave the colony. Quickly.

The war between Bligh and Foveaux intensified, Foveaux pushing him to go and Bligh insisting on staying. As Bligh petitioned Lord Minto to send armed forces to quell the subversion, Foveaux was proving an unpopular ruler, mostly due to his harsh and unscrupulous nature. Many settlers were still faithful to Bligh and resented Fovaux's new regime. When he ordered a muster of all landowners one of them, George Suttor, refused to obey and was tried. Dragged to court and facing the Judge Advocate, Suttor refused to acknowledge its legality.

'Gentlemen, I deny the legality of this court; you may do with myself as you please; my unfortunate wife and family I leave to the mercy of God, until peace shall be restored in the colony: I have nothing more to say.'

'Mr Sutter, you are called upon to plead to your indictment; and whatever you may have to offer ibn your defence will be attentively considered. I again ask: are you guilty or not guilty?'

'Sir, all that I have to say I have already said. My allegiance is due to Governor Bligh, and Governor Bligh alone; and every drop of blood within my veins prevents me from ever acknowledging the legality of this court. You may do with me as you think proper.'

'Mr Sutter, it is my duty to acquaint you, that it is provided by act of parliament, that in case a prisoner shall refuse to plead to this indictment, the effect will be the same as if he pleads guilty. Once more I call upon you – are you guilty or not guilty?'

'I stand as before: I have said all I have to say; you are to do with me as you think proper.' [5]

He was sentenced to six months' imprisonment and fined one shilling.

In January 1809, Paterson finally decided to sail to Sydney and Bligh was little inclined to have warm feelings towards the man who had ignored his pleas for assistance. Still head of the Navy, he ordered that Paterson be placed under arrest as soon as he landed. On hearing this, Paterson decided not to disembark in town but landed the *Porpoise* before he arrived. As Bligh expected, Paterson had made up his mind not to interfere with the state of things and he took over the reins of government, appointing Foveaux and Abbott as his advisors.

Bligh's insistence on hanging on to the command of the Navy – as ordered by His Majesty's Government – was a thorn in Paterson's side as he wished to use the *Porpoise* for the evacuation of Norfolk Island and the *Admiral Gambier* to sail to England. Bligh was obdurate so Paterson resorted to menaces, threatening to deport Bligh if he continued to resist. He sent Johnston and Abbott to parley with him but got nowhere:

'I will never comply with any orders from you; and it is at your peril, and at the peril of anyone else, to take that ship, with my broad pendant, from me, sir; you shall not have her.'

Johnston replied: 'I am very sorry, sir, but I have orders, that unless you comply with his Honour's request, you are to proceed with us up to a subaltern's barrack, which is prepared for you at the barracks.'

Bligh was not allowed the original order, but Griffin was permitted to copy it. Then Abbott and Johnston forced him into a one-horse chaise. When Mary Putland saw what was happening to 'Papa', she followed him to the barracks and there they were taken to a small barrack with two rooms – they were the quarters of Lieutenant Finucane, Foveaux's Secretary. After a while Johnston joined them.

'Sir, I am directed by His Honour to inform you that you are to hold yourself in readiness to embark on board the *Estramina*, schooner, when she arrives.'

'Where am I to go?'

'I really cannot say…' [6]

For a week he was kept prisoner, suffering indignities from his captors. He wrote to Admiral Pellew and asked for military assistance, informing him of the town's fortifications and a minute description of the armed capabilities of the *Porpoise*.

On 4 February Paterson and Bligh came to an agreement. Bligh agreed to leave New South Wales on board the *Porpoise* under conditions; he would sail straight to England, he would not land at or return to any part of the territories without orders from His Majesty; he would not interfere in the colonial government; and he would not impede the fitting of the ship. He could return to Government House and would be allowed to sail off with his family and any of his friends he cared to name. Bligh pledged to this on 'his honour as an officer and a gentleman.' Here is the document in full:

The conditions upon which Colonel Paterson gives Governor Bligh, pledging himself to proceed to England in the Porpoise:-

Sydney, New South Wales, 4th of February, 1809.

It being deemed, by Lieutenant-Governor Paterson, absolutely essential to his Majesty's service, and the interests of this colony, to send Governor Bligh immediately to England, and it being the intention of Lieutenant-Governor Paterson to take up the ship Admiral Gambier for his conveyance; and in the interests of this colony, Governor Bligh has represented that it would, in many accounts, be much more desirable to him to be allowed to return home in his Majesty's ship Porpoise.

Lieutenant-General Paterson, anxious to contribute as much as possible to the convenience of Governor Bligh, consents to his proceeding to Europe in the Porpoise, on the following conditions, to the strict and unequivocal observance of which Governor Bligh hereby solemnly pledges his honour as an officer and a gentleman, viz:

That he will embark with his family on the board the Porpoise on the 20th instant, and will put to sea as soon after as the wind and weather will admit. That he will proceed to England with the utmost despatch; and that he will neither touch at, nor return to, any part of this territory until he shall have received his majesty's instructions, or those of his Ministers. That he will not in any manner or under any pretence whatever, while he remains in this colony, interfere in the government of affairs thereof, and that he will not throw any impediment in the way of the Porpoise being equipped and proceeding with him or her voyage at the stipulated time.

In consequence of the above pledge, Lieutenant-Governor Paterson consents to remove the additional restraints which have been laid upon Governor Bligh since the 27th of last month, and to permit him to return to Government House, and to communicate with his friends in the same manner as previous to that day; to make such arrangements as he may deem necessary for his voyage, and to allow such persons to accompany him as he may think proper to name, agreeable to the proposition contained in the Lieutenant-Governor's letter of the 28th ult.

Signed William Paterson

Signed William Bligh [7]

Bligh did not keep his word, although the fact that Palmer was not allowed to sail with him was a breach of the pledge and so technically Bligh could plead that he was no longer bound by it. It is doubtful whether Bligh ever intended to keep his promise; once on the deck of the *Porpoise*, he felt he was Governor again. He certainly acted like it. He arrested the ship's Lieutenant Kent but kept the Captain, John Porteous. Then Bligh declared war – he sent out a proclamation denouncing the revolutionaries and forbidding any ship to carry out any of the mutineers – especially members of the New South Wales Corps. He even aimed his guns at the *Admiral Gambier* and ordered her Captain not to take Johnston on board. [8] When Paterson found out about Bligh's activities he made a proclamation of his own, in which he ordered that no-one should communicate with Bligh, on pain of being arrested as an 'abettor of sedition'. [9]

On 28 March the *Admiral Gambier* defied Bligh's order and sailed out to Rio de Janeiro with Johnston, Macarthur, Harris and Jamison. Johnston was happy to go – he had fallen out with Paterson over his decisions concerning Bligh. For his part, Paterson must have been glad to see both Johnston and the troublesome Macarthur out of sight. He could now get on with the government – or lack of it. He praised the New South Wales Corps and gave extravagant land grants – 67475 acres and after that his regime was marked by indolence, drunkenness and inaction. The phenomenal amount of land distributed was done in something of a hurry – before a new Governor could arrive from Britain.

Bligh looked for help from the Governor of New Zealand, David Collins and so sailed the ship he had won 'by finesse' and reached the Derwent. All went well – Collins welcomed him, accepted his authority and offered him his own residence to stay at. Bligh declined, preferring to stay on the ship, but Mary took two apartments in Government House. [10] There was only one thing which made Bligh and his daughter uneasy – Collins had a 'kept woman' and he would shamelessly walk with her arm in arm around the town. Each day he would bring her to his office, an annex to the main house, right in full view of Mary. For the British *mores* of the day, this was scandalous.

Back in England, Betsy had learned of her husband's troubles and turned frantically to Banks for advice and information. Banks turned to Under Secretary Cooke, who told him that nothing of Bligh's conduct had given the slightest reason for a recall although the insurrection made it impossible for Governor Bligh to continue his position with ease or being of any further help to the colony. On 13 May Banks wrote to Bligh, telling him that the rebellion had all the hallmarks of the French Revolution and was 'treason of the deepest dye'. [11] He told him that the rebels had accused him of cowardice, which he could not believe. The next day the Government chose Colonel Lachman Macquarie as his successor. His orders were to replace Bligh for twenty-four hours, as a token gesture; to send Johnston to England for trial; to try Macarthur in New South Wales;

to declare all appointments made by Johnston as invalid; the New South Wales Corps was to be recalled; Atkins was to be sent back to England; land grants made by Paterson declared invalid and Bligh's papers were to be restored.

Collins knew nothing of the Government's decision and neither did Bligh, who had found out about Paterson's proclamation and set about writing another of his own, denouncing the revolutionary government.

Paterson's words hit home with Collins, who knew that by ignoring the orders from the interim government he was playing with fire and he now realised that Bligh was a spent force. He had allowed the settlers to write letters to Bligh but now he forbade it and refused to broadcast Bligh's new proclamation. He had been unable to have it printed as the ink conveniently disappeared. Finding that his host had now turned against him, Bligh played hardball and threatened Collins with dire consequences if he heeded Paterson and enforced his illegal orders. He then commanded Porteous to open fire on any ships who refused to acknowledge to *Porpoise*'s signals. Bligh was determined to prove that he was still Governor and could act like one, but his behaviour lost him Collins' respect – and aid.

Collins finally acted and ordered the Reverend Robert Knopwood to publicly read out Paterson's proclamation. Bligh now took his daughter to the ship and there they lived while relations between Collins and Bligh deteriorated past the point of return. Having no means of support but the ship's supplies they were dependant on the kindness of several settlers, who aided them in defiance of the orders. Some of them paid dearly for their daring; according to Bligh, one man was given four or five hundred lashes for bringing meat to his daughter. They sailed about the coast and ended up in Adventure Bay, which must have brought many old memories back to Bligh. By the end of December, he learned that a new Governor had arrived in Sydney – Macquarie.

Macquarie arrived on board the *Dromedary*, accompanied by the *Hindostan*, both of which contained the 73rd regiment which was to replace the disgraced New South Wales Corps. They were under the command of Lieutenant Colonel O'Connell. The new Governor was met by Foveaux who went out to the Heads for an official greeting. Later he was joined by Paterson. The official landing took place on 31 December and the next day Macquarie delivered his first proclamation was to express His Majesty's displeasure at the rebellion and to explain that Bligh would regain his former position for twenty-four hours. This was followed by others, hoping for future harmony and action to be taken to repeal the land grants and declaring all trials which took place in the Governor's absence as void. He then recalled Bligh.

It was music to Bligh's ears and he made his way to Sydney, arriving on

17 January 1810. He was given a thirteen-gun salute and was met by Macquarie's aide-de-camp, Captain Antill. Bligh disembarked with his daughter and Griffin, his secretary, being escorted to Government House by Lieutenant Colonel O'Connell. They then rode out two miles to the barracks where the 73rd Regiment fired in honour of their arrival. [12] While this was going on, O'Connell had been enchanted by the young widow and before they came back to town he had invited her and her father to dine with him and they had accepted.

The New South Wales Corps might have been sent home, but they had not sailed yet and they continued to do their duty, as Bligh put it, 'in great glee.' Bligh was also unhappy to see that Foveaux still held a position of trust, which he himself would have ended immediately. While awaiting a ship to take him home, Bligh busied himself by gathering evidence for the Johnston trial; he and his daughter had hired a cottage for ten pounds per month. He also visited the Hawksbury settlers, which must have been a happy reunion and spent many evenings holding parties at which his old friends and some new ones from the 73rd Regiment were invited. He also wrote to his wife, sending her his 'blessing and affectionate love.'

The relationship between Bligh and Macquarie, which had begun so harmoniously, began to fray. Most of the trouble seemed to stem from Macquarie's reliance on his new sidekick Foveaux, Bligh's inveterate enemy. Macquarie wrote to Castlereagh exculpating Bligh from any indiscretion which may have led to the mutiny and stated that he had heard very few complaints against him 'and even those few are of rather a trifling nature.' Privately he began to detest Bligh's overweening demeanour and his determination to interfere. He considered his temper as 'uncommonly harsh' and concluded that he was 'a very improper person to be employed in any situation of trust or command.' Strong words; and born from a slowly-growing resentment and an impatience to see Bligh go.

Macquarie, as per his orders, helped Bligh as much as he could in collecting evidence against Johnston but unfortunately some of it was made public, which created quite a stir. The letter which gave much offence was the first report to Castlereagh, in which Macarthur complained of the behaviour of the citizens. Immediately Bligh's friends rallied – those of the settlers and those at Sydney including Palmer, Fulton and Suttor. They demanded a general meeting at which condolences and praise would be given to the departing Governor and to refute the charges made by Johnston.

The meeting went ahead in Sydney and all went well until the chairman, Gore, read the offensive passages from Johnston's missive and asked:

'Will anyone here avow whether he or they had a design to massacre the Governor and the officers in whom he confided, if Colonel Johnston had not seized and imprisoned the Governor?'

It was a foolish question and met with cries of 'no!' Gore cannot but have seen that Bligh's old enemies, including officers from the NWS Corps as well as Blaxcell, Lord and Wentworth, were in attendance. After the congratulatory resolution was passed, most left, leaving Bligh's opponents who were waiting for a chance to mar proceedings. They insisted on two amendment, one that the meeting was planned to stir up discord in the colony and another pledging support for Macquarie's first proclamation. Gore refused, but after this was reported to Macquarie he ordered Gore to go back and hear them. Forced back in the chair and faced with none but Bligh's enemies, he was compelled to add four amendments, the two as previously proposed and another that Gore should sign these amendments and that they had been carried unanimously.

Eight days later Bligh left Australia, after an address was made to him by his supporters and signed by 460 people. As he made his preparations for departure O'Connell came to see him and dropped a bombshell; his relations with Mary had bloomed so strongly and so quickly that he had proposed to her – and she had accepted. Stunned, Bligh listened to O'Connell's story and when he asked for Mary's hand he flatly refused until he had had a chance to speak with her. Bligh later explained his actions to his wife:

What will you not my dear Betsy feel for my situation at the time, when you know that nothing I could say had any effect; at last overwhelmed with a loss I could not retrieve, I had only to make the best of it – my consent could only be extorted, for it was not a free gift. However, on many proofs of the Honour, Goodness and high character of Colonel O'Connell, and his good sense which had passed under my own trial, I did, like having no alternative, consent to her marriage, and gave her away at the ceremony consummated at Government House.... [13]

The celebration was one of gaiety and joy. Government House was decorated with flowers and the Reverend Samuel Marsden performed the ceremony. The couple were not to be wanting for a place to live – Macquarie gave them Riverstone farm as a gift. There was much rejoicing around the colony and the following soon went the rounds:

To Putland, amiable and fair,
Soft as her manners pour the warbled lay;
Another – bolder strain prepare.
For brave O'Connell on his nuptial day!
In Australasia's genial clime proclaim,

That Love and Valour blend their spotless flame. [14]

On 12 March Bligh sailed from Sydney on the *Hindostan* accompanied by the *Porpoise* and the *Dromedary*, which contained the New South Wales Corps and the defendants, including Paterson and Johnston, as well as many witnesses for the coming Court Martial. Paterson did not live long enough to see England – he was weakened by excess of alcohol and died off Cape Horn. On 11 August 1810, at Rio de Janeiro, Bligh took time to write a long letter to his wife, part of which has been quoted. It is interesting as it shows Bligh in the role of loving husband and father.

I have bought for you and our Dear Girls some Gold Beads in strings for Necklaces or Bracelets, and six handsome crosses, but not of the Malta kind as you desired – no such sort could I find – the amount of all is £56 6s which I have given 3 Bills of Exchange in favour of Rundle and Bridge to a Mr Maiden here who obligingly carried me through all the Portuguese shops in the City. – The late intercourse of the English have foolishly made every Article of Jewel kind extremcly dear... [15]

Bligh arrived at Spithead on 25 October and made his way to London.

Chapter Sixteen. Finem Respice

It must have been a happy reunion between Bligh, Betsy and his 'darling girls.' When that was done, he turned his thoughts to that which was occupying his mind – the Court Martial of Johnston.

There was much manoeuvring between the parties. After Edward Macarthur's efforts, Johnston found a strong ally in the Duke of Northumberland; meanwhile Samuel Marsden had published an article on the whole rebellion, supporting Bligh and painting the resurrectionists – including Macarthur – in the blackest shades. Macarthur was furious at the tirades given by the 'honest, immaculate priest' and hurried to write a rejoinder. His spirits rose when Lord Minto's brother told him that 'only one opinion now prevails on this subject — it is universally acknowledged that the measure was indispensable for the preservation of everything worth saving in the Colony.' Boosted by his support, Macarthur even considered taking private action against Bligh – 'My damages will be laid at twenty thousand Pounds.' [1]

As the two parties jostled for favour, the Court Martial was held against Lieutenant William G C Kent on 8 January 1811. It took place on board the

HMS Gladiator and Kent was arraigned on the following charges: having sailed from Port Jackson without Bligh's orders; for hauling down Bligh's broad pendant on board the *Porpoise* and again sailing off without orders; and for allowing Lieutenant James Symons to carry dispatches to England from the rebel government. Bligh only called one witness, Griffin, and Macarthur acted as Kent's advisor. The Court took his difficulties into account and understood his perplexity, so having found that he showed a sincere wish to perform his duty, he was acquitted.

Macarthur was jubilant, but Bligh was still popular in government circles – and higher ones too. Porphyria had again attacked the King, leading to a period of insanity during which the Prince Regent took over office. On 27 February he held his first levee at which Bligh was invited. He was third on that eminent list and it is clear that if he had been under a cloud for his actions in Australia, he would not have been admitted at all. His favour at Court troubled Macarthur and while optimistic at the outcome and buoyed up by Bligh's seeming unpopularity elsewhere, by April 1811 he was harbouring doubts:

Our Counsel give us hopes of Victory—but I know not what to think—Atkins is no where to be found, and his written evidence will not I fear be admitted—the other party I suspect have been somehow instrumental in smuggling him away, well knowing that his testimony would be most powerful against them:—all the evidence who are to support Bligh receive daily pay from Government, many of them (amongst the number Devine) a Guinea a day—they are all in high spirits, or affect to be so. I say affect for they are well aware of the strong tide of Public prejudice which runs against them, and that they and their Chief Mr. Bligh is universally execrated—Sir Joseph Banks certainly supports their cause with all his interest. [2]

On 2 May 1811, the Court Martial was convened at Chelsea Hospital on 7 May 1811. For the prosecution, Bligh called on twenty-three witnesses, including Palmer, Campbell, Fulton, Griffin, Suttor, Gore and Oakes. The defence relied on nineteen witnesses including Macarthur, Kent and several officers and men from the New South Wales Corps. Atkins had turned tail and joined the defence, probably because a secret estimation of his character had been leaked and was to be used in evidence:

He has been accustomed to inebriety; he has been the ridicule of the community; sentence of death has been pronounced in moments of intoxication; his determination is weak; his opinion floating and infirm; his knowledge of the law is insignificant, and subject to private inclination; and in confidential causes of the Crown, where due secrecy is required, he is not to be trusted with. [3]

Bligh began with an opening speech, explaining the history of his Governorship until the time of his arrest. The defence paid special attention to his penalties for rum-trafficking, then alleged that when he had discovered his own bailiff was guilty of the same offence, he remitted his sentence. When he was asked if the bailiff had indeed been convicted and did he not remit the penalty, Bligh visibly squirmed:

'The latter part of the question is, 'And did you not remit the penalty?''

'No; I recollect nothing of the kind, of remitting the penalty; I was so incensed, I thought the penalty too light: he had been guilty of a breach of faith, which I thought deserving of the highest punishment....'

'Was the penalty remitted by the magistrates?'

'Really I cannot positively speak to that.'

'You have stated, that after he was in the hands of the magistrates you had nothing more to do with him?'

'I do not believe it was remitted at all, I know nothing of its being remitted; but, sir, the magistrates will be forthcoming as witnesses to speak to the fact.'

'Will Captain Bligh add to that, that he did not remit it?'

'I really cannot call the thing to recollection, but the magistrates will be forthcoming; I do not recollect, upon my oath, that it was remitted: on the contrary, upon my oath I should declare that it was not remitted; that is my idea of it, but the magistrates will be forthcoming to prove the facts.' [4]

Naturally enough, the witnesses for the prosecution unanimously declared that Bligh had been an able and successful Governor. On the point of law and order, Gore stated that Bligh had put an end to many bad practices, preventing anyone from being arrested without a Magistrate's warrant and stopping torture as a method of extracting confessions, for example by flogging. Some soldiers testified as to the burning of Bligh in effigy and some of the free settlers described similar events in Green Hills, where men were threatened with imprisonment if they did not sign a support for Johnston. One man called Martin Mason was severely cross-examined by Johnston, who tried hard but did not succeed in blackening the witness's name.

In his defence, Johnston questioned the legality of bringing a court case after three years. He replied to Bligh's petition from the settlers with his own for redress on the day of 26 January, although his bill originally had eight or nine signatures whereas Bligh's had 833 names. As for depriving people of their homes, he declared that this vow was 'hourly uttered in the lowest and coarsest terms, accompanied by the threats of the privation and destruction of their property, and declarations that appeals to law or justice from the mandates of his will should be useless and unavailing.' He exaggerated the extent of his injury in falling from the chaise and his doctor (Jamieson) had unfortunately died and so could not attest to that.

Johnston attacked Crosley:

'There was no crime in which he had not been implicated: perjury and subornation, conspiracy and forgery.' [5]

Of all the defence witnesses, Atkins was the most virulent and it is clear that Bligh's insult had wounded him. When asked about Wentworth's suspension, he stated that Johnston had reprimanded him; then later, Bligh stated that he intended to dismiss him. When Atkins remonstrated that it was against the law to condemn a man twice, Bligh – according to his testimony – stormed:

'The law, sir! damn the law: my will is the law, and woe unto the man that dares to disobey it!' [6]

Macarthur was looking forward to his time in the dock, imagining that he would be free to pour execrations on Bligh's mismanagement of the colony. It did not work out that way and he found himself on the wrong side of a barrage of tricky questions which he fenced as best he could. Minchin described Bligh's arrest as his cowardly concealment under a bed and that he begged Minchin for protection, looking terrified. Blaxland got so confused under questioning that his testimony was worth little. Several witnesses testified to Bligh's methods of wresting people from his homes.

Both parties – Johnston and Bligh – were allowed to make observations in the summing-up. A central argument revolved around Bligh's hiding under the bed, which was surely out of all proportion. However, it was a matter of honour; the military saw this as an ignoble, base and cowardly act, not in keeping with that of a gentleman. This was the evidence given by Sergeant John Sutherland:

'He was under the bed, supporting himself forward upon his two hands, with one foot placed against each of the two posts, either on one side or at the bottom of the bed, with his back pressed upwards against the bottom of the bed. I saw the cover of the bed, which was hanging down, move, which made me think that something was under the bed. I put my piece under the bed, and moved it along to see if there was anything. I found nothing under the bed when I first put my piece under it.'

'Afterwards did you see him?'

'The second time I put my piece under the bed, the piece struck his boot; the boot went from the post of the bed, and made a slip on the boards.'

'Did you find him under the bed?'

'I found him under the bed, in the same form I have told the honourable Court.'

'How long had the Governor been searched for when you found him?'

'To the best of my knowledge, it was an hour and a half before we found him, from the time we went there first.'

'What sort of room was it, in which you found the Governor under the bed?'

'It was a room at the back of the house, formed the same as a skilling, for the steward to sleep in. When we got up stairs, we asked the steward what was in that room; the steward said there was nothing but his bed and some lumber.'

'Did you see any papers with him?'

'No, sir, I did not, indeed. I saw some dirt that came from the bottom of the bed hanging on his epaulets and skirts, that was the first sight I got of him.'

'Describe the situation of the bed?'

'The bed had no top or curtains to it, and it was pretty high underneath.'

'How high was it from the floor?'

'I cannot tell exactly how high; it was that high that Governor Bligh had room to keep himself close to the bottom of it, and I had room to move my piece along under it without touching his feet.'

'Who was in the room besides yourself, and saw the situation of the Governor?'

'Colonel Marlborough and William Wilford; they both spoke to him, as I did.' [7]

In fact, the good sergeant could do little else but give this testimony. Macarthur had stated it in the very first despatch describing Bligh's arrest and to deny it would have been tantamount to branding him and the military as liars. Even had the incident been true, few could have blamed Bligh; he carried papers which had to be concealed at any cost and his plans to put down the mutiny would have failed if he had been discovered. It says much that Bligh did not entertain any notion of confirming the report; instead it filled him with indignation and he replied to the accusation as follows:

'Just before I was arrested, on learning of the approach of the regiment, I called for my uniform (which is not a dress adapted for concealment); and going into the room where the papers were kept, I selected a few which I thought most important either to retain for the protection of my character, or to prevent from falling into the hands of the insurgents: - among the latter were copies of my private and confidential communications to the Secretary of State, on the conduct of several persons then in the colony: with these I retired upstairs, and having concealed some about my person, I proceeded to tear the remainder.'

'In the attitude of stooping for this purpose, with my papers about the floor, I was discovered by the soldiers on the other side of the bed. As to the situation in which it is said I was found, I can prove by two witnesses that it was utterly impossible; and I should have done so in the first instance, had I not thought that Colonel Johnston was incapable of degrading his defence by the admission of a slander, which, if true, affords him no excuse, and, if false, is highly disgraceful. I know that Mr

Macarthur wrote the despatch in which this circumstance is mentioned with vulgar triumph; but I could not anticipate that Colonel Johnston's address to the court would be written in the same spirit; and that after being the victim of Mr Macarthur's intrigues he would allow himself to be made the tool of his revenge.'

'It has been said that this circumstance would make the heroes of the British Navy blush with shame and burn with indignation. I certainly at such a suggestion burn with indignation, but who ought to blush with shame I leave others to determine.'

'The court will forgive me if I intrude a moment on their time, to mention the services in which I have been employed. For twenty-one years I have been a post-Captain, and have been engaged in services of danger, not falling within the ordinary duties of my profession: - for four years with Captain Cook in the Resolution, and four years more as a commander myself, I traversed unknown seas, braving difficulties more terrible because less frequently encountered. In subordinate situations I fought under Admiral Parker at the Dogger Bank, and Lord Howe at Gibraltar. In the Battle of Camperdown, the Director, under my command, first silenced and then boarded the ship of Admiral de Winter; and after the Battle of Copenhagen, where I commanded the *Glatton*. I was sent for by Lord Nelson to receive his thanks publicly on the quarter-deck.'

'Was it for me then, to sully my reputation and to disgrace the medal I wear by shrinking from death, which I had braved in every shape? An honourable mind will look for some other motive for my retirement, and will find it in my anxiety for those papers, which during this enquiry have been occasionally produced to the confusion of those witnesses who thought they no longer existed.' [8]

It was a good defence and perhaps if the speaker had been any other than Bligh it would have silenced the ugly accusation once and for all. However, after this mountain grown from a molehill, it was time for the Judge to consider the evidence. The verdict followed:

That Lieut.-Col: George Johnston, Major as aforesaid, did, on or about the 26th day of January, 1808, at Sydney, in the colony of New South Wales, begin, excite, cause, and join in, a mutiny, by putting himself at the head of the New South Wales Corps, then under his command and doing duty in the colony, and seizing and causing to be seized and arrested, and imprisoning and causing to be imprisoned, by means of the above-mentioned military force, the person of William Bligh, Esq. then Captain General and Governor in Chief in and over the territory of New South Wales.

The Court having duly and maturely weighed and considered the whole of the evidence adduced on the Prosecution, as well as what has been offered in defence, are of opinion that Lieut.-Col. Johnston is guilty of the act of Mutiny as described in the charge, and do therefore sentence him to be Cashiered. [9]

It was condemnation for Johnston, but it did not affect him materially. He was allowed to return to New South Wales and continue with his private employment. The Prince Regent was not happy with the outcome:

The Court, in passing a sentence so inadequate to the enormity of the crime of which the prisoner has been found guilty, have apparently been actuated by a consideration of the novel and extraordinary circumstances, which, by the evidence on the face of the proceedings, may have appeared to them to have existed during the administration of Gov. Bligh, both as affecting the tranquillity of the colony, and calling for some immediate decision. But although the Prince Regent admits the principle under which the court have allowed this consideration to act in mitigation of the punishment which the crime of, mutiny would otherwise have suggested, yet no circumstances whatever can be received by His Royal Highness in full extenuation of an assumption of power, so subversive of every principle of good order and discipline under which Lieut.-Col. Johnston has been convicted. [10]

To mark the Admiralty's support for Bligh and to demonstrate that the name of their erstwhile Governor was to be respected, on 31 July 1811 he was promoted to Rear Admiral of the Blue, backdated by one year. The next year another promotion followed and he became Rear Admiral of the White.

These successes were marred by tragedy. His beloved Betsy died on 15 April 1812, aged sixty, and was buried in Lambeth Churchyard. It was a great blow for Bligh and the house seemed no longer a home. He planned to move immediately and on 7 May Anne Hallet accompanied him and his daughter to Sydenham, where they did some house-hunting. At last they found a cottage which Bligh decided on straight away, planning to have repairs done the week following.

In June a Select Committee was convened under the chairmanship of the Honourable George Eden to examine transportation of convicts and alleged abuses. Two ex-Governors were invited to give evidence, Hunter and Bligh. Bligh gave a long and well-reasoned account of the subject, including observations on administration, legal matters, the judiciary and rum trading. With some pride he told the meeting that his door was always open to the convicts so that they could air any grievances and spoke of shocking immorality among them. He told of his encouragement to have them marry and his assistance in providing them homes, be they ever so humble. In particular he discussed the conditions of labour and the allocation of prisoners among the settlers and the army. [11]

Soon after, Bligh had moved to Sydenham and in the summer the Hallets took a cottage nearby. Bligh had escaped the bustle of city life and tried to forget Betsy as he absorbed himself in the countryside. The Hallets sometimes joined him, when they would go for 'delightful rambles' together. Bligh remained very protective of his daughters, especially Fanny and Ann, whom he kept a close eye on, not even allowing them to dine with the Hallets on occasion.

By April of 1813, Bligh was nearing the age of sixty and was thinking about his retirement. Having been offered half of his salary as a condition of serving as Governor, he wrote to the Admiralty asking them to fulfil their promise. His payment of £1000 per year was awarded. A month later the Admiralty asked for his opinion on the fees of Admiralty Courts as compared with the courts in Australia.

Living in Sydenham without his beloved Betsy must have been hard that year; besides, he now had the wherewithal to live in more substantial surroundings. He therefore retired to the Manor House in Farningham, Kent and took with him four of his daughters: Elizabeth, the twins Frances and Jane and his mentally handicapped, epileptic girl Anne. Mary had stayed in New South Wales, while his other daughter, Harriet, had married Henry Aston Barker.

He had hardly settled in to his new home when he was summoned again by the Admiralty, this time to report on a new design of ship pioneered by Lord Stanhope. Along with Rear Admiral Thomas Hamilton, Captain Huddart, Henry Peake, Mark Beaufoy and a Mr Allen they agreed that the construction would be beneficial to the Navy. Bligh reported:

I believe this ship will draw 7 feet less water than in our common way of construction. Her wear and tear, as it is called, will be less. Her building will require very little curved Timber, her run both forward and abaft, altho a flat bottom, will be very good, and she will sail fast and lie easy at her anchors, besides her being easy at sea ... Her great lateral resistance united with her progressive motion we expect will make her more weatherly than any of our Ships of War, and she will wear and stay in as little space as a ship of that length can do. She will be highly useful in getting near the shore landing and covering troops, which with every other consideration induces me to wish she may be built. [12]

Bligh now settled down to enjoy his retirement. Banks knew the area well and mentioned that two of his friends were living nearby – a cousin called Sir Henry Hawley and his wife. The Blighs and the Hawleys got along very well, Bligh remarking on their 'warm welcome' and hospitality. Bligh was given full rein to wander over their estates. Other friends included the Gattys and Bligh entertained their child Alfred by showing him the shot he had used to weigh out food on board the *Bounty*'s launch. Bligh now rested and none could blame him after his long and often turbulent life; he retained an interest in botany and local agriculture, watching the harvest and commenting now and then on the state of the crops and hops.

On 4 June 1814, Bligh was given his final promotion – to Vice Admiral of the Blue, but he never saw active service again. [13] His enemies gloated that it was because of his behaviour while Governor of New South Wales, but the truth is, he was getting too old for that kind of lifestyle. Little is told of his last three years, but he developed an illness for which he would often visit London for treatment. He was probably suffering from cancer, but he lived until the time his daughter Elizabeth married her cousin Richard Bligh of Lincoln's Inn who had written several legal books.

On one of his visits to London, in Bond Street, Bligh died at the age of sixty-five. He was buried next to the remains of his wife in St Mary's Church. On one side an inscription was engraved:

SACRED TO THE MEMORY OF

WILLIAM BLIGH, ESQ., F.R.S.

VICE-ADMIRAL OF THE BLUE

THE CELEBRATED NAVIGATOR WHO FIRST TRANSPLANTED
THE BREAD-FRUIT TREE FROM OTAHEITE TO THE WEST INDIES

BRAVELY FOUGHT THE BATTLES OF HIS COUNTRY

AND DIED BELOVED, RESPECTED AND LAMENTED

ON THE 7TH DAY OF DECEMBER 1817

AGED 64 [14]

The mortal body perished but the memory of William Bligh lingered on. Today few would even know of his stirring battles under Nelson and Duncan, his first voyage of discovery under Captain Cook, his own discoveries in Tasmania and the Fiji Islands or of his attempts to bring peace and order to the colony of New South Wales. Edward Christian sowed the seeds of disdain in his notorious *Appendix* and since then the Mutiny on the *Bounty* has been virtually all anyone is aware of; Hollywood added its knife-wounds and the spectre of the sadistic monster Bligh is known as a household truth. Of all British naval heroes, Bligh is surely the most undervalued and certainly the most traduced and stained by history.

We are left to wonder how Bligh's reputation would have fared if things had been otherwise. He had been sent to Tahiti with an armed vessel but no marines, resulting in a mutiny. When sent to Australia, he had been given a sheriff's badge and told to clean up Dodge, but without backing. The Admiralty had been advised that the Bounty was too small and that it needed marines, but they ignored it. Past Governors of Australia had warned the Government about the New South Wales Corps and the Macarthur Gang, but again they had been ignored. When they gave Bligh marines in his second breadfruit voyage, the task was completed; when the Government disbanded the New South Wales Corps, the colony was governed in peace. However, the mistakes made by the authorities had cost Bligh dear – they had endangered his life on several occasions and had ruined his reputation.

Had Bligh been given the appropriate means to perform his tasks, the future would have looked on him with a completely different eye. He would have succeeded on the *Bounty* and the subsequent court martial would never have occurred. He would have dealt with the racketeers in Australia and continued to develop the colony and bring prosperity to the settlers. His successes in sea battles and his discoveries would more than likely have made him a national hero. Edward Christian and John Macarthur would have shrunk into insignificance. Nobody knows how high his star would have risen. His bad temper would have been overlooked, as had been the case with Cook and so many other sea captains before him.

However, such speculation is fruitless. History cannot be changed; and it is doubtful whether any future generations will think of William Bligh with anything but disdain, to be forever associated with the fictions of the mutiny on the *Bounty*.

FOOTNOTES

1. A SMELL OF THE SEA

1. All details of Cook's first two voyages are taken from his own accounts.
   Details of all voyages may be found in *Three Voyages of Captain James Cook*, 7
   vols, Longman, Hurst, Rees, Orme, and Brown, London 1821.
2. Bligh, William, *A Voyage To The South Sea*, pp11-12
3. See *Navy and Army Illustrated,* Hudson and Kearns, 1901, p243
4. Reported in *The Gentleman's Magazine,* Vol 23, John Bowyer Nichols and Son,
   1845, p155
5. *Rule, Britannia!* originated from the poem "Rule, Britannia" by James Thomson
   and set to music by Thomas Arne in 1740, see Scholes, Percy A, *The Oxford
   Companion to Music (tenth Edition)*, Oxford University Press 1970, p. 897.
6. See Fiennes, Celia, *Through England On A Side Saddle*, Folkcustoms, reprinted from
   1888 edition, p203-5
7. Mackaness, George, *The Life of Vice-Admiral Bligh,* vol 1, p7
8. Bligh, John H, *Vice Admiral Bligh FRS*, p19
9. Mackaness, *ibid,* vol 1, p8
10. See *Navy and Army Illustrated,* vol 1, Hudson and Kearns, 1895.
11. Thompson, George, *A Documentary History of the African Theatre*, p138
12. Born in 1715, Miguel de Muesas was a Spanish soldier who held the positions of
    Lieutenant Governor of Santiago de Cuba and Governor and Captain General of
    Puerto Rico between 1770 and 1776.
13. *The London Chronicle for the Year 1773*, No 33, p 78, J Wilkie, London 1773
14. Kennedy, Gavin, *Bligh,* p3.
15. The *Albion* saw her first taste of action in the American War of Independence at
    the Battle of Grenada 1779.
16. Cook, James, *Voyage to the Pacific Ocean*, Dublin 1784, p5

2. TOOTE AND BRY

1. Polwhele, R, *Biographical Sketches in Cornwall,* p19
2. See Thomas Busby, *Concert Room and Orchestra Anecdotes of Music and Musicians,*
   Ancient and Modern, Volume 1, Clementi, 1825, p81
3. Genealogy was gleaned from parish records.
4. Mackaness, *ibid,* vol 1, p4
5. Cook, James, *A Voyage To The Pacific Ocean,* vol 1, p33
6. Cook, *ibid,* pp58-9
7. Cook, *ibid,* 976
8. Cook, *ibid,* p xxxvii
9. Cook, *ibid,* pp182-3
10. Bligh's marginal note on his copy of *A Voyage To The Pacific Ocean.*
11. Cook, *ibid,* p270
12. Bligh's marginal note on his copy of *A Voyage To The Pacific Ocean.*
13. Cook, *ibid,* p263
14. Bligh's marginal note on his copy of *A Voyage To The Pacific Ocean.*
15. Cook, *ibid,* p276
16. Cook, *ibid,* p327
17. Cook, James, *A Voyage To The Pacific Ocean,* vol 2, p15
18. Cook, *ibid,* p15
19. Cook, *ibid,* p47
20. Cook, *ibid,* p70
21. Sturma, Michael, *South Sea Maidens: Western Fantasy and Sexual Politics in the*
   South Pacific, p-p 25-30
22. Cook, *ibid,* p100
23. Cook, *ibid,* p125
24. Cook, *ibid,* p216
25. Cook, *ibid,* pp359-60
26. Cook, *ibid,* p363
27. Cook, *ibid,* p363
28. Cook, *ibid,* p482
29. Bligh's marginal note on his copy of *A Voyage To The Pacific Ocean.*
30. Cook, *ibid,* pp506-7
31. Cook, *ibid,* p536
32. King, James, *A Voyage To The Pacific Ocean,* vol 3, p31-2
33. Cook, *ibid,* p548
34. King, *ibid,* p49
35. King, *ibid,* p155
36. King, *ibid,* p36
37. King, *ibid,* p40

38. Bligh's marginal note on his copy of *A Voyage To The Pacific Ocean.*
39. King, *ibid,* 53-4
40. King, *ibid*, p57
41. King, *ibid*, p137
42. King, *ibid*, p98
43. King, *ibid*, p283
55. Mackaness, *ibid,* vol 1, pp24-5

3. A TASTE OF POWDER

1. Allen, Kenneth S, *That Bounty Bastard*, p38
2. Mackaness, *ibid,* vol1, p 35
3. Mackaness, *ibid,* vol 1, p36
4. Kennedy, *ibid,* p10
5. Parker's account of the Battle may be read in Ekins, Charles: *The Naval Battles of*
   Great Britain, pp137-145
6. Rawson, Geoffrey, *Bligh of the 'Bounty'*, p43
7. Mackaness, *ibid,* vol 1, p55
8. Frederick Sayer, *The History of Gibraltar and of Its Political Relation to Events*
   in Europe Notes And Queries, Oxford University Press, 1890, p262.
9. Wahlroos, Sven, *Mutiny and Romance in the South Seas*, Salem House Publsihers
   1989, p245
10. Mackaness, *ibid,* vol 1, p41
11. Mackaness, *ibid,* vol 1, p225
12. Dening, Greg, *Mr Bligh's Bad Language, Passion, Power and Theatre on the Bounty,*
   Cambridge University Press, 1994, p70
13. Mackaness, *ibid,* vol 1, p46
14. Mackaness, *ibid,* vol 1, p49

4. SCUDDING BEFORE THE FORESAIL

1. Valentine Morris (1727-89) was the son of sugar plantation magnate Colonel
   Valentine Morris. He became Governor of the island of St. Vincent's in 1763 but
   negotiated its surrender to France in 1779.
2. Mackaness, *ibid,* vol 1, pp45-6
3. Mackaness, *ibid,* vol 1, p60
4. Mackaness, *ibid,* vol 1, pp64-5
5. Bligh, William, *A Voyage To The South Sea*, p9

6. Bligh's log for 24 Dec 1787
7. Bligh, *ibid*, p16
8. Bligh, *ibid*, p21
9. Bligh's log for 23 Jan 1788.
10. Keynes, Richard Darwin, *The Beagle Record*, p34
11. Mackaness, *ibid*, vol 1, p72
12. Bligh, *ibid*, pp26-7
13. Bligh's log for 29 March 1788.
14. Bligh's log for 13 April 1788.
15. Bligh, *ibid*, p31
16. Bligh's log for 24 May 1788.
17. Bligh, William, *A Voyage To The South Sea*, p17
18. Bligh, *ibid*, p47
19. Bligh, *ibid*, pp47-8
20. Bligh, *ibid*, p56
21. Bligh's log for 24 Oct 1788.

5. A TYO OF OTAHEITE

1. Bligh, William, *A Voyage To The South Sea*, p65
2. Bligh, *ibid*, p69
3. Bligh, *ibid*, p69
4. Bligh, *ibid*, p73
5. Bligh, *ibid*, p75
6. Bligh, *ibid*, p78
7. Bligh, *ibid*, p85
8. Bligh, *ibid*, p87
9. Bligh, *ibid*, pp87-8
10. Bligh, *ibid*, p91
11. Bligh, *ibid*, p96
12. Bligh, J H, *Vice Admiral Bligh FRS*, p55
13. Bligh's log for 10 Dec 1788
14. Bligh, *ibid*, p111
15. Bligh, *ibid*, p113
16. Bligh's log for 15 Jan 1789
17. Bligh's log for 17 Jan 1789
18. Bligh, *ibid*, p119
19. Bligh, William, *An Answer to certain assertions contained in the appendix [to a*
   pamphlet by E. Christian], p1

20. Bligh, *ibid*, p124
21. Bligh's log for 11 Feb 1789
22. Bligh, *ibid*, p128
23. Mavor, William Fordyce, *A General Collection of Voyages and Travels*, p54
24. Bligh's log for 8 March 1789
25. Bligh, *ibid*, p141

6. SHARKS

1. Bligh, William, *A Voyage To The South Sea*, p149
2. Bligh, *ibid*, p152
3. Rutter Owen, *The Court Martial of the Bounty Mutineers*, p71
4. Rutter, *ibid*, p72
5. Rutter, *ibid*, p142
6. Bligh, William, *Dangerous Voyage of Captain Bligh*, p22
7. Rutter, *ibid*, p23
8. Rutter, *ibid*, p27
9. Bligh, William, *A Voyage To The South Sea*,pp157-8
10. Rutter, *ibid*, p75
11. Bligh, William, *Dangerous Voyage of Captain Bligh*, p25
12. Bligh, *ibid*. p23
13. Bligh, *ibid*, p24
14. Mackaness, *ibid*, vol 1, p162

7. THE EVER-ROLLING OCEAN

1. Bligh, William, *Dangerous Voyage of Captain Bligh*, p34
2. Bligh, *ibid*, pp34-5
3. Bligh, *ibid*, p41
4. Bligh, *ibid*, p42
5. Bligh, *ibid*, p46
6. Bligh, *ibid*, p48
7. Bligh, *ibid*, p48
8. Bligh, *ibid*, p50
9. Bligh, *ibid*, p52
10. Bligh, *ibid*, p54
11. Bligh, *ibid*, p56
12. Bligh, *ibid*, p57
13. Bligh, *ibid*, pp59-60

14. Bligh, *ibid,* p60
15. Bligh, *ibid,* p65
16. Bligh, *ibid,* p71
17. Mackaness, *ibid,* vol 1, pp218-9
18. Mackaness, *ibid,* vol 1, pp217
19. Bligh, *ibid,* p75
20. Bligh, *ibid,* pp76-7
21. Bligh, *ibid,* p79
22. Bligh, *ibid,* p80
23. Bligh, *ibid,* p81
24. Bligh, bid, p82

8. 'PROSPER THEREFORE OUR UNDERTAKINGS'

1. Belcher, Diana Jolliffe, *Mutineers of the Bounty,* pp120-1
2. Mackaness, *ibid,* vol 1, p317
3. Bligh's log for 15 Sept 1791
4. Bligh's log for 30 Oct
5. Bligh's log for 20 Dec
6. In his log, Bligh adds: 'Near our fires we had little birds like robins, except the want of a red breast, that visited us as domestically as in England.'
7. Bligh's log for 19 Feb 1792
8. Bligh's log for 16 March and 19 March
9. Bligh, William, *An Answer to certain assertions contained in the appendix [to a pamphlet by E. Christian],* p4
10. Bligh's log for 9 April
11. Noted in Bligh's log for 10 April
12. Bligh's log for 10 April include the dialogue.
13. *Sydney Gazette and New South Wales Advertiser,* Saturday, 17 July 1819.
14. The narrative is based on Bligh's logs and Mackaness.
15. Belcher, Diana Jolliffe, *Mutineers of the Bounty,* p80
16. Belcher, ibid, p85
17. Belcher, ibid, p86
18. Belcher, ibid, p91
19. Bligh's log for 14 April
20. Bligh's log for 16 April
21. Bligh's log for 19 April
22. Bligh's log for 27 April
23. Bligh's log for 2 May
24. Bligh's log for 19 May

25. Bligh's log for 2 June
26. Bligh's log for 18 July

9. THE ROCKY ROAD

1. Bligh's log for 18 July 1792
2. Bligh's log for Aug 5-10 describes his naming method
3. Bligh's log for 19 Aug
4. Bligh's log for 31 Aug
5. Bligh's log for 6 Sept
6. Bligh's log for 11 Sept
7. Scott, Ernest, *The Life of Captain Matthew Flinders*, p33
8. Bligh's log for 17 Sept
9. Bligh's log for 18 Sept
10. Scott, ibid, p34
11. Mackaness, *ibid,* vol 2, p23
12. Bligh's log for 6 Nov
13. *Transactions of the Society Instituted at London for the Encouragement of Arts, Manufactures, and Commerce,* Volume 12, pp312-3
14. Bligh's log for 9 Aug, 4 Sep and 6 Sept 1793.

10. THAT BOUNTY BASTARD

1. Fiske, Nathan Welby, *Aleck, The Last of the Mutineers*, p64
2. Belcher, Diana Jolliffe, Mutineers of the *Bounty*, p103
3. Belcher, *ibid,* p109
4. Belcher, *ibid,* p114
5. Tagart, Edward, *Memoir of the Late Captain Peter Heywood, R.N.*, p127
6. Rutter Owen, *The Court Martial of the Bounty Mutineers*, p80
7. Rutter, *ibid,* p83
8. Rutter, *ibid,* p87
9. Rutter, *ibid,* p108
10. Rutter, *ibid,* p128
11. *Chronicles of the Sea,* vol 1, p198
12. Tagart, *ibid,* p127
13. Tagart, *ibid,* p146
14. Bligh, William, *An Answer to certain assertions contained in the appendix [to a pamphlet by E. Christian],* pp16-7
15. Rutter, *ibid,* p16
16. Rutter, *ibid,* p16
17. Morrison, James, *After The Bounty*, p12
18. Morrison, *ibid,* p13
19. Morrison, *ibid,* p14

20. Morrison, *ibid*, p22
21. Morrison, *ibid*, p28
22. Bligh, *ibid*, p1
23. Bligh, ibid, p3
24. Christian, Edward, *A Short Reply to Capt. William Bligh's Answer*, p7
15. Christian, *ibid,* p10

11. A VERY DELICATE BUSINESS

1. Mackaness, *ibid*, vol 2, p33
2. Mackaness, *ibid*, vol 2, p33
3. Kennedy, ibid, pp231-4
4. Polwhele, ibid, pp376-7
5. Neale, William Johnson, *History of the Mutiny at Spithead and the Nore*, p125
6. Mackaness, *ibid*, vol 2, p39
7. Kennedy, ibid, p243
8. Kennedy, ibid, pp243-4
9. Kennedy, ibid, p245
10. Gill, Conrad, *The Naval Mutinies*, p241
11. Irving, Terry and Cahill, Rowan, *Radical Sydney*, p265
12. Mackaness, *ibid*, vol 2, p49
13. Mackaness, *ibid*, vol 2, p45
14. Mackaness, *ibid*, vol 2, p47

12. A HEART OF OAK

1. Wolfe Tone, William Theobald, *The Life of Theobald Wolfe Tone*, p427
2. Kennedy, ibid, p249
3. Ekins, Charles: *The Naval Battles of Great Britain*, p257
4. Brenton, Edward Pelham, The Naval History of Great Britain, p117
5. Mackaness, *ibid*, vol 2, p50
6. Mackaness, *ibid*, vol 2, p50
7. Padfield, Peter, *Nelson's War,* p103
8. Mackaness, *ibid,* vol 2, p51
9. Padfield, Peter, *Nelson's War,* p103
10. James, William, *Naval History of Great Britain,* p111
11. Duncan, Robert Adam Philips Haldane, *Admiral Duncan*, p359
12. Mackaness, *ibid,* vol 2, pp52-3
13. Lloyd, Christopher, *St Vincent and Camperdown*, p163
14. Mackaness, *ibid,* vol 2, p59
15. Mackaness, *ibid,* vol 2, p60
16. Mackaness, *ibid,* vol 2, p61

13. BLIND EYE

1. Feldbaek, Ole, *The Battle of Copenhagen 1801: Nelson and the Danes*, p45
2. Bligh's log for 2 April 1801
3. Southey, Robert, *The Life of Nelson*, p230
4. Grimshaw, *William, History of the Wars of the French Revolution*, p370
5. Grimshaw, *ibid,* p371
6. Southey, *ibid,* p217
7. Grimshaw, *ibid,* p371
8. Bligh's log for 3 April 1801
9. Mackaness, *ibid,* vol 2, p64
10. Mackaness, *ibid,* vol 2, p91
11. Mackaness, *ibid,* vol 2, p69-93 for full account.
12. Mackaness, *ibid,* vol 2, p96
13. Rundle, Rob, *Bligh, Master Mariner*, p209
14. Rundle, *ibid*, p209

14. A QUESTION OF RUM

1. Macarthur Onslow, Sibella, *Some Early Records of the Macarthurs of Camden*, p44
2. Macarthur, *ibid,* p59
3. Macarthur, *ibid,* p57
4. Macarthur, *ibid,* p101
5. Lang, John Dunmore, An Historical and Statistical Account of New South
    Wales, vol 1, pp96-7
6. Macarthur, *ibid,* pp137-8
7. Lang, *ibid*, p100
8. Lang, *ibid*, p101
9. Lang, *ibid*, pp438-9
10. Lang, *ibid*, p108-9
11. Lang, *ibid*, pp110-1
12. Lang, *ibid*, p112
13. Lang, *ibid*, p112
14. Lang, *ibid*, p116
15. Lang, *ibid*, p117
16. Lang, *ibid*, pp117-8
17. Lang, *ibid*, p119
18. Lang, *ibid*, p120
19. Lang, *ibid*, p121
20. Lang, *ibid*, p112
21. Lang, *ibid*, p124
22. Lang, *ibid*, p124

23. Lang, *ibid*, pp124-5
24. Macarthur, *ibid,* p125
25. Lang, *ibid*, p127
26. Mackaness, *ibid,* p191
27. *Proceedings of a General Court Martial held at Chelsea Hospital,*417
28. Lang, *ibid*, p138
29. Macarthur, *ibid,* p153
30. Lang, *ibid*, p139
31. Lang, *ibid*, p139

15. IN LIMBO

1. Bonwick, James, *Curious Facts of Old Colonial Days,* p188
2. Bennett, Samuel, *The History Of Australian Discovery and Colonisation Part 4*, p386
3. Lang, *ibid*, p142
4. Mackaness, *ibid,* vol 2, p280
5. O'Hara, James, *The History of New South Wales*, p322
6. Mackaness, *ibid*, vol 2, p285
7. Bennett, *ibid*, p385
8. Bonwick, *ibid,* p212
9. Bonwick, *ibid*, p214
10. Mackaness, *ibid*, vol 2, p297
11. Mackaness, *ibid*, vol 2, p301
12. Mackaness, *ibid,* vol 2, p305
13. Mackaness, *ibid*, vol 2, pp317-8
14. Bonwick, *ibid*, p180

16. FINEM RESPICE

1. Mackaness, *ibid*, vol 2, p324
2. Macarthur, *ibid,* p220
3. *Proceedings of a General Court Martial held at Chelsea Hospital*, p60
4. *Proceedings of a General Court Martial held at Chelsea Hospital*, p50
5. *Proceedings of a General Court Martial held at Chelsea Hospital*, p150
6. *Proceedings of a General Court Martial held at Chelsea Hospital*, p161
7. *Proceedings of a General Court Martial held at Chelsea Hospital*, p371-2
8. *Proceedings of a General Court Martial held at Chelsea Hospital*, p390-1
9. *Proceedings of a General Court Martial held at Chelsea Hospital*, p408
10. *Proceedings of a General Court Martial held at Chelsea Hospital*, p408-9
11. Mackaness, *ibid*, vol 2, p335-6
12. Mackaness, *ibid*, vol 2, p339
13. Mackaness, *ibid*, vol 2, p339
14. Mackaness, *ibid*, vol 2, p341

BIBLIOGRAPHY

A Description of England and Wales: Containing a Particular Account of Each County ... Embellished with Two Hundred and Forty Copper Plates, of Palaces, Castles, Cathedrals,etc... Newbery and Carnan, London, 1769

Alison, Archibald, *History of Europe from the Commencement of the French Revolution,* Baudry's European Library, Paris, 1841m vol 3

Belcher, Diana Jolliffe, *Mutineers of the Bounty,* John Murray, 1870

Bennett, Samuel, *The History Of Australian Discovery and Colonisation Part 4,* Hanson and Bennett, Australia, 1865

Bligh, J H, *Vice Admiral Bligh FRS,* John Bligh, Rochester, Kent, 2001

Bligh, William, *A Voyage To The South Sea,* George Nichol, London, 1792

Bligh, William, *An Answer to certain assertions contained in the appendix [to a pamphlet by E. Christian] entitled: Minutes of the proceedings on the Court Martial held August 12th 1792 on ten persons charged with mutiny on board His Majesty's Ship the Bounty,* G Nichol, London, 1794

Bligh, William, *Dangerous Voyage of Captain Bligh, In An Open Boa, Over 1200 Leagues Of the Ocean, In The Year 1789,* T Courtney, Dublin, 1820

Bonwick, James, *Curious Facts of Old Colonial Days,* Sampson Low, Son and Marston, London, 1879

Brenton, Edward Pelham, *The Naval History of Great Britain: From the Year MDCCLXXXIII to MDCCCXXII,* C Rice, London, 1823

Christian, Edward, *A Short Reply to Capt. William Bligh's Answer,* J Deighton, London 1795

Chronicles of the Sea, vol 1, William Mark Clark, London, 1838, p198

Cook, James, *A Voyage To The Pacific Ocean,* vol 1, printed for H Chamberlaine W Watson, Potts, Williams, Cross, Jackson, Moncrieffe, Walker, Jenkin, Burnet, Wilson, Wogan, Exshaw, valance, Beatty, White,

Whitestone, Burton, Byrne, Mills, J Porter, Stewart, Wallace, Higly, Cash, Herey and McKenzie, Dublin, vol 1(1784),

Cook, James, *A Voyage To The Pacific Ocean*, vol 2, W and A Straton, London, 1784

Cook, James, *Three Voyages of Captain James Cook*, 7 vols, Longman, Hurst, Rees, Orme, and Brown, London 1821.

Dening, Greg, *Mr Bligh's Bad Language, Passion, Power and Theatre on the Bounty,* Cambridge University Press, 1994

Duncan, Archibald, *The British Trident, or, Register of Naval Actions,* James Cundee, London, 4 vols, 1805

Duncan, Robert Adam Philips Haldane, *Admiral Duncan*, Longmans, Green and Co, London, 1898

Ekins, Charles: *The Naval Battles of Great Britain*, Baldwin and Cradock, London, 1828

Feldbaek, Ole, *The Battle of Copenhagen 1801: Nelson and the Danes*, Leo Cooper, Barnsley, 2002

Fiske, Nathan Welby, *Aleck, The Last of the Mutineers*, Benjamin Perkins and
Co, Boston, 3rd ed, 1848

Gill, Conrad, *The Naval Mutinies*, University Press, Manchester, 1913

Grimshaw, William, *History of the Wars of the French Revolution*, Bangs, Brother and Co, New York, 1852

Heywood, Perter and Heywood, Nessy, *Innocent on the Bounty*, McFarland and Co., Jefferson, Morth Carolina and London, 2013, p165

Irving, Terry and Cahill, Rowan, *Radical Sydney,* University of New South Wales Press, Sydney, 2010

James, William, *Naval History of Great Britain,* Harding, Lepard and Co., London, 1826

Kennedy, Gavin, *Bligh*, Duckworth, London, 1978

Keynes, Richard Darwin, *The Beagle Record*, Cambridge University Press 2011

King, James, *A Voyage To The Pacific Ocean*, vol 3, H Hughs, London, 1785

Lang, John Dunmore, *An Historical and Statistical Account of New South Wales,both as a Penal Settlement and as a British Colony*, 2nd Edn, A J Valpy, London, 1837

Lee, Ida, *Captain Bligh's Second Voyage to the South Sea,* Longmans. Green and Co, London, 1920

Lloyd, Christopher, *St Vincent and Camperdown*, Macmillan, 1963

Macarthur Onslow, Sibella, *Some Early Records of the Macarthurs of Camden*, Angus and Robertson, Sydney, 1914

Mackaness, George, *The Life of Vice-Admiral William Bligh,* Farrar and Rinehart, New York, 1931

Mavor, William Fordyce, *A General Collection of Voyages and Travels, Vol 13*, Mathews, Sherwood, Neely & Jones, London, 1813

Morrison, James, *After The Bounty,* Potomac Books, Dulles, Virginia, 2010

Neale, William Johnson, *History of the Mutiny at Spithead and the Nore*, Thomas Tegg, London, 1842

O'Hara, James, *The History of New South Wales*, J Hatchard, London, 1818

Padfield, Peter, *Nelson's War*, Granada, London, 2015

Polwhele, R, *Biographical Sketches in Cornwall,* W Polyblank, London, 1831

Proceedings of a General Court Martial held at Chelsea Hospital, for the Trial of Lieut.-Col. Geo. Johnston, Sherwood, Neely and Jones, London, 1811

Rawson, Geoffrey, *Bligh of the 'Bounty'*, P Allan, 1930

Rodger, N.A.M., *Commissioned Officers' Careers in the Royal Navy, 1690–1815,* Journal for Maritime Research, 3:1, 85-129, DOI: 10.1080/21533369.2001.9668314, 2001

Rundle, Rob, *Bligh, Master Mariner,* Pen and Sword Books Ltd., Barnsley, 2012, p206

Rutter Owen (ed.), *The Court Martial of the Bounty Mutineers*, William Hodge and Company, Glasgow and Edinburgh, 1931

Rutter, Owen, *Turbulent Journey,* Ivor Nicholson and Watson, London, 1936

Sayer, Frederick, *The History of Gibraltar and of Its Political Relation to Events in Europe: From the Commencement of the Moorish Dynasty in Spain to the Last Morocco War,* Saunders, Otley and Co., London, 1862

Scott, Ernest, *The Life of Captain Matthew Flinders*, Cambridge University Press, New York, 1914

Southey, Robert, *The Life of Nelson*, Bell and Daldy, London, 1861

Sturma, Michael, *South Sea Maidens: Western Fantasy and Sexual Politics in the South Pacific*, Greenwood Publishing Group, 2002

Tagart, Edward, *Memoir of the Late Captain Peter Heywood, R.N.,* Effingham Wilson, London, 1832

Thompson, George, *A Documentary History of the African Theatre*, Northwestern University Press, 1998

Transactions of the Society Instituted at London for the Encouragement of Arts, Manufactures, and Commerce, Volume 12, T Spilsbury and Sin,. London, 1794

Wahlroos, Sven, *Mutiny and Romance in the South Seas*, Salem House ~ Publishers 1989

Wolfe Tone, William Theobald, *The Life of Theobald Wolfe Tone*, Gales and Seaton, 1826

Printed in Great Britain
by Amazon